WBL

The Bahamas

A Great Destination

The Bahamas

A Great Destination

Chelle Koster Walton
with photographs by the author

The Countryman Press ✳ Woodstock, Vermont

FIRST EDITION

Interior photographs by the author unless otherwise specified
Maps by Erin Greb Cartography, © The Countryman Press
Book design by Bodenweber Design
Composition by PerfecType, Nashville, TN

Published by The Countryman Press, P.O. Box 748, Woodstock, VT 05091

Distributed by W. W. Norton & Company, Inc., 500 Fifth Avenue, New York,
NY 10110

The Bahamas: A Great Destination

978-1-58157-125-7

Printed in the United States of America

10 9 8 7 6 5 4 3 2 1

To my son, Aaron, who lost his fear of the water
on his first trip to the Bahamas at age 4,
mesmerized by the clear-clear seas.

EXPLORE WITH US!

Here's how this book works: I have organized the island chapters of this book starting with the two most popular destinations: Nassau/Paradise Island and Grand Bahama Island. From there I proceed with seven major Out Islands in alphabetical order, followed by one chapter devoted to six other less-visited islands or group of islands.

Other sections deal with the Bahamas' history as a whole, transportation, and nitty-gritty information

A series of indexes at the back of the book provide easy access to information. The first, a standard index, lists entries and subjects in alphabetical order. Next, it categorizes hotels, inns, and resorts price. Restaurants are organized in two separate indexes: one by price, one by type of cuisine.

WHAT'S WHERE

In the beginning of the book you'll find an alphabetical listing of special highlights and important information that you may want to reference quickly. There you'll find everything from where to find Bahamian blue holes to the lowdown on lobster.

LODGING

I've selected lodging places for mention in this book based on their merit alone; we do not charge innkeepers to be listed. The author always checks every property personally.

PRICES

Rather than give specific prices, this guide rates dining and lodging options within a range.

Lodging prices are normally based on per person/double occupancy for hotel rooms and per unit for efficiencies, apartments, cottages, suites, and villas. Price ranges reflect the difference in the off-season and high season (usually Christmas through Easter, but some islands such as Bimini have a high season of spring through summer).

Generally, the colder the weather up north, the higher the cost of accommodations here. Many resorts offer off-season packages at special rates. Others close down completely from one to three months. Pricing does not include taxes and gratuities, which can add up to 12 percent or more to a tab.

Dining cost categories are based on the range of dinner entrée prices or, if dinner is not served, on lunch entrées. Most restaurants in the Bahamas add 10 percent gratuity to the tab. Satisfied diners are expected to tip between 15 and 20 percent, except when the server happens to be the restaurant owner, which happens more than you'd think.

KEY TO SYMBOLS

⚭ **Weddings**. The wedding-ring symbol appears next to lodging venues that specialize in weddings.

🎗 **Special value**. The blue-ribbon symbol appears next to selected lodging and restaurants that combine quality and moderate prices.

✎ **Child-friendly**. The crayon symbol appears next to lodging, restaurants, activities, and shops of special interest or appeal to youngsters.

♿ **Handicapped access**. The wheelchair symbol appears next to lodging, restaurants, and attractions that are partially or completely handicapped accessible.

"ᵼ" **Wireless Internet**. The wireless symbol appears next to lodging, restaurants, and attractions that offer wireless Internet access.

✪ **Author's Favorites**. These are the places we think have the best to offer in each region, whether that means great food, outstanding rooms, beautiful scenery, or overall appeal.

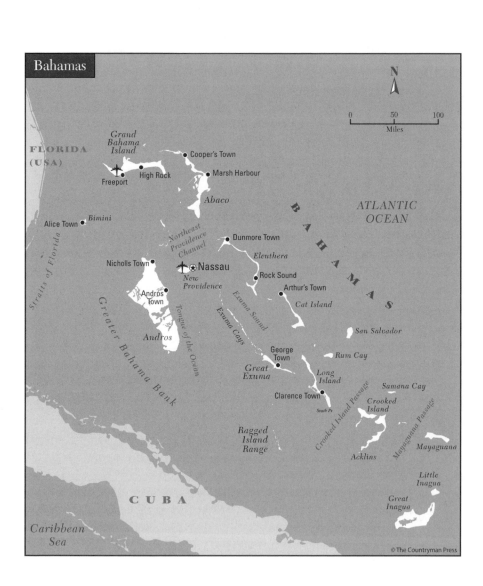

Bahamas

N

0   50   100
Miles

FLORIDA
(USA)

Grand
Bahama
Island

Cooper's Town

Freeport High Rock

Marsh Harbour

Abaco

ATLANTIC
OCEAN

Alice Town ● Bimini

Nicholls Town

Northeast
Providence
Channel

Dunmore Town

Eleuthera

B
A
H
A
M
A
S

Nassau

New
Providence

Rock Sound

Arthur's Town

Straits of Florida

Andros
Town

Andros

Tongue of the Ocean

Exuma Sound

Exuma Cays

Cat Island

San Salvador

Greater Bahama Bank

George
Town

Great
Exuma

Rum Cay

Long
Island

Clarence Town

South Pt

Crooked Island Passage

Samana Cay

Crooked
Island

Mayaguana Passage

Mayaguana

Ragged
Island
Range

Acklins

Little
Inagua

CUBA

Great
Inagua

Caribbean
Sea

© The Countryman Press

CONTENTS

10 LIST OF MAPS
11 INTRODUCTION
13 WHAT'S WHERE IN THE BAHAMAS
24 HISTORY
39 TRANSPORTATION

1 Nassau/Paradise Island / 49

51 NASSAU/PARADISE ISLAND: Colonial Heritage, Modern Vibe
    (Including Cable Beach and Outlying Settlements)

2 Grand Bahama Island / 83

85 GRAND BAHAMA ISLAND: City Mouse, Country Mouse
    (Including Lucaya, Freeport, West End, and East End)

3 Abaco / 107

109 ABACO: Boater's Wet Dream
     (Including Marsh Harbour/Great Abaco Island, Elbow Cay,
     Green Turtle Cay, and Other Cays)

4 Andros / 133

135 ANDROS: Blue Holes & Bonefish
     (Including Andros Town/Fresh Creek, Nicholl's Town, Behring Point,
     Cargill Creek, and South Andros)

5 Bimini / 155

156 BIMINI: Fishing. Legends.
     (Including Alice Town/North Bimini and South Bimini)

6 Cat Island / 173

174 CAT ISLAND: Old Bahamia
     (Including The Bight and Port Howe)

7 Eleuthera / 185

187 ELEUTHERA: Beaches Is We
     (Including Harbour Island, Governor's Harbour, Gregory Town,
     and South Eleuthera)

8 Exuma / 205

207 EXUMA: So Many Isles, So Little Time
     (Including George Town, Williams Town, and Emerald Bay)

9 Long Island / 221

223   LONG ISLAND: Keeper of Tradition
       (Including Deadman's Cay, Clarence Town, Stella Maris, and Oneil's)

10 Other Out Islands / 237

238   OTHER OUT ISLANDS: Remote & Dreamy
       (Including Berry Islands, San Salvador, and Great Inagua)

11 Information / 247

248   Practical Matters

254   INDEX

MAPS

8   OVERALL MAP
50   NEW PROVIDENCE/NASSAU
84   GRAND BAHAMA ISLAND
108   ABACO
134   ANDROS
157   BIMINI
186   ELEUTHERA
206   EXUMA
222   LONG ISLAND

INTRODUCTION

Once upon a time, I believed the Bahama Islands were all about casinos and cruise ships, which is why I snubbed them for many years as I went on to explore the diverse culture of the Caribbean Islands. Two separate press junkets completely flipped my mind, however, and in the past 17 years I've returned to the islands more times than I can count.

The first trip took me to Grand Bahama Island in its casino heyday. Aha! Just as I suspected! But then I discovered that Freeport and Lucaya, the island's pre-fab tourism centers, were a minute part of the 96-mile-long island's makeup. The rest consists of vast stretches of deserted beach, piney forest, limestone caves, and small, time-stunted fishing villages. Like all of the Bahamas, fishing, boating, and diving the intoxicatingly gin-clear waters attract a specialty tourist, much different from the mobs of gamblers and shoppers I'd envisioned.

Preconceptions dropped, I ventured next to Nassau with a side trip to the Abacos. The focus of this visit was the arts. In Nassau, we talked to local artists, visited Junkanoo Expo, heard a boys choir, danced to the Baha Men long before "Who Let the Dogs Out," watched a straw-plaiter's magic fingers, and toured art galleries. In the Abacos, we met an expert model-shipbuilder and visited the foundry of late sculptor Randolph Johnston. That, my first Out Island experience, introduced me to the islands' British genes, West Indian culture, and seawater blood. I tasted johnnycake, chicken souse, raw conch, stew fish, and guava duff. I fell in love. Since then, the islands continue to tantalize with a diversity that ranges from cosmopolitan airs and big-time tourism to conch-blowing contests and pink-sand beaches.

In this book, I will share with you my favorite discoveries on Bahama soil so that you, too, will come to fully appreciate the complexity of this scattering of isles in all shapes, sizes, and character.

My most heartfelt thanks goes to the Bahamian people, who throughout my months of research proved not only polite and helpful, but shored my spirit with their humor, rich traditions, and help where I never expected to find it.

The Bahamas Ministry of Tourism (MOT) came through with amazing support for this project at a time when money was tight and its public relations people did not feel confident in taking a small gamble. Special thanks go to MOT agents Ben Pratt on Andros Island, Debra Pinder in Nassau, Terrance Roberts and Karen Seymour on Grand Bahama Island, Donnalee Miller in Eleuthera, and Charles Robins in Bimini. Others within the agency who were a tremendous help include Prescott Young, Charity Armbrister, Salena Burrows, Marshaleise Levarity, Kevin Wallace, and Jeritzan Edwards. They all patiently answered my endless questions without the teeniest sign of exasperation. They're either excellent actors or superb public servants.

I cannot possibly name all of the other people who were helpful above and beyond the call of duty while I was on my research mission, but these I cannot

RANDOLPH JOHNSTON'S SCULPTURE *TRIBUTE TO BAHAMIAN WOMEN* GREETS GUESTS ALONG NASSAU'S HARBOR.

overlook: Jeff Birch at Small Hope Bay Lodge on Andros Island, Jackie Higgins and Michael McKnought-Smith at Long Island Breeze Resort on Long Island, Samuel R. Zabawsky and Britney Lolley representing Wyndham Nassau, Roberta and Paolo Garzaroli at Graycliff Hotel in Nassau, Lorianne Lacey representing Atlantis on Paradise Island, Greg Romanelli with Our Lucaya Resort on Grand Bahama Island, the Armbristers and staff at Fernandez Bay Village on Cat Island, Beth Watson-Jones and Stephen Kappeler at Cape Eleuthera Resort & Yacht Club, Danielle Dunfee and Anva Roberts representing Bimini Bay Resort, and Frank Cooney and Grant Johnson at Bimini Bay Sands.

I owe a huge debt of gratitude to Leesa Fountain, my on-the-ball, on-the-spot, Eleuthera-based fact checker; Kim Grant, who has helped me through this project from conception to completion; Lisa Sacks with Countryman Press, who was ever-encouraging; and my thorough but gentle editor, Kathryn Flynn. Finally, thanks to my husband, Rob, who has always shared my love of the Bahamas, yet tried not to pout when I took off on research trips without him.

AREA CODE The 242 area code applies throughout the Bahamas. Many lodging listings also include a U.S. number; either their owners live part time in the States or they maintain an office or phone line there. You often need to be persistent when trying to reach businesspeople in the Out Islands, sometimes even in Nassau and Grand Bahama. No answer doesn't necessarily mean a wrong number, so try, try again. Numbers prefixed with 800, 888, 866, and 877 are toll free from the United States. Note that calling a toll-free number from a Bahamas hotel will incur an extra, hefty fee.

ART, PERFORMANCE (see also MUSIC) Although more traditional forms exist, Junkanoo rules the islands' performing arts scene. Its brand of street theater, music, dance, and costumes is pure Bahamian. One of the earliest forms of Bahamian dance is the quadrille—a precursor to square dancing descended from colonial times. In Nassau and Freeport, dance and theater embrace their African and British heritage while appealing to a broader audience with modern interpretations. The **National Dance Company of the Bahamas** (242-328-7588; www.ndcbahamas.com) performs in Nassau. Also in Nassau, the **Dundas Centre for the Performing Arts** (242-393-3728) and the **National Centre for the Performing Arts** (242-393-2884) host concerts, dance, and theater. On Grand Bahama Island, the **Freeport Players' Guild** (242-352–5533) and **Grand Bahama Players** (242-352-9851) perform. **Port Lucaya Marketplace** (242-373-8446) is a good place to catch musical acts from calypso to gospel.

ART, VISUAL The islands have inspired artists since Winslow Homer. In more modern times, great artists have ascended from the ranks of both British- and African-descended Bahamians to demonstrate a richness of color and diversity. Landscape and Junkanoo most inspire local painters, such as the late Brent Malone and Stanley and Jackson Burnside, the latter two of whom operate important Nassau and Paradise Island galleries called **Doongalik Studios** (242-363-1313; www.doongalik.com). New Providence's other galleries include The **National Art Gallery of the Bahamas** (242-328-5800; www.nagb.org.bs), **Anthaya Art Gallery** (242-

327-1045; www.anthayaart.com), and
Nassau Glass Art Gallery (242-393-
8165; nassauglass.com/art-gallery.htm).
Look for the art of the late **Amos
Ferguson,** the islands' leading intuitive art. Their most high-profile and
prolific artist resides outside Nassau,
however, on tiny Green Turtle Cay.
Alton Lowe is known for his island
portraits, many of which have graced
the nation's postage stamps. In Little
Harbour on Great Abaco, the studio
and foundry started by sculptor **Randolph W. Johnston,** whose famous
Bahamian Woman graces Nassau
Harbour, now operate under his son's
direction as **Pete's Pub & Gallery**
(242-366-3503; www.petespuband
gallery.com). **Harbour Island** and
Hope Town (Elbow Cay) are also
known for their artists and galleries.

BEACHES Several islands claim to
have the most beautiful beaches in
the Bahamas. **Harbour Island** in
Eleuthera is known for its peachy-
pink sand. Grand Bahama Island's
Taino Beach ranks high for its beauty and accessibility, but the island
boasts some 90 miles of beachfront,
much of it relatively unexplored.
Many of the small, uninhabited cays
scattered around **Abaco** and **Exuma**

are the most delightful, including
Munjack Island in Abaco and **Sandy
Cay** in Exuma. Day charters take you
to these outposts. For the beach-lover
looking for less seclusion, more activity, **Paradise Island** is the answer.

BIRDS The Bahamas hosts species of
birds—some year-round, some seasonal—that include those not found
anywhere else in the world. The
endangered **Bahama parrot,** which
is found in Great Inagua and Abaco,
is most signature, along with the **pink
flamingo,** the national bird, which
inhabits Great Inagua and other
southernmost islands. Other species
include the Bahama swallow in the
northern islands, Cuban bananaquits,
painted buntings, smooth-billed ani,
flycatchers, red-legged thrushes,
Bahama woodstar, a variety of hummingbirds, green herons, yellow-
crowned night herons, egrets,
limpkins, mangrove cuckoos, white-
cheeked pintail ducks, burrowing
owls, and various woodpeckers (called
"peckerwoods" in local parlance).
Summer brings the gray kingbird,
Greater Antillean nighthawk, and
black-whiskered vireo.

BLUE HOLES Both offshore and inland, sinkholes in the limestone have created the islands' dramatic blue holes. Some are so deep divers have been unable to reach the bottom. Andros is known for its wealth of blue holes. Those inland and easily accessible (if you don't mind a short hike) include **Captain Bill's** (Small Hope), **Rainbow Blue Hole** (Small Hope), and **Uncle Charlie's** (North Andros). Offshore Andros, divers explore others from 40 to 200 feet deep. Exuma's **Thunderball Grotto** starred in a James Bond movie and remains a popular dive site. South Eleuthera has its popular inland **Ocean Hole Park.** One of the islands' most renowned, **Deal's Blue Hole** on Long Island, is said to the deepest and is certainly one of the prettiest—surrounded by beach and sheer cliffs. It is the site of a biannual international free-diving competition.

BOATING The islands' earliest means of transport has survived and expanded to a favorite pastime for visitors. Many, in fact, arrive by boat. **Bimini** especially caters to the summer South Florida boating crowd because of its close proximity. **Bahamas Boating Flings** (800-32-SPORT) is the Bahamian equivalent of a road trip, when a caravan of boats crosses the Gulf Stream and island-hops through Bimini and surrounding islands for a week or so. To see boats in the making on Bimini, hook up with **Bonefish Ansil Saunders** (242-347-2178). **Abaco** is another boating hot spot—both as a destination and a boatbuilding capital. Marinas are plentiful, as are boat rentals and charters. In addition, a dependable ferry service transports locals and visitors to the outlying cays, such as **Man-O-**

War Cay, where you can also find boatbuilders and model boat-crafters at work. **Regatta,** usually in summer, is the biggest event next to Junkanoo on most of the islands.

BREAD It perfumes the morning air and ranks as a matter of pride on every Out Island. Islanders make their own bread or patronize a favorite bakery where the cook puts her culinary thumbprint on every loaf. In general, Bahamian bread is white and sweet, and some has a hint of coconut flavor. Certain islands boast a signature, such as **Bimini Bread,** which shares its sweetness with the dough made for pizza locally. The most regal of Bahamian breads, however, comes from **Sands Bakery** (242-332-6143) in Eleuthera—once a favorite of Princess Diana and Prince Charles during their stays on the island. Cousin **johnnycake** is a dense, unleavened bread baked in loaves and usually served steaming hot for breakfast.

BREAKFAST, TRADITIONAL
Move over, ham and eggs. In the Bahama Islands, breakfast favorites take a turn toward the unusual. Most well-loved are chicken souse and boil' fish, both also known as Bahamian penicillin and a hangover cure. They are brothy concoctions seasoned with lime juice, hot peppers, and onions. Variations include conch, pig's feet, mutton, and sheep tongue souse—all best sopped up with hot johnnycake, which is baked in loaves with a hint of sweetness. Stew fish is another favorite—hearty with a tomato-based gravy. If you're lucky, you'll find stew conch on the menu or a dish known as "fire engine"—corned beef hash and grits with a spicy red sauce. Look

for traditional breakfast menus at home-cooking restaurants, usually named for the owners such as **Becky's** (242-352-5247) and **Geneva's Place** (242-352-5085) in Freeport, **Café Skan's** (242-322-2486) in Nassau, and **Sam's Place** (242-336-2579) in George Town, Great Exuma.

BUSH MEDICINE In recent years, islanders have resurrected the old-time cures of their grandmothers by making teas out of the leaves, berries, bark, and other components of native plants. On some of the Out Islands, you can find tours that explain to you what plants are good for what ailments, such as fever grass to bring down high temperatures, strongback to strengthen back muscles, kamalame leaves for diarrhea, and stiffcock—well, I think you can figure that one out. You can self-tour the **Bush Medicine Trail** on Andros Island with a booklet from **Small Hope Bay Lodge** (242-368-2013 or 800-223-6961; www.smallhope.com). At **Nettie's Different of Nassau** (242-327-8153; www.nettiesplace .com, changing to www.netties differentofnassau.com), you can get a tour of the gardens, learn the plants' uses, and sip hot, sweetened fever grass tea. Ask your hotel staff on other islands for similar tours.

CAVES The Bahamas' honeycombed limestone foundation means a boon for spelunkers. Whether you explore them by foot or fin, they divulge secrets and mysteries, including a rare crustacean found nowhere else, nesting bats, Indian drawings, and, in the past, even prehistoric skeletons. The **Burial Cave,** in fact, is one of two you can descend at **Lucayan National**

Park (242-352-5438; www.bnt.bs) on Grand Bahama Island. It is part of one of the world's longest mapped underground cave systems. On Long Island, explore **Deadman's Cay Cave** (if you dare, given the name), **Dunmore's Cave,** and **Hamilton's Cave.** Ask around to find a guide who will take you.

CHURCHES Highly religious, Bahama islanders dress up in finery and put on their best voices to attend Sunday services. The **Baptist** religion is high on the list, and its services are probably the most vocal and colorful. **Anglicanism** and **Catholicism** generally rank second and third. The islands' plentiful churches and religious sites include some historic beauties. Most famous is **The Hermitage** on Cat Island, built as a religious retreat for a priest-architect known as Father Jerome, who designed several churches in the 1940s on **Cat Island** and **Long Island. Nassau** has its share of beautiful old churches, as well, most notably circa-1670 **Christ Church Cathedral** (242-322-4186), circa-1802 **St. Matthew's Anglican Church** (242-323-8220), and circa-

1886 **St. Francis Xavier Cathedral**
(242-322-8528; www.stfrancisxavier
cathedral.com), the first Catholic
Church in the Bahamas.

COMMUNICATIONS Telephone
calls to and from the Bahamas can be
quite costly using regular land-line
and international cell phone plans.
Avoid using the long-distance phone
machines you'll see all over the
islands—they are crazy expensive.
Also be aware that making toll-free
calls from your hotel phone will be
charged at a per-minute rate. That
said, the best way to communicate
with and from the islands is by Internet. Most resorts and hotels, even the
smallest, have wireless access. Some
charge—mainly the larger, chain
properties. In the Out Islands people
often don't answer their phones, so
try, try again. Also in the smaller
islands, TV is not a given, especially in
the rooms (many of which also have
no phones). Small properties often
have one satellite TV in the lobby
area.

CONCH The queen conch reigns as a
cultural symbol, culinary trademark,
and economic mainstay of the islands.
Practically every restaurant prepares
it in one way or another. Most popular are tomato-based conch chowder
and a cevichelike dish made fresh
before your eyes and known simply as
conch salad. Cracked conch is tenderized, breaded, and deep-fried. Stew'
conch or conch souse appear on true
Bahamian breakfast menus. **Toni
Macaroni's** (242-533-6766) on Grand
Bahama Island is known for its roasted conch, while **Billy Joe's** (242-373-
1333), also on Grand Bahama, is
known for its grilled conch. Throughout the islands, you'll find conch in
everything from omelets and pizza to
sushi and stir fry.

CRAB As far as the dinner table goes,
there are two kinds of crab in the
Bahamas. They couldn't be further
apart in habitat, taste, and prepara-
tion, however. The **stone crab** lives
in the sea, where fishermen relieve
them of their rock-hard claws, which
regenerate in a year's time. Diners
enjoy them cold and dipped in mus-
tard sauce or warm dipped in drawn
butter. **Land crabs,** on the other
hand, live most of their lives, as their
name suggests, on terra firma,
although they lay their eggs and hatch
in seawater. Islanders, particularly on
Andros Island and other old-
Bahamian style islands, harvest them
as they make their trek across island,
migrating from low-lying areas when
they're flooded by summer rains.
Islanders cook up the crustaceans in
favorite folk-food dishes such as crab
soup or crab 'n' rice.

FILMING Movie-makers had a special contraption built along Grand
Bahama Island's shoreline to simulate

the motion of a sailing ship for the filming of the *Pirates of the Caribbean* movies. Many James Bond movies were filmed in and around Nassau, including *Thunderball*, *The Spy Who Loved Me*, *Moonraker*, *You Only Live Twice*, and *Casino Royale*. Other movies that take advantage of the Bahamas' inimitable natural stage set: *Cocoon*, *Jaws: the Revenge*, *Splash*, *Flipper*, *The Insider*, and *Into the Blue*.

FISHING **Grouper, snapper, mahimahi** (dolphinfish, dorado), and **wahoo** are the mainstays of Bahamian food fish. **Hog snapper** (aka hogfish), a deepwater species that must be spear-fished, is gaining popularity in restaurants. In the Out Islands, large **mutton snapper** feed islanders. In addition, deepwater game fish such as the national fish, **blue marlin,** challenge anglers. **Bonefish** provide the ultimate test for fly and other specialized fishermen. The Bahamas depend heavily on their fish populations both for food and economic reasons that go well beyond commercial fishing. They draw recreational fishermen, snorkelers, and divers looking for guides, accommodations, and all that goes along with a sporting vacation to the Bahamas. In fact, the islands' reefs, blue holes, and grass flats—home to the coveted bonefish—are the main reason visitors love the Out Islands.

HAIR-BRAIDING As iconic of a Bahamas vacation as a suntan and rum hangover, hair-braiding is especially prevalent in the major tourism areas of Nassau and Grand Bahama Island. Government-licensed braiders congregate around **Nassau's cruise ship docks,** in **straw markets,** and

at **Port Lucaya Marketplace** (242-373-8446) on Grand Bahama. They typically charge $2 per braid up to 15 and about $120 for a full head.

HUNTING On **Long Island,** September marks the opening of bird hunting season, when sportsmen beat the bush for coot, whistling ducks, and white-crowned pigeons. It runs through December. On **Andros Island,** wild boar hunting and land crab harvesting offer visitors a true island adventure. Ask your resort staff or talk to the people at the tourist office for information.

JUNKANOO In one word, the spirit of the Bahamas is expressed in Junkanoo. Holiday-time festivities that started in the slavery era, Junkanoo was forced underground during certain periods, but gained a new exuberance and significance in local culture as tourists begin showing their appreciation. The grandest celebration takes place in **Nassau** on Boxing Day—the day after Christmas—and again on New Year's Day. Year-round, small Junkanoo bands—dressed in colorful crepe-paper or fabric-strip costumes and playing bells, whistles, drums, and brass instruments—appear at clubs and attractions for entertainment. Practically every island stages its own Christmastime version of Nassau's all-day, highly competitive affair. At any island festival and during summertime Goombay festivities, a Junkanoo rush-out (street party) is the entertainment de rigueur. The rich, old, African-based tradition has informed and inspired every aspect of life and culture in the islands. Its influence can never be overestimated.

LANGUAGE Bahamians speak their own brand of English, influenced equally by early British and African settlers. The result: British pronunciation with a musical lilt and often humorous twist. Their speech is easily enough understood, when they want it to be. Get some Bahamians talking among themselves in a group, though, and you might get lost.

LOBSTER Known as **Caribbean spiny lobster** or locally as crawfish, the species *Panulirus argus* has no claws, but its tail meat is tender and sweet—more so than the Maine lobster, some insist. Lobster season in the Bahamas runs August 1 through March 31, when you'll find it fresh and plentiful in local restaurants.

KID STUFF Most kids will be thrilled with the islands' natural attributes—their beaches, shallow and clear seas, and marine creatures. At age 4, my son was much more impressed with snorkeling at Andros' Small Hope Bay than whooshing down a water slide at **Atlantis Resort** (242-363-3000; www .atlantis.com) on Paradise Island. Atlantis, however, is the ultimate family attraction in the Bahamas, with endless aquariums, slides, animal encounters, kids programs, and other activities to keep them enthralled and sensory-overloaded. If you're not staying there, you can buy day passes. Nassau's **Ardastra Gardens and Zoo** (242-323-5806; www.ardastra .com) has some hands-on bird interactions in addition to cool animals that kids love. Children age 6 and older will most appreciate **Pirates of Nassau** (242-356-3759; www.pirates -of-nassau.com). **Dolphin and sting ray encounters** throughout the islands are also popular with families.

MUSEUMS Nassau claims the majority of Bahamian museums, including the **Balcony House** (242-302-2621), **Bahamas Historical Society Museum** (242-322-4231), **Nassau Public Library & Museum** (242-322-4907), and **Pompey Museum of Slavery & Emancipation** (242-356-0495). Many of the Out Islands hold small museums often sit-

uated in historic homes, such as **Wyannie Malone Historical Museum** (242-366-0293; www.hopetown museum.com) and **Albert Lowe Museum** (242-365-4094) in Abaco, the **Long Island Library, Museum, and Community Centre** (242-337-0500), **Bimini Museum** (242-347-3038), and **Erickson Museum & Library** (242-339-1863) on Great Inagua.

MUSIC, INDIGENOUS The most indigenous form of music in the islands, **rake 'n' scrape** employs household items such as old saws along with goatskin drums and, in more sophisticated bands, accordions and tambourines. In its bygone days, goat's jawbones sometimes were involved. **Cat Island** is credited as the birthplace of the form. Other types of Caribbean music such as **calypso, soca** (a soul-calypso hybrid),

and **reggae** also influence local styles. The greatest historic influence, however, is the high-energy sound of **Junkanoo**—bells, whistles, and brass instruments. **Gospel** is another popular form of music, along with the sounds of the **Royal Bahamian Police Band.** The Bahamas' greatest claim to musical fame was the short-lived popularity of **Baha Men** in the U.S. with their hit, "Who Let the Dogs Out."

NATIONAL PARKS The **Bahamas National Trust** (242-393-1317; www .bnt.bs) has created and maintains a number of national preserves throughout the chain. **Lucayan National Park** (242-352-5438) on Grand Bahama Island is one of the most easily accessible. Here you can take a staircase down into its caves and hike to a secluded beach. **Clifton Heritage National Park** (242-362-5360) on New Providence offers a glimpse of history at its plantation and other ruins. Others require guides, a boat, or sometimes even a snorkel and mask. **Abaco National Park** (no phone) on Great Abaco calls for a four-wheel-drive vehicle and a guide. You'll need a boat to explore **Exuma Cays Land & Sea Park.** You must prearrange a tour with the local warden of **Inagua National Park** (242-339-1616) on Great Inagua, home to the islands' largest flamingo colony.

PEOPLE-TO-PEOPLE PROGRAM To experience Bahamian culture one-on-one, the Ministry of Tourism's **People-to-People Program** (242-324-9772 or 242-356-0435; www .bahamas.com/peopletopeople) can match visitors with Bahamian families who will share their careers, hobbies, and other interests. Call prior to your visit. The program also hosts teas and other visitor opportunities on some of the islands. On the last Friday of the month from January through August, Nassau's program hosts a free tea party for visitors in the **Government House** (242-323-1853) ballroom.

PLANTATIONS Ever since the Loyalists arrived on the islands with their slaves after the American Revolutionary War, farming has sustained islanders. Early 18th-century plantations grew sugar, cotton, sisal, and pineapple. Ruins of these plantations stand as stark reminders of a cruel chapter in history. The best-preserved are those of **Clifton Heritage National Park** (242-362-5360) on New Providence. Long Island has its share you can visit: **Adderley's Plantation, Dunmore's Plantation,** and **Gray's Plantation.** On Great Exuma, there are **Crab Cay Ruins** and **Hermitage Estate Ruins.**

PRIVATE ISLANDS Many of the smallest Bahamian islands are privately owned, some by celebrities, others by resorts—including **Little Whale Cay** in the Berry Islands and **Musha Cay** in Exuma. Some tour operators have their own islands where they

take guests to recreate for the day, such as **Blackbeard's Cay** near Nassau. Many of the cruise ships maintain private island destinations for their passengers. Disney's **Castaway Cay** and Royal Caribbean's **CoCo Cay** are part of the Berry Islands. Norwegian stops at **Great Stirrup Cay,** also in the Berrys. Holland America's **Half Moon Cay** lies between south Eleuthera and Cat Island.

RUM DRINKS Like their counterparts in the Caribbean, the islands of the Bahamas are synonymous with rum. Whereas you'll find all the typical rum punches, piña coladas, and daiquiris, the Bahamas also claim a couple of their own signature rum concoctions. Most well-known, the **Bahama Mama** gets every party started with its mix of gold rum, coconut rum, and orange and pineapple juice. More enigmatic, the **Goombay Smash** was invented at **Miss Emily's Blue Bee Bar** (242-365-4181) on Green Turtle Cay in Abaco. Miss Emily's daughter, who now runs the colorful establishment, continues to keep the recipe a secret, but many places try to emulate the potent quaff.

SETTLEMENTS Bahamians use this word as we might use "villages," basically anything too small to be considered a town. Here's where visitors can experience the true Bahamian way of life centered around the church and fishing or farming. Many of the settlements are "generational land," meaning anyone related to the families that own land there can rightfully claim unclaimed land.

SNORKELING & SCUBA DIVING
It's just wrong to visit the Bahamas without doing some underwater sight-

seeing, because you'll not find any prettier waters and vibrant marine life anywhere. It doesn't matter which island you decide upon, snorkeling and diving will be available. Some of the tiniest, most remote islands might not have rentals, tours, or certification courses, but the major islands have lots of options from which to choose. Shops and tours take care of everyone, from novice snorkelers to experienced divers. If you're not a certified diver, you may want to consider completing the advance class work at home and scheduling your certification dives for the warm, swimming-pool-clear waters of the Bahamas. Islands specifically known for their diving include **Grand Bahama Island,** where **UNEXSO** (242-373-1244 or 800-992-3483; www.unexso .com) has a reputation for excellence and shark and dolphin diving; and **Andros Island,** where **Small Hope Bay Lodge** (242-368-2013 or 800-223-6961; www.smallhope.com) dives take you "over the wall." For snorkeling, I recommend **Brendal's Dive Center** (242-365-4411; www.brendal .com) in Green Turtle Cay and **Stuart Cove's Snorkel Bahamas** (242-362-4171; www.stuartcove.com) in Nassau. If you yearn to see the reefs without getting wet, Stuart Cove's also offers personal submarine expeditions, where you navigate your own sea-horse-shaped underwater vessel. Glass-bottom boat tours are another option, and you'll find them in Nassau and Grand Bahama Island.

STRAW WORK Straw markets fill the islands, ranging from a stand or two to Nassau's massive downtown spread. Most carry cheap-imitation baskets from Asia along with T-shirts and other cheesy souvenirs. For the

true brand of hand-plaited straw work that originally gave the islands its reputation for baskets, look for work that comes from **Long Island** and **Andros.** In Nassau, **The Plait Lady** (242-363-1416) carries these artisan baskets. On Long Island, visit the settlement of **Oneil's** to watch plaiters at work and buy their wares. On Andros, **Red Bay** is home to a community of Seminole Indian descendants who weave their baskets with Androsia Batik fabric also made on the island.

TOURIST INFORMATION The **Bahamas Ministry of Tourism** (800-448-3386; www.bahamas.com) oversees matters on all of the main islands. For specific information on the Out Islands, contact the **Bahamas Out Island Promotion Board** (305-931-6612 (U.S.) or 800-688-4752; www.myoutislands.com). For phone numbers to tourism offices on individual islands, see chapter 11, *Information.*

TRANSPORTATION, BY AIR & BOAT Nassau is the main hub for commercial airlines flying into the Bahamas, although there are also direct flights from Florida and other U.S. cities to Grand Bahama Island, Abaco, Bimini, Eleuthera, and Exuma. **Bahamasair** is the country's national airline, plus a few U.S. airlines make regular flights. Smaller commercial planes fly between Nassau and the Out Islands. Besides commercial flights, the Bahamas see a great deal of charter and private jet traffic. All the major islands have an airport, and the smaller ones and some resorts have their own airstrip. Many arrivals to the Bahamas are by boat, whether by cruise ship into Nassau or Freeport or by private boat. **Bimini** is most popular with boaters from South Florida because it is the closest island to shore.

TRANSPORTATION, GETTING AROUND Roundabouts, driving on the left, and no-name roads: Driving can be a challenge for first-time visitors to the Bahamas. Maps are inexact and directions—given, again, that some roads have no or many names—can be even iffier. Nassau is the scariest for the unaccustomed, but driving is a great way to get out of the city to New Providence Island's less-visited beaches, restaurants, and attractions. First-timers may want to consider taxi, bus, or tours. Grand Bahama

Island is easier to navigate, with less traffic and straight, long roads. On many of the Out Islands, one road— usually named either King's or Queen's Highway—runs from end to end, with occasional turnoffs to settlements that merit leaving the main thoroughfare. Small islands have little to no vehicular traffic, and you travel instead by golf cart, bike, or foot. The ultimate way to explore island groups is by boat—a rental if you're good at reading charts, or a charter if you're not.

WEDDINGS Take the plunge from a trapeze or at the bottom of the sea. Choose a garden backdrop, a barefoot beach wedding, or a historic setting. You can even opt for a dolphin ring bearer! The choices are endless in the Bahamas. Some of the most popular settings include **Versailles Gardens at One&Only Ocean Club** (242-363-2501 or 800-321-3000; www.one andonlyresorts.com) on Paradise Island, historic **Graycliff Hotel** (242-302-9150; www.graycliff.com) in Nassau, and **Garden of the Groves** (242-374-7778) on Grand Bahama Island. The trapeze wedding? Check out **Breezes Bahamas** (242-327-5356 or 800-GO-SUPER; www.super clubs.com) on New Providence Island. Within the book we note properties that are popular wedding spots with the ring symbol ♂.

HISTORY

Like the very tides that wash its shores and dictate much of its daily schedule, the nation known as the Bahama Islands tells its past in terms of ebb and flow, boom and bust, halcyon and turbulence. So close to American mainland shores, but so isolated by their vast dispersal and limited resources, the islands have a history of welcoming refugees, rebels, and transients.

A difficult culture to define because of the influences that have swept through with the tides, the Bahamas get lumped into the Caribbean ball of wax, mostly because they share a strong African-based heritage. The nation, however, does not border the Caribbean Sea and differs from Caribbean islands by its makeup and extreme internal diversity. The Bahama Islands is like no other place, and each of its 14 major islands—even many of its minor cays—tells a story all its own. So here I will only overview the islands' peaks and valleys and introduce the major players, while going into more depth within each chapter on each major island's historical and cultural perspective.

NATURAL HISTORY & GEOGRAPHY

"Having landed, they saw trees very green, and much water, and fruits of diverse kinds."

—Bartolome de las Casas, Columbus's biographer

ROCKY PAST Believed to be the remains of an ancient mountain range, the Bahamas' 700 major islands and thousands of smaller cays lie distributed on either side of the Tropic of Cancer. Made up principally of coral limestone, the islands' inherent flatness is interrupted by the karst cliffs and caves that the topography creates. Its highest point, 206 feet above sea level, "towers" over Cat Island and is known as Mount Alvernia.

Nearly as important as its landside complexion, Bahama waters fill the valleys of yore—deep channels such as the Gulf Stream, Crooked Island Passage, and the Tongue of the Ocean. Of the nearly 100,000 square miles the archipelago occupies, most of it is the liquid Bahamas. Its land mass accounts for only 5,380 square miles, roughly the size of Connecticut.

WIND-CARVED LIMESTONE CLIFFS LEND STRONG CLUES TO THE BEDROCK FOUNDATION OF THE BAHAMA ISLANDS.

Water and culture are the Bahamas gifts to the world, and the two are inextricably intertwined.

Through the eras, the sea has provided inhabitants with sustenance and livelihood, from commercial fishing to diving and snorkeling charters. Its estimated 900 square miles of coral reefs include the world's third longest and one of its most vital. It caches 5 percent of the entire world's supply of coral.

Both offshore and inland, sinkholes in the limestone have created the islands' dramatic blue holes. Some are so deep divers have been unable to reach the bottom. Eerily beautiful and mysterious, they have inspired local legends of the "lusca," an octopuslike monster that pulls sailors who enter its world to their death.

In Grand Bahama Island's Lucayan National Park, divers explore one of the world's most extensive cave systems, where they have found Lucayan skeletons and other artifacts, plus a rare species of crustacean.

SPECIES OF THE BUSH Most of the islands' land acreage remains unsettled, even on populated islands such as Grand Bahama and Abaco. Bahamians call the natural lands "the bush"; the plants and herbs that grow there are made into teas or applied externally as "bush medicine." Yellow

BAHAMA TALK
Cay: It's not OK to say "kay." Every time you do, you'll have to take a swig of Bahama Mama. (Stop: That's supposed to *deter* you from mispronouncing it.) It is pronounced "key." Technically a cay, from the Spanish word *cayo,* is a small, low-lying island or reef formed from sand or coral.

THE TASTY, CHERISHED CUSTARD APPLE BEARS FRUIT IN THE LATE SUMMER.

pines and casuarinas grow tallest in the bush, followed by coconut and cabbage palms. Many different fruiting plants have been introduced to the islands over the centuries, including mangoes, sapodillas (called "dilly" here), citrus, guava, various types of plums, custard apple, tamarind, and mamey. About 120 species of its 1,370 different kinds of plants are native to the Bahamas, including the yellow elder bush, the national flower, which blooms October through March. Lignum vitae, the national tree, is cherished for its hard wood and the medicinal properties that earn it its name "tree of life."

The environment generally falls into five different categories: beach, sandy or whiteland coppice (hardwood forest), mangroves, rocky coppice, and pine forest. The different habitats host rare species of birds not found elsewhere. The endangered Bahama parrot (*Amazona leucocephala bahamensis*) clings to existence in preserves on Great Inagua and Great Abaco Island. Specific to the northern Bahamas, the Bahama swallow (*Tachycineta cyaneoviridis*) is a year-rounder. The country's national bird, the pink flamingo, mostly inhabits Great Inagua, home to the western hemisphere's largest breeding colony, but can be found from time to time at the south end of Long Island and on other southern cays. Other life-list sightings include Cuban bananaquits, painted buntings, smooth-billed ani, flycatchers, red-legged thrushes, Bahama woodstar, humming-birds, green herons, yellow-crowned night herons, egrets, limpkins, mangrove cuckoos, white-cheeked pintail ducks, burrowing owls, and various woodpeckers

THE IRIDESCENT BIMINI BOA IS A SUBSPECIES OF THE BAHAMA BOA.

(called "peckerwoods" in local parlance). In the summers, the gray kingbird, Greater Antillean nighthawk, and black-whiskered vireo visit.

Besides birds, the Bahamas hosts various reptiles including iguanas, freshwater terrapins, three species of boa constrictors, Cuban tree frogs, and the iconic curly tailed lizard (*Leiocephalus carinatus*). A couple of lower islands are the last holdout for a rare, large (8- to 24-inch) rodent known as the Bahamian hutia (*Geocapromys ingrahami*). Butterflies (or "flutterbys," as some islanders call them) are the stars of the insect world, including the Mexican fritillary, Bahama swallowtail, and common buckeye. Spiders such as the big, colorful banana spider live in the bush and generally don't bother anybody. At least not as much as the mosquitoes, sand flies (aka no-see-ums), and doctor flies do.

Indigenous mammals include raccoons, but wild horses and wild boars still roam some of the Out Islands, descendants of animals left by early settlers.

UNDER THE SEA In the crustacean world, the land crab is one of few species that begins its life as a marine creature before becoming terrestrial. It is a favorite form of folk cuisine in the islands, celebrated at an annual festival on Andros.

Grand Bahama Island claims its own rare species of crustacean, the blind, colorless remipedia known as *Speleonectes lucayensis,* discovered in its underwater caves. In surrounding salt waters, the spiny lobster, also known as crawfish, and the queen conch are the most emblematic of sea creatures because of their food value and importance to the culture. Conch is so crucial to the Bahamian diet that islanders protest against suggestions to limit harvesting as populations become weakened. To a lesser degree, shrimp also figures importantly into restaurant menus, but not so much Bahamian home cooking.

GREEN TURTLES, ONCE AN IMPORTANT FOOD SOURCE IN THE BAHAMAS, ARE NOW PROTECTED BY LAW.

In September 2009, the Bahamas Ministry of Agriculture and Marine Resources enforced an official ban on "harvesting, possession, purchase, and sale of turtles, their part and eggs." The measure protects the entire nation's populations of green, loggerhead, and hawksbill turtles, the latter of which have been protected since 1986.

Grouper, snapper, mahimahi (dolphinfish, dorado), and wahoo are the mainstays of Bahamian food fish. Hog snapper (aka hogfish), a deepwater species that must be spear-fished, is gaining popularity in restaurants. In the Out Islands, mutton fish or mutton snapper feed islanders. In addition, deepwater game fish, such as the national fish, blue marlin, challenge anglers. Bonefish provide the ultimate challenge for fly and other specialized fishermen.

The Bahamas depend heavily on their fish populations both for food and economic reasons that go well beyond commercial fishing. They draw recreational fishermen, snorkelers, and divers looking for guides, accommodations, and all that go along with a sporting vacation to the Bahamas. In fact, the islands' reefs, blue holes, and grass flats—home to the coveted bonefish—are the main reason visitors love the Out Islands.

Geographywise, the islands are divided between the two main metropolitan islands and the Out Islands, known also as the Family Islands. **New Providence** and **Paradise Islands** are the Bahamas' governmental and resort centers. **Grand Bahama Island** ranks second for tourism. The remainder of the islands range from resort meccas for boaters to quiet little islands with a few bonefish lodges and lots of nature.

SOCIAL HISTORY

> *"They go as naked as when their mothers bore them, and so do the women, although I did not see more than one girl. They are very well made, with very handsome bodies, and very good countenances."*
>
> —Admiral Christopher Columbus, Oct. 12, 1492

LUCAYANS TO LOYALISTS The first known inhabitants of the Bahama Islands were a tribe known as the Lucayans, a subset of the Caribbean Arawaks. Some estimated 40,000 populated the islands at one time. Their peaceful existence erupted on Oct. 12, 1492, when Christopher Columbus made his first New World landfall on their island of Guanahani. He renamed it after the Holy Savior, San Salvador. The name "Bahamas," historians believe, came from the Spanish words *baja mar*, shallow sea—obviously by sailors approaching from the leeward side of the islands.

Shortly after Columbus burst onto the scene, the Lucayan population was wiped out due to enslavement, relocation, and disease. They left in their wake some vocabulary words such as hurricane and iguana, plus a scattering of artifacts and art found in caves.

The Bahamas remained unsettled for 100 years before the French established a colony on Abaco in the 1500s, but it was short-lived. In 1647 a group of British settlers arrived to another Out Island, escaping Cromwellian religious persecution. They called themselves the Company of Eleutheran Adventurers, after the Greek word for "freedom," and named the island where they settled Eleuthera, which became the first Bahama island to have a written constitution.

The biggest population influx came, however, on the tails of the American Revolutionary War in the late 1700s. American settlers who had supported the British government found themselves in a dangerous situation, so more than 8,000 of these British Loyalists—from New England to the Carolinas—fled to the Bahamas, bringing with them their African slaves. They settled largely on the islands of Exuma, Abaco, and Eleuthera.

King Charles II had granted the Bahamas to six lord proprietors a century earlier, and so the colony already existed under the broad British Commonwealth umbrella. Before the Loyalists arrived, the town of Nassau had been thriving, first as a pirate's haven and later, with the appointment of Captain Woodes Roger as governor in 1717, as a government-ruled entity with two forts protecting its harbor.

American warships and the Spanish military both made attacks on Nassau in the late 1700s. The U.S. was successful the first time, 1776, and held Fort Montagu for a short while. A second attempt in 1778 failed. As for the Spanish, their brief possession ended with a treaty in 1783.

The British Loyalists introduced a plantation economy to the island, first growing cotton, which failed due to the islands' rocky, thin soil and an infestation of the chenille bug. Many forsook their plantations, leaving the land and their names to the slaves they also abandoned. With the abolition of slavery in 1838, any hope of agricultural success withered on the vine.

A MONUMENT IN THE SCULPTURE GARDEN ON GREEN TURTLE CAY PAYS HOMAGE TO LOYALIST SUBJECTS WHO FLED FROM AMERICA TO THE BAHAMAS FOLLOWING U.S. INDEPENDENCE.

FLUCTUATIONS The American Civil War sparked a brief flash of prosperity for Nassau, a major supply base for the Confederacy. Its first resort opened and Nassau's future was sealed. While it developed as a fashionable winter destination, the Out Islands' populations struggled for subsistence. Some made a living growing sisal to make rope, but Mexican competition strangled that prospect. The sponging industry brought a flush of prosperity until it succumbed to fungus. Lumbering, the salt industry, pineapple fields, and other farming enterprises came and went. Pineapple growing on Eleuthera, farming on Andros and Long Island, and the salt industry on Great Inagua continue to contribute to the economy. Commercial fishing steadily provided income for the Out Islanders and even residents of Grand Bahama Island and Nassau.

As the resort trade grew in Nassau, the more intrepid visitors made their way to Grand Bahama Island and the Out Islands, and starting in the 1940s small guest houses, fishing lodges, and resorts popped up. Some, such as Jack Tar Village in Grand Bahama Island's West End, Bimini Bay Rod & Gun Club and the Compleat Angler on Bimini, Cape Eleuthera in South Eleuthera, and Andros Beach Hotel in North Andros, later became the haunts of the wealthy and famous. Names such as Ernest Hemingway, John Steinbeck, Ian Fleming, Rockefeller, and Charlie Chapin filled guest books.

In the 1950s, American financier Wallace Groves developed Freeport on Grand Bahama Island as a cargo and cruise ship port, and the extravagant Princess Resort grew in its wake. The Bahamas reached its zenith as a resort destination in the 1960s and '70s.

Then, in 1973, the Bahamas declared its independence from the British government, creating its own nation and government on July 10, and ending 325 years of British rule. A deep national pride grew, and many of the rich traditions, music, dance, arts, and local language that persisted in the Out Islands were revived in Nassau. Holiday-time Junkanoo festivities, which started in the slavery era and were, during certain periods, forced underground, gained a new exuberance and significance in local culture.

Nassau resorts grew ever grander. First came the $300 million Crystal Palace Resort and Casino on Cable Beach in 1990. Five years later, Atlantis on Paradise Island raised the bar for megaresorts in the Americas. The opening of Our Lucaya on Grand Bahama Island marked another landmark occasion for Bahamas tourism, upon which the nation has now become primarily dependent.

That's good news when the American economy is strong, as the majority of visitors come from the U.S. At press time, the Bahamian people, especially in Grand Bahama Island and some of the Out Islands, were experiencing yet another ebb from the halcyon days of the past decade, when corporate jet-in business bolstered the economy. Plans for expansions, including a new megaresort where Crystal Palace first opened, are in a holding pattern as the next chapter of Bahamian history waits to be written.

BAHAMIAN PEOPLE

"Even in this small black settlement on the coast of an island isolated on the western edge of the Atlantic Ocean the people still reaches back instinctively to an almost forgotten heritage that still shone through the complex imposition of everything else that had happened to them in the centuries since Africa had been their home."
—Samuel Charters in The Day Is So Long and the Wages So Small

The complexion of the Bahamas, 338,000 people strong, has been influenced by many cultures, but none so much as the African slaves brought to the islands by their American mainland plantation masters. The presence of the British Loyalists lurks still in certain settlements such as Harbour Island and Spanish Wells in Eleuthera, and Green Turtle Cay and Elbow Cay in Abaco, where old island families such as the Lowes, Malones, and Armbristers still live.

Other cultures, from Canadian and Greek to Seminole Indian and Haitian, have stirred their flavor into the melting pot. Exotic traditions have stewed in the pot over time, many still found in the Out Islands and even revived in the cities.

Islanders all speak English, but with a bit of a British lilt and some colloquialisms and shortcuts that can be difficult to understand if you're listening from the outside.

To experience Bahamian culture on a one-on-one basis, the Ministry of Tourism's **People-to-People Program** (242-324-9772 or 242-356-0435; www .bahamas.com/peopletopeople) can match visitors up with Bahamian families who share careers, hobbies, and other interests. Call prior to your visit. The program also hosts teas and other visitor opportunities on some of the islands.

ART & ARCHITECTURE

Nassau holds the richest trove of historic architecture along Bay Street and its side streets, where churches, forts, and other buildings—built in Georgian styles that reflect their British roots—date from the 18th and 19th centuries. You'll also see a bit of U.S. Southern plantation, classic revival influence in the public buildings.

In the Out Islands, the gingerbread and shipwright architecture of New England shows in picket fence settlements with pitched roofs, storybook gables, and clapboard siding painted in pastels.

The Bahamas have had a strong visual arts tradition since the early 19th century, when Winslow Homer came here to paint the magically hued colors of the sea and flora flooded with tropical light, light that makes the colors pop with an intensity exclusive to these latitudes.

Alton Lowe, the best known and most successful Bahamian artist in history, paints realistic portraits of all aspects of Bahamian life from his home on Green Turtle Cay in the Abaco Islands. Much of his work is available for pennies on the postage stamps he creates.

Junkanoo has greatly influenced the arts in the Bahamas, far beyond performance art. The late Brent Malone fathered the tradition of art imitating street festivals with a detailed, realistic style that jumps from the canvas. More interpretative, John Beadle and Jackson and Stanley Burnside also create with Junkanoo colors and exuberance.

Other notable Bahamian visual artists include Maxwell Taylor, known principally for his haunting woodcut images, and the late Amos Ferguson, whose "Paints by Amos" combine Bahamian spirituality with intuitive simplicity.

Artists of another kind work in the

BAHAMA TALK

Bahamians often switch W and V sounds in their speech. For instance, an example Patricia Glinton-Meicholas gives on the cover of her *Talkin' Bahamian* book: "Ve is straw wendors." They also replace the th consonant blend with a simple T, dropping the h, as in "t'ree" instead of "three."

HARBOUR ISLAND EPITOMIZES THE BAHAMAS' TRADEMARK NEW ENGLAND-STYLE
COTTAGES.

medium of "straw"—actually the tops of the silver thatch or coconut palm tree.
You won't see their work in the straw markets, which typically import products
from abroad rather than hand-plait, as the old artisans in the Out Islands—particularly Long Island and Andros—do.

Woodcarvers, potters, shell crafters, model-boatbuilders, and other artisans
too keep alive age-old traditions born out of utilitarian need but raised to an art
form.

As far as performance art, there's that word again: Junkanoo. The African-
retained tradition informs and inspires nearly every type of music, theater, and
dance on the islands. At its basic, original form, it consisted of goat skin drums,
whistles, cowbells, and costumes. The instruments have stayed the same, with
the addition of brass backup, but the costuming has gone over the top (see side-
bar). Traditionally, it happens in Nassau and throughout the islands on Boxing
Day (the day after Christmas) and New Year's Day. Today, summertime Goombay Festivals and almost any special occasion call for at least one Junkanoo band,
if not the fierce competition of many that takes place in Nassau.

The goatskin drum and other improvised instruments gave rise to rake 'n'
scrape bands. Cat Island gets the credit for this art form that has spread
throughout the islands. Tambourines, saws and screwdrivers, and animal jawbones all have been used by these popular, colorful bands.

Local bands also play calypso and reggae music. Entirely Bahamian, gospel
music can be heard in bandstands and at special occasions as well as in churches.
The spit-and-polish Royal Bahamian Police Band reminds us of the islands'
strong British roots. It performs at major events throughout the islands.

The purest form of Bahamian dance is the quadrille—a precursor to square
dancing descended from colonial times. In Nassau and Freeport, dance and theater embrace their African and British heritage while appealing to a broader
audience with modern interpretations.

In 1994, the Smithsonian Institution's Festival of American Folklife Exhibit

JUNKANOO

"If you're losing control 'cause of the rhythm in your soul,
If you should be in bed, but you're on the street instead . . .
Junkanoo."

—Bahamian Junkanoo tune

Haunting rhythms thump softly on goatskin drums tightened over impromptu fires. Whistles scream shrilly, bells *ka-lik,* and color explodes in a combustion of feathers, sequins, and streamers: The images of Junkanoo today.

Throughout the Bahamas, Junkanoo translates as a cavalcade of costumed pageantry. Through the years, the festival has evolved from a ragtag celebration of a slave's day off, to a British-influenced mummers show, to an instrument of intimidation and revolt, then an underground tradition denounced as vulgar, and finally it paraded on to today's carnival-like extravaganza.

Masks, stilt dancers, drums, fifes, and costumes made of locally harvested sponge, fabric, and paper scraps typified the late-19th-century genesis of Nassau's Junkanoo. When outlawed in the 1920s, it went into hiding in the city backstreets and rural areas. The demands of visitors who had enjoyed the festive holiday scene effected the parade's reinstitution only a couple of years later as "John Canoe." There are many conjectures about the name, which eventually adopted a more islandy spelling as it came under tourism board auspices.

JUNKANOO TOUCHES THE LIVES OF BAHAMIANS IN COUNTLESS WAYS, INSPIRING ART, VIBRANCY, AND PRIDE. THIS METAL SCULPTURE OUTSIDE THE NATIONAL ART GALLERY OF THE BAHAMAS IN NASSAU REALISTICALLY DEPICTS A JUNKANOO REVELER.

Today massive local bands with names like The Valley Boys, Prodigal Sons, and Saxons compete. The bands dress in bright fringes of crepe paper and sequins layered onto cloth or gigantic cardboard or wooden headdress and shoulder frames. The party begins before daybreak on Boxing Day and continues in a burst of energy that is self-perpetuating.

gave Bahamian arts the shot in the arm needed to revive traditions that were on the verge of extinction by ridicule and shame. The Bahamian program showcased boat building, kite-making, Junkanoo, market crafts, music, religious practices, cuisine, bush medicine, and more during its duration.

ISLAND CUISINE

"Apart from talking about our health, no pastime is as dear to the heart of a Bahamian as eating."

—*Patricia Glinton-Meicholas in* How To Be a True-True Bahamian: A Hilarious Look at Life in the Bahamas

Perhaps how we eat tells the most about our history and heritage. Surely that's true in the Bahamas, where not surprisingly seafood and chicken are the culinary protein main course. Conch heads the list of seafood specialties. Most commonly cooks prepare it as crack' (cracked) conch—tenderized, breaded, and deep-fried. For a conch burger, slap it between a bun. Conch fritters and conch salad are equally popular, the latter made to order and "cooked" cevichelike with lime and orange juice, flavored with bell and hot peppers and onions. Wash it down with a Kalik beer, and you've got the Bahamian equivalent of "fast food."

More unusual and creative conch uses include everything from stew conch for breakfast to stir-fry conch, conch pizza, roasted or grilled conch, and even a conch omelet.

On the subject of stew conch, let's explore a bit what Bahamians call "traditional breakfast," usually enjoyed on the weekends. Besides stew conch, there's stew fish—prepared with a thick tomato-based gravy and usually served with grits. You'll never hunger for eggs at breakfast again.

Most emblematic of this class of breakfast dish are chicken souse and boil' fish, both also known as Bahamian penicillin and a hangover cure. They are brothy concoctions seasoned with lime juice, hot peppers, and onions. Variations include conch, pig's feet, mutton, and sheep tongue souse—all best sopped up with hot steaming johnnycake, baked in loaves with a hint of sweetness.

Other breakfast favorites cling to a prerefrigeration era and include "fire engine," corned beef hash and grits with a spicy red sauce; tuna (salad) and grits; and canned sardines and grits. If there's potato bread on the menu, don't pass it up. It's actually a puddinglike dish made with sweet potatoes.

CONCH CHOWDER AT FERNANDEZ BAY VILLAGE—TOMATO-BASED WITH JUST THE RIGHT AMOUNT OF SPICE.

Another sweet not to miss: guava duff. Used to be you could only get this jelly-roll-like confection topped with rum-spiked cream sauce in the summer during guava season. Now it's generally available year-round. Fancier restaurants do guava soufflé, crème brûlée, and cheesecake.

But here I am eating dessert before the main course is finished. Besides seafood—lobster, stone crab (lobster season runs August 1 through March 31; unlike Florida, stone crab season is year-round), snapper, grouper, mahimahi, wahoo, shark—and chicken, you'll find mutton (which really means goat) in the Out Islands and a lot of pork. Land crab is a home-cooked specialty, prepared with rice or as a soup.

Rice has an important place in the Bahamian kitchen, especially in the iconic peas 'n' rice. Made with pigeon peas, white rice, salt pork, and spices, it comes with practically every lunch or dinner. Other common side dishes include baked macaroni and cheese, slaw, and potato salad.

Bahamians eat heartily at lunch and dinner, so you may want to ask for a "snack" at lunchtime, which means the kitchen won't load your plate up to quite the capacity it normally would. When looking for good home cooking, steer to the "name" restaurants such as Geneva's Place, Becky's, and Toni Macaroni's.

Resort and other major restaurants take reservations. For small restaurants in the Out Islands and outside of town on New Providence and Grand Bahama Islands, it's a good idea to call ahead to make sure they're open. Often they require that you order your dinner ahead of time from the two or three selections they may offer that evening.

As for drinking, this is a male-dominated sport in the Bahamas, where they love their Kalik, Sands, and manly Strongback beer and maybe some rum. Tourists go for the sweet sticky signature drinks like Goombay Smash and Bahama Mama, plus the usual daiquiris and coladas.

SHOPPING

Straw markets, iconic of Bahamian shopping, can describe anything from a stand set up outside a hotel or attraction to a city block filled with vendors. Originally they sold handmade local goods, but these days you're more likely to find straw baskets, hats, and jewelry made in Asia. You get what you pay for in these markets, so if you buy T-shirts at three for $10, don't expect them to hold up beyond one washing. Vendors expect you to barter, so they'll start off with a high price. Take small bills for the best bargaining power. For more genuine souvenirs, ask around for galleries or Out Island settlements where artisans might congregate, such as Red Bays on Andros and Oneil's on Long Island.

Duty-free shopping is the other form of buying most associated with the Bahamas. Liquor, perfume, watches, jewelry, cameras, leather wares, linen, crystal, and china are among the most popular buys on which you can save anywhere from 20 to 40 percent. If you're used to duty-

BAHAMA TALK

Kalik: The Bahamas' first home-brewed beer, it gets its name onomatopoeically from the clang of Junkanoo cowbells.

free shopping in the Caribbean islands, you'll find the Bahamas slightly more expensive. Duty-free shops are in Nassau-Paradise Island, Freeport-Lucaya, and a couple of the Out Islands.

Each U.S. resident, including minors, is allowed to bring back duty-free purchases up to $800 if he has been out of the country for more than 48 hours and has not taken the exemption in 30 days. Exemption includes up to 2 liters (67.6 ounces) of liquor per person age 21 or older if 1 liter is manufactured in the Bahamas or Caribbean; 200 cigarettes and 100 cigars per person age 18 or older. Cuban cigars are not allowed in the U.S.

Most stores, with the exception of Atlantis's and other resort shops, close on Sunday. Be aware that usually if you charge purchases on a credit card, a foreign transaction fee will be added to your monthly statement.

WHICH ISLAND FOR YOU?

Here's a short guide to picking which island or islands are most suited to your Bahama vacationing interests. The destinations are listed from most visited to least visited.

Nassau/Paradise Island

Many pick this for their first-time Bahamas experience, and that's a good idea if you plan to combine it with an Out Island side trip. The Nassau area is for people who need to have a lot of vacation options and action. It has all the fishing, diving, boating, and beaches of the Out Islands, but it also has a lot of traffic, hype, and crime. Known mostly for its big theme resorts, it also has some small gems in and outside the city where you can get an authentic Bahamian experience. If casinos, fine restaurants, duty-free shopping, and nightlife are important

RENT A BOAT TO ISLAND-HOP TO GREEN TURTLE CAY AND ABACO'S OTHER DAY-TRIP CAYS.

Grand Bahama Island

Once a destination for the same kind of thrill-seeker Nassau attracts, it has
changed its focus of late toward golfing, diving, and ecotourism. It still has one
casino at its one megaresort. But with 96 miles of length, its attractions appeal to
people looking for kayaking, birding, and hiking adventure as well as the exploration of its remote beaches and old-island settlements, known as "generational
lands"—throwbacks to post-slavery days.

Abaco

The favorite activity here is renting a boat (or taking a ferry) to island-hop
around the various cays and settlements. Of course, fishing and diving are great
(with a little surfing thrown in), but not to quite the same reputation of other
Out Islands. It's the most developed of the Out Islands and has one golf course.

Eleuthera

Beaches, that's the number one reason. Surfing is another—it has the Bahamas'
best waves. Most people who visit stay on or at least day-trip to Harbour Island.
On the main island, you can get a sense of belonging in its small settlements.
Capital George Town has a movie theater, if that's important to you. There's also
a lot of good dive sites.

Exuma

Oddly, it attracts both people looking for a big, all-inclusive resort experience
and those who prefer becoming part of the local scene. Head north to Sandals
for the former, south to capital George Town for the latter. Aside from Sandals,
the accommodations are small and intimate; the restaurants "true true" Bahamian;
the bonefishing excellent.

Bimini

Most of its visitors are boaters, fishermen, and party-types from South Florida
who zip over during the spring and summer months. Two big resorts and a handful of smaller ones take care of their docking and landside needs. North Bimini
is packed with shops, restaurants, clubs, homes, and people. South Bimini, with
its one big resort, is more laid-back and natural, geared toward kayaking, ecotourism, and diving.

Andros

Bonefishing and diving: This island lives and breathes both. If that's the whole of
what you want, this is where you need to go. Most of the lodging revolves
around either or both, with all-inclusive meal and fishing packages. The biggest,
most undeveloped of the islands, it's also a good place to explore nature—especially its plethora of blue holes—and local culture.

Long Island

Islanders here still raise goats, farm fruit and vegetables, and plait straw work by
hand, meaning it's best for those who love the quiet, island way of life. Small
inns cater to boaters and beach-lovers; resorts at the north end are modern, full-
service complexes, but not in a hustle-bustle way.

Cat Island

Like Long Island, this is a retreat from fast pace to a slower lifestyle. It has all the beaches, diving, fishing, and even historic attractions. It doesn't have fancy restaurants or much in the way of shopping or nightlife except the rake 'n' scrape bands that originated here.

Other Out Islands

In the Berry Islands, like in neighboring Andros and Bimini, it's all about bonefishing and diving, with some very pretty beaches thrown in for good measure. Crooked and Acklins Islands and the Inagua Islands appeal to hard-core nature-lovers who come for the flamingos and other birds. Fishing and diving are good, but there's little or no service infrastructure other than a few small inns. San Salvador, on the other hand, is home to full-service, all-inclusive Club Med, known for its diving. Plus there's the historic hubbub over Columbus's landfall here.

SUGGESTED READING

The Bahamas: A Family of Islands, by Gail Saunders, a respected Bahamian historian. History and highlights with beautiful color photography.

Bahamas Saga: The Epic Story of the Bahama Islands, by Peter Barratt. A dense, detailed history; available through Amazon and other outlets. $19.95 paperback.

Bahamas: Independence & Beyond, edited by Wendall K. Jones. With color photography.

Bahamian Art, edited by Basil Smith. A quincentennial (1992) celebration of modern island art with fabulous illustrations.

Bush Medicine in Bahamian Folk Tradition, by Martha Hanna-Smith. Photographic field guide to medicinal plants.

How To Be a True-True Bahamian: A Hilarious Look at Life in the Bahamas, by Patricia Glinton-Meicholas. Available locally.

I Come to Get Me! An Inside Look at the Junkanoo Festival, by Arlene Nash Ferguson, John Beadle, and Pamela Burnside. Beadle and Burnside are the "royal" names of Junkanoo artistry. Exuberantly illustrated, it's available in Nassau outlets.

Junkanoo: Festival of the Bahamas, by E. Clement Bethel, illustrated by the late Brent Malone, famed Junkanoo artist.

The Lucayans, by Sandra Riley, paintings by Alton Lowe. The history of the indigenous, long-gone natives of the Bahamas, available in local stores.

Talkin' Bahamian: A Useful Guide to the Language of the Islands, by Patricia Glinton-Meicholas. Available locally.

TRANSPORTATION

Historically, by-boat ranked as the primary mode of transportation in the Bahama Islands, and that hasn't changed much over the centuries. The first visitors arrived in vessels named *Nina, Pinta,* and *Santa Maria.* Later, sailing ships brought religious and Loyalist American Revolutionary War refugees.

Today, those seeking refuge from mainland rigors arrive by both plane and boat. Once they get to the islands, they often get around by foot, bike, golf cart, or boat, but taxis, rental cars, and tour companies also stand at the ready. No matter how you travel to and around the Bahamas, remember that the time mind-set here ticks to a different clock. Island time is no mere exotic turn-of-phrase, it's a cultural difference, and a refreshing one at that.

So stop looking at your watch and checking your e-mail. Get on island time and learn to live island life the way the locals do—at the pace of tides, winds, sunsets, and seasons.

GETTING TO THE ISLANDS *By air:* All of the major Bahama Islands have international airports. Some of the smaller Out Islands, however, require a connection through Nassau or, to a lesser degree, Freeport/Grand Bahama Island. Below are descriptions of air service to the major islands. Dozens of private airstrips accommodate private planes.

Nassau International (NAS): Nassau/Paradise Island is only 2½ hours by air from New York, little more than 3½ hours from the Midwest, and only 30 minutes from Miami. The following airlines provide service to Nassau from the U.S: **Air Canada, American Airlines, Bahamasair, Continental, Delta, JetBlue Airways, US Airways, Spirit Airlines,** and a number of charter airlines.

Grand Bahama International (FPO): Only 55 miles east of the coast of Florida, Grand Bahama Island is convenient and accessible through the following airlines: **American Eagle, Bahamasair, Continental/Gulfstream International Airlines, Delta Airlines, Spirit Airlines,** and **US Airways.** From Nassau, **Bahamasair** flies to FPO.

Abaco: About 175 miles east of Palm Beach and 106 miles north of

SIGN ALERT
Seen on Grand Bahama Island:
Undertakers Love Overtakers.

Bahamas Ministry of Tourism.

FROM PREHISTORIC TIMES TO THIS DAY, BOATING TRANSCENDS MEANS OF TRANSPORT AND CONSTITUTES A WAY OF LIFE IN THE BAHAMAS.

Nassau, Abaco's two airports receive flights for a number of airlines from South Florida and St. Petersburg: **American Eagle, Bahamasair, Continental Connection, Locair, Twin Air, US Airways, Yellow Air Taxi.** The following airlines serve Abaco from Nassau: **Bahamasair, Cat Island Air, Sky Bahamas,** and **Southern Air.**

• **Marsh Harbour International** (MHH)

• **Treasure Cay** (TCB)

Andros: Four airports serve Andros. (Keep in mind that Andros consists of three islands not connected by bridges.) The following are options for scheduled flights from South Florida: **Continental Connection** and **Lynx Air.** From Nassau: **LeAir** and **Western Air.**

• **Andros Town** (ASD)

• **Congo Town** (COX)

• **Mangrove Cay** (MAY)

• **San Andros** (SAQ)

South Bimini International (BIM): About 50 miles from South Florida, it services flights from Fort Lauderdale: **Gulfstream International** and **Island Air Charters;** Nassau: **Sky Bahamas** and **Western Air** twice a week; and Grand Bahama Island: **Regional Air** twice a week. Visitors to North Bimini must take a taxi and ferry from the airport (see "Getting Around," below).

Cat Island (CAT): A number of airlines service Cat Island from South Florida, including **Continental Connection** and **Lynx Air.** Two airlines fly in from Nassau: **Bahamasair** and **Cat Island Air.**

Eleuthera: Three airports serve this long island. Air transport from South Florida includes **American Eagle, Continental Connection, Continental/Gulf Stream International Airlines, Lynx Air, Twin Air,** and **US Airways Express.** From Nassau: **Bahamasair** and **Southern Air.**

• **North Eleuthera** (ELH) serves the north along with offshore Harbour Island and Spanish Wells.

• **Governor's Harbour Airport** (GHB)

• **Rock Sound/South Eleuthera** (RSD)

Exuma International (GGT): Receives flights from Miami on **American Eagle;** from Nassau on **Bahamasair.**

Long Island Airport (LGI): Service from South Florida is provided by

Locair twice weekly; from Nassau: **Bahamasair, Pineapple Air,** and **Southern Air** (242-377-2014).

Other Islands: Small airlines service the more remote islands of Berry (GHC and CCZ), San Salvador (ZSA), Inagua (IGA), Crooked and Aicklins (CRI), and Mayaguana (MYG) on flights from Nassau: **Island Air Charters.**

Note: Flights to the Bahamas and their frequencies change often according to demand.

AIRLINE INFORMATION

Air Canada (888-247-2262; www.aircanada.com)

American/American Eagle (800-433-7300; www.aa.com)

Bahamasair (800-222-4262; www.bahamasair.com)

Cat Island Air (242-377-3318)

Continental Connection (800-525-0280; www.continental.com)

Continental/Gulf Stream International Airlines (800-231-0856; www.continental.com)

Delta Airlines (800-241-4141; www.delta.com)

Island Air Charters (800-444-9904; www.islandaircharters.com)

JetBlue Airways (800-538-2583; www.jetblue.com)

LeAir (242-377-2356; info@leaircharters.com)

Locair (877-359-4160; www.locair.net)

Lynx Air (888-LYNX AIR; www.lynxair.com).

Pineapple Air (242-377-0140 Deadman's Cay, 242-338-2070 Stella Maris; www.pineappleair.net)

Regional Air (242-352-7121, 242-367-0446)

Sky Bahamas (242-377-8777; http://skybahamas.net)

Southern Air (242-377-2014; www.southernaircharter.com)

Spirit Airlines (800-772-7117; www.spiritair.com)

Twin Air (954-359-8266; www.flytwinair.com)

US Airways (800-622-1015; www.usairways.com)

US Airways Express (800-428-4322; www.usairways.com)

Western Air (242-347-4100 Bimini, 242-369-2222 Congo Town, 242-369-0003 Mangrove Cay, 242-351-3804 Freeport, 242-367-3722 Marsh Harbour, 242-377-2222 Nassau, 242-329-4000 San Andros; www.westernairbahamas.com)

Yellow Air Taxi (888-YELLOW4; www.flyyellowairtaxi.com)

By sea: A good share of Bahama visitors arrive to the islands by boat, whether cruise ship or private launch.

By cruise ship: Nassau is a major cruise ship port, accommodating up to 16 ships on any given day. Cruise lines that dock in Nassau include **Carnival, Celebration, Costa, Disney, Holland America, MSC Italian, Norwegian, Regal**

CRUISE SHIPS IN PORT AT NASSAU HARBOR.

Empress, Royal Caribbean (including its newest *Oasis of the Sea* megaship, for which the harbor had to be newly dredged), and **Voyages of Discovery.**

Freeport/Grand Bahama Island is a smaller cruise ship port; island tourism officials have plans to build two additional docks in a separate location. Carnival and Norwegian cruise lines call on Freeport. In March 2010, **Celebration Cruises** debuted a two-night cruise from West Palm Beach to Freeport.

A same-day, four-hour cruise out of Fort Lauderdale aboard **Discovery Cruises** (800-259-1579; www.discoverycruiseline.com) sails daily except Wednesdays. Passengers have the option of spending four hours on the island or paying more to extend and return a different day. Meals and drinks are included in the price.

Many of the cruise ships maintain private island destinations for their passengers in the Bahamas. Princess Cays is actually a gated area on the south end of Eleuthera. Disney's Castaway Cay and Royal Caribbean's CoCo Cay are part of the Berry Islands. Norwegian stops at Great Stirrup Cay, also in the Berrys. Holland America's Half Moon Cay lies between south Eleuthera and Cat Island.

To bid on cruise ship vacations to the Bahamas, contact **Cruise Compete** at www.cruisecompete.com.

By private boat: Seasoned yachtsmen with local knowledge spend their days, especially when the weather turns cold up north, hopping from island to island. They often sail in groups. In spring and summer, many make the short (50-mile) crossing from South Florida to Bimini for weekend visits or longer. **Top Gun Charters** (305-361-8110 U.S.; www.miamifloridafishingcharters.com) out of Miami does charters to Bimini, specifically with fishing in mind.

All of the major islands have at least one port of entry with Customs and Immigration facilities. All passengers must have a passport and complete an immigration card. See each chapter for individual information on anchorages. Entry fee for vessels up to 35 feet is $150 for four persons or less, valid for 90 days; over 35 feet, $300. There is an extra $15 per person departure tax for more than four passengers.

GETTING AROUND THE ISLANDS Let me start out by saying that there are no logistics. Unless you have a month or so to kick around the islands, there's no easy way of hopping to more than a couple major islands or island groups in a week's time, because usually it means a flight or boat trip back to Nassau or Florida.

Your first option is a scheduled flight on the major airlines, which leaves out the smallest islands and only offers a couple of airlines at best for each flight. Option two: Charter a flight—expensive. Option three: by boat, which still requires backtracking to Nassau to depart for other ports.

You would think, in a country where boats are nearly as common as cars, you could get from one island to the next without any trouble. Deep passageways between the islands, however, mean waters can be treacherous for small craft, especially in the winter months, when most people come to visit. So, the bad news: Even getting transportation from the main Andros Island to South Andros requires some advance planning and string-pulling.

The good news: Officials understand they need to address the problem for short-term (one-week) visitors. The other good news is that some island groups, particularly Abaco, have excellent ferry service to its smaller cays. In Abaco, it's also easy to rent or charter a boat and go island-hopping on your own; the same is true of Exuma. Because Exuma is so close to Nassau, there are also fast ferries that make day trips between the two.

Slower ferryboats depart from Nassau for a number of the Out Islands.

By interisland ferries: **Nassau:** The Paradise Island ferry departs from a small wharf under the bridge—not the fancy day excursion terminal—starting at 9:30 and every half-hour thereafter for $3 each one way. It's a cool, breezy spot where stands sell snacks, Bahama Mamas, and straw market goods. Return ferries from

SEA PLANES AND OTHER SMALL PRIVATE AIRCRAFT HAVE LONG BEEN THE WAY MANY VISITORS ARRIVED TO THE OUT ISLANDS. THE RECENT CRACKDOWN ON CORPORATE SPENDING HAS PUT A HURT ON THESE ISLANDS FOR THAT REASON.
Bahamas Ministry of Tourism.

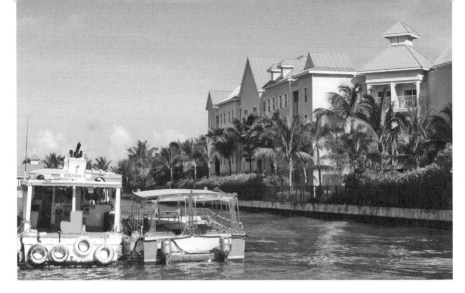

FERRYBOATS TAKE YOU THE SHORT DISTANCE BETWEEN PARADISE ISLAND AND
DOWNTOWN NASSAU IN MINUTES.

the Nassau wharf run on roughly the same half-hour schedule.

Fast ferries depart from Potter's Cay, Nassau, for several of the Out Islands on a set schedule that ranges in frequency from once a week to twice daily, depending on demand and distance. Routes include round-trip from Nassau to Abaco (Sandy Point), Andros (Fresh Creek, Morgan's Bluff), Eleuthera (Harbour Island, North Eleuthera, Current, and Governor's Harbour), and Exuma (George Town). Some ferries transport vehicles as well as passengers. Cost for adult passengers ranges from $50 to $75 one way. Most trips take two to three hours. Contact Bahamas Ferry Services (242-323-2166, 242-323-2165; www .bahamasferries.com) for current schedules, which change seasonally, and fares.

Abaco: The Green Turtle Cay Ferry (242-365-4166) crosses between the dock in Treasure Cay and New Plymouth eight times daily. Cost is $11 one way, $17 same day round-trip. Albury Ferry Service (242-367-0290 or 242-359-5851; www.alburysferry.com) provides service to Elbow Cay (Hope Town) from downtown Marsh Harbour with seven round-trip schedule times. The 20-minute one-way ride is $15, $25 for round-trip. It also makes transfers to Man-O-War Cay and Guana Cay; schedules vary. Pinder's Ferry Service (242-365-2356 or 242-557-6060) makes the one-hour trip between Crown Haven in Abaco to McLean's Town in Grand Bahama Island twice daily; cost is $50 one way.

Andros: A free government ferry (242-369-0331) makes the crossing between Mangrove Cay and South Andros twice daily.

Bimini: The ferry between South and North Bimini costs $2 each way. It begins about 7 AM and runs until 11 PM or later—sometimes 3 or 4 AM on weekends, depending upon need.

Eleuthera: Ferries run continuously between North Eleuthera and Harbour Island (from Three Island Dock, $10 round-trip, seven to 10 minutes) and Spanish Wells (from Gene's Bay dock, $8 round-trip, seven minutes).

Grand Bahama Island: Pinder's Ferry Service (242-365-2356 or 242-557-6060) makes the one-hour trip between McLean's Town to Crown Haven on Great Abaco Island twice daily; cost is $50 one way.

Crooked & Acklins Islands: A government ferry connects the two islands daily, about every hour 9–4. One-way fare is $5.

By mailboat: Out Islanders depend on the mailboats to ship their produce, fish, and meat to Nassau, and to receive goods they've ordered. They depart from Potter's Cay Dock in Nassau to run weekly round-trips to more than 30 islands. Passengers are invited to ride along; one-way passage ranges from $30 to $100, depending on the distance. Voyages can take up to 12 hours. For rates and schedules, contact the dockmaster at 242-393-1064. Then be prepared for a leisurely, not necessarily comfortable, but thoroughly Bahamian experience.

By car: Ironic in a nation where "island time" means slowing down the pace, driving is at flat-out speed with no sign of patience whatsoever. When you're riding along, try to let the scenery calm you—that and the knowledge that a great percentage of accidents in the islands are caused by tourists.

The pace is particularly grueling in **Nassau,** where traffic can be unnerving, particularly downtown. Avoid the Bay Street area, especially when there are a lot of cruise ships in port, which increases pedestrian, carriage, and taxi traffic. Between downtown Nassau and Paradise Island is the worst. The toll to cross the bridge to Paradise Island is $1 each way.

Grand Bahama Island traffic, between the airport, Freeport, and Lucaya, can be brisk. If you're driving from the airport, ask for a map and follow the back roads (avoiding Mall Drive and Sunrise Highway) to get to Lucaya.

To explore the larger Out Islands such as **Andros, Great Abaco, Cat Island, Eleuthera, Exuma,** and **Long Island,** you'll need a rental car—unless you want to do a one-day overview tour and veg or do water sports the rest of the time. Most of these islands have one main road, usually named Queen's Highway. The main roads are typically well-maintained. Side roads leading to beaches, resorts, and off-the-beaten-path settlements and natural attractions can be torturous. Some require four-wheel drive.

GOLF CART IS THE MOTORIZED MODE OF TRANSPORT ON MANY OF THE SMALLER OUT ISLANDS.

CAR & GOLF CART RENTALS
REMEMBER: Drive on the left-hand side of the road. If you have trouble making that transition, do what I do and chant the whole time (especially when making a turn): keep left, keep left, keep left. Don't forget to look both ways whenever turning; this will break you of the habit of only looking in one direction when turning right.

In Nassau and Grand Bahama Island, you'll find major car rental companies such as Hertz, Budget,

Dollar, and Thrifty. A day's rental runs about $60–$75 a day in the cities. Check your insurance to make sure you are covered in the islands. If you have American Express and the rental firm accepts that card, use it. It will cover any damage not covered by your regular automobile insurance. Local rental firms are also available, but you take a risk as far as insurance coverage should you have an accident. The quality of the vehicle can also be iffy—even from the "reputable" companies. Check your car thoroughly; drive it around a bit to check for major problems. (I ended up with a flat tire in the middle of nowhere on Grand Bahama Island with a recent rental .) Ask your rental agent to make note of damages to the car before you drive away.

The Out Islands are a totally different story. Rental firms are all locally run and cars typically cost more—up to $90 a day. Some rental companies don't take credit cards. Most are located near the airport or deliver. Cars sometimes have steering wheels on the right and come in various states of disrepair. Often, it's best to arrange rentals through your hotel or resort, but that may result in a higher charge. Arrangements are lackadaisical at best. I've been asked to just leave the car at the airport with the keys under the seat, for instance. Renters don't seem to worry much about details like driver's license, nicks, and dents. It's all a matter of rural-based trust in the Out Islands.

Some Out Islands, such as Bimini, Elbow Cay, Green Turtle Cay, Harbour Island, and Staniel Cay, run on gas- or electric-powered golf carts. They cost about $20 an hour or $70 to $90 a day. Renting carts and cars is often a sideline business in the Out Islands.

Grand Bahama Island: Besides name rental firms, the following local agencies rent out of the airport: Cartwright's Rent-A-Car (242-351-3002; www.cart wrightsrentacar.com), Island Jeep & Car Rental (242-373-4002); KSR Car Rental (242-351-5737; www.ksrrentacar.com).

Abaco: A&P Auto Rentals (242-367-2655; Don McKay Blvd./Airport Rd., Marsh Harbour), Bargain Car Rentals (242-367-0500; Don Mackey Blvd./Airport Rd., Marsh Harbour), Central Wheels Cars & Vans (242-367-4643; Bay St., Marsh Harbour), Island Cart Rentals (242-366-0448; www.islandcartrentals.com; Hope Town, Elbow Cay), Kool Karts (242-365-4140 or 954-246-3193 in U.S.;

I'LL BE A ROUNDABOUT

Roundabouts are common traffic control mechanisms in the Bahamas, particularly in the larger metropolitan areas. They can be confusing, especially because driving on the left tends to throw off your sense of who has the right-of-way. Just remember the Bahamas mind-chant: Keep left, keep left. And also remember that whoever is already in the roundabout has the right-of-way. Look to your right for cars you must merge with.

As far as when to leave the roundabout, think of it this way: If you want to make a left-hand turn, leave the roundabout at the first exit; to go straight, the second; to make a right-hand turn, the third; to return the way you were coming from, the last.

New Plymouth, Green Turtle Cay at the ferry dock), Quality Star Car Rentals (242-367-2978; www.qualitystarrentals.com; Marsh Harbour), Sea Side Cart Rentals (242-365-4147; Green Turtle Cay at the waterfront).

Andros: Adderley's Car Rental (242-537-2149; Fresh Creek), Executive Car Rental (242-329-2636 or 242-329-4081 after hours; Nicholl's Town), Lenglo Car Rental (242-369-1702; Congo Town).

Bimini: Elite Golf Cart Rentals (242-473-8125; North Bimini); Sunshine Golf Cart Rental (242-347-2757; North Bimini).

Eleuthera: Gateway Rentals (242-335-0455; Gregory Town), Morley's Transportation Services (242-470-3888), T.W. Auto Rentals (242-335-6173; Governor's Harbour).

Exuma: Airport Car Rental (242-345-0090), Don's Rent A Car (242-345-0112), Exuma Transport (242-336-2101, George Town), Thompson's Rental (242-336-2442, George Town), Up Town Rent A Car (242-336-2822, George Town). On Staniel Cay, rent carts from Staniel Cay Yacht Club (242-355-2024).

Long Island: Seaside Car Rental (242-338-0041; Salt Pond, Long Island) Alton Fox is the man to see for cars midisland.

Other Islands: Happy People's (242-367-8117; Great Harbour Cay, Berry Islands) rents golf carts, jeeps, and cars. Ingraham Rent-A-Car (242-339-1677; Great Inagua).

TAXIS & TOURING Airport taxis are available on practically every island where there's an airport. In the big cities, the government fixes fares, but it's always a good idea to ask before getting in.

In Nassau, fare from the airport to Cable Beach is $18, to downtown $25, to Paradise Island $32. From Cable Beach to downtown costs $15. Cabs wait in front of most major resorts, otherwise ask your hotel to call or phone 242-323-5111 yourself. For touring, try Romeo's Limousine Service and Executive Taxi (242-363-4728).

On Grand Bahama Island, cabbies charge $3 for the first ¼ mile and 40 cents for each additional ¼ mile. Additional passengers over two are $3 each. You can find a cab outside the Our Lucaya Resort or across the street near Pelican Bay, or call the GB Taxi Union (242-352-7101) for a pickup.

In Marsh Harbour on Great Abaco Island, "Abaco Joe" (242-359-6248) is the guy you want to see for colorful narration and a smooth ride. On Cat Island, you can get insider information from Reverend Cyril T. Ingraham, Ingraham's Taxi Service (242-342-3115 or 242-464-6284; New Bight).

In Andros, taxis meet airplanes and ferries; fare to resorts ranges about $10–$30. To arrange transportation, call 242-329-2273 in North Andros, 242-368-2333 in Central Andros, 242-382-0312 in Mangrove Cay, and 242-554-0011 in Congo Town.

Taxis in South Bimini deliver you to the ferry landing for North Bimini for $3 each. (Ferry is an additional $2 one way.) The Bimini Tram (242-473-

SIGN ALERT

Seen in Freeport—these instructions for navigating a roundabout: SQUEEZE. Filter Turn. In case you weren't confused enough! Translation? Merge.

2055 or 242-359-8407; North Bimini) covers all of North Bimini from Alice Town to Bimini Bay Resort with frequent stops; $3 per pickup and drop-off.

In south Eleuthera, the same guy who sells you conch salad at Coco's in Rock Sound will provide tour or taxi service (no credit cards accepted): Morley's Transportation Services (242-470-3888; South Eleuthera). Others include Amos at Your Service (242-422-9130; North Eleuthera), Neville Major Taxi & Car Rental (242-333-2361; Harbour Island), or Sunshine Tours (242-332-1575; Governor's Harbour).

On Great Exuma, call Ballsound's Taxi Service (242-336-2375), Exuma Transit Services (242-345-0232), Junior Taxi Service (242-336-2509), Leslie Dames Taxi Service (242-357-0015), or Luther Rolle Taxi Service (242-345-5003).

Taxi service is available from the Crooked Island airport, but hotels often send a driver to meet guests.

BUSES & OTHER TRANSPORT In Nassau, you can hire a horse and surrey for a 25-minute ride for up to three people through town. The horses take a break for an hour or so around 1 PM. Cost is $10 for adults, $5 for children.

To get around and out of town on New Providence Island, jump aboard a jitney bus. Cost is $1.25 in the Nassau area and $1.50 to Compass Point and Adelaide Village. Correct change is required.

Shuttle vans in the Freeport-Lucaya area of Grand Bahama Island cost $1 each one way. Buses from Freeport to the West End cost $5 each way; to the East End, $15. Exact change is required.

Many resorts on Grand Bahama Island provide free shuttle buses or boats to beaches or shopping. Some beach bars, tours, and attractions include free pickup in their prices. Several tour companies schedule regular island sight-seeing excursions; ask your hotel concierge or front desk for information.

Nassau/
Paradise Island

NASSAU

PARADISE ISLAND

CABLE BEACH

OUTLYING SETTLEMENTS

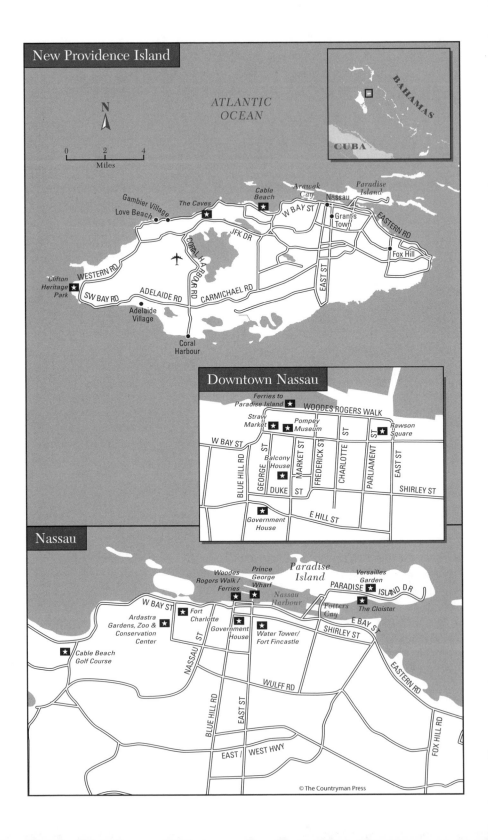

New Providence Island

ATLANTIC OCEAN

BAHAMAS

CUBA

N

0   2   4
Miles

Gambier Village
Love Beach
The Caves
Cable Beach
Arawak Cay
Nassau
Paradise Island
W BAY ST
Grant's Town
EASTERN RD
JFK DR
Fox Hill

CORAL HARBOUR RD

Clifton Heritage Park
WESTERN RD
SW BAY RD
ADELAIDE RD
CARMICHAEL RD
EAST ST

Adelaide Village

Coral Harbour

Downtown Nassau

Ferries to Paradise Island
WOODES ROGERS WALK
Straw Market
Pompey Museum
Rawson Square
W BAY ST
BLUE HILL RD
GEORGE ST
Balcony House
DUKE ST
MARKET ST
FREDERICK ST
CHARLOTTE ST
PARLIAMENT ST
EAST ST
SHIRLEY ST
Government House
E HILL ST

Nassau

Paradise Island
Woodes Rogers Walk / Ferries
Prince George Wharf
Versailles Garden
PARADISE ISLAND DR
Nassau Harbour
Potters Cay
The Cloister
W BAY ST
Fort Charlotte
Ardastra Gardens, Zoo & Conservation Center
Government House
Water Tower/ Fort Fincastle
E BAY ST
SHIRLEY ST
Cable Beach Golf Course
NASSAU ST
BLUE HILL RD
EAST ST
WULFF RD
EASTERN RD
FOX HILL RD
EAST / WEST HWY

© The Countryman Press

NASSAU/PARADISE ISLAND

COLONIAL HERITAGE, MODERN VIBE

"New Providence and its wild harbor town were in many ways a pirate heaven as well as a pirate haven. Free from all laws other than the laws of piracy, it made available all the rough joys that the outlaw brother-hood held dear."

—*Frank Sherry in* Raiders & Rebels: The Golden Age of Piracy

My taxi driver dropped me at the wrong spot, so I ended up tugging my luggage through a mammoth casino with all the blinking glitz of Vegas, then a towering atrium decorated with outrageous mythical sculptures, painted ceilings, an over-sized throne where people were taking turns snapping each other's pictures, and a mass of humanity. Welcome to Atlantis, no longer a lost world, but one found on Paradise Island by a million each year.

The scene differed upon my arrival to Graycliff, perched quaintly upon a limestone hillside overlooking downtown Nassau. Doris checked me in at a small office in a corner of a gracious circa-1776 mansion. She insisted that her bellman would park my car in the hotel's private lot, unload my suitcase, and carry it through the lush fountain gardens to my second-floor, antique-decorated suite.

Atlantis in Paradise Island and Graycliff in Nassau are just a 15-minute drive from one another, but light-years away in style, age, and philosophy. They represent the yin and yang of the destination that combines two islands and hundreds of years of history.

Tightly bound to the bygones of colonial America, Nassau's **New Providence Island** became a British possession shortly after its citizens settled into the mainland, awarded to the six lord proprietors of South Carolina by King Charles II in 1670. The lords

> **BAHAMA TALK**
> Nassau: Originally named Charles Towne for King Charles II, the city was renamed Nassau in 1695 to honor King William III, formerly Prince of Orange-Nassau.

RAWSON SQUARE GREETS SEA ARRIVALS TO NASSAU.

immediately set about protecting their possession by building Fort Nassau in Charles Towne.

Despite the fortifications, a tribe of pirates made themselves at home in a makeshift shantytown they set up on today's Nassau Harbor. Here they came to count and spend their booty and raise a little buccaneer hell. In fact, it was often said of Caribbean pirates that when they slept, they dreamed not of dying and going to heaven, but of returning to New Providence Island.

The appointment of Capt. Woodes Rogers in 1717 finally put an end to their marauding in British waters, and Nassau became the administrative headquarters it remains today. Work began on Fort Montagu in 1741 to further protect the harbor, which it effectively did until 1776, when American warships captured it briefly. Fort Charlotte and Fincastle followed in 1789 and 1793, respectively.

Nassau rose in status as a center of trade, including the slave trade, which centered at the Vendue House on Bay Street until emancipation put an end to that in 1838.

During the Civil War, Nassau played an important role in supplying Confederate troops and was discovered, then developed for the resort destination it was destined to be. Today, **Nassau** is the first name tourists equate with the Bahamas. At its genesis, tourism centered around the harbor. Later, it spread west to **Cable Beach,** named for a submarine cable that came ashore there. After a bridge connected **Paradise Island,** formerly known as Hog Island, to the main island, development proceeded there also. Originally owned by A&P heir Huntington Hartford II, the island still holds vestiges of his estate in addition to one of the world's most highly touted megaresorts.

Besides being a mecca for vacationing tourists arriving by airplane, Nassau has become a major cruise ship destination. In 2009 it made history after dredging its harbor from 35 to 45 feet deep to accommodate Royal Caribbean's bigger-than-ever *Oasis of the Seas* ship.

SIGN ALERT
"Welcome to Cable Beach, the Bahamian Riviera."

Nassau continues to thrive despite economic downturns elsewhere in the country. Whereas other islands have cut back on hotel and restaurant rates, Nassau continues to price at high-dollar figures. Although it has a distinct British island character, signs of American influence—McDonald's, Burger King, et al—make some statesiders feel at home, others disturbed.

Most visitors stick to the main resort areas these days, as crime makes the news. Other more intrepid and culture-cued travelers make their way around the 21-mile-long New Providence Island to **Grant's Town,** just "over the hill" from Nassau, for a taste of local urban life. Or they head west to beach settlements such as **Gambier Village** and **Adelaide Village,** more akin to the Out Islands than Nassau proper, where more than one-third of the country's population resides in a space that hovers between the historic and the ultramodern.

BAHAMA TALK

Titta: An endearing term for sister (usually an older sister), it often gets shortened to one syllable, so don't be shocked—especially if you see it on a sign for a restaurant-bar called Lil Tits.

Viewpoint: Not someone's outlook on life, but spots marked throughout New Providence Island where you may want to stop, admire the view, and take pictures. In other words: Scenic overlook.

DON'T MISS
- Conch salad at Arawak Cay or Potter's Cay.
- The plantation ruins at Clifton Heritage National Park.
- A special-occasion lunch or dinner at Graycliff Hotel.
- Fort Fincastle followed by a climb down Queen's Staircase.
- The Dig and other Atlantis aquariums.

SUGGESTED READING *Nassau Guardian* (www.thenassauguardian.com) Established in 1844, it is THE source for local news and gossip.

Nassau's Historic Landmarks, by Gail Saunders and Linda M. Huber. More than 170 color photos, plus etchings and maps.

✳ To See

MUSEUMS Bahamas Historical Society Museum (242-322-4231), Shirley St. and Elizabeth Ave., Nassau. Open 10–4 Mon., Tues., Thurs. and Fri. Admission by donation. Reaching back into pre-Columbian history and the Lucayan culture, the museum displays artifacts from various eras of Bahamian history. Exhibits include the history of Christopher Columbus, the Eleutheran Adventurers, native Indians, and colonial and other historic artifacts.

Balcony House (242-302-2621), Market St. (off Bay St.), Nassau. Open 9:30–1 and 2–4:30 Mon.–Fri. (closed Thurs. afternoon and weekends). $1 adults, 50 cents children ages 5–18. A prime example of 18th-century colonial architecture, circa 1788, Balcony House claims to be Nassau's oldest wooden residential structure. Its restored rooms hold period furnishings and other museum artifacts.

Shipwrights influenced the style of the wooden home; its mahogany staircase came right off a salvaged ship.

Nassau Public Library and Museum (242-322-4907), Shirley St., Nassau. Open 10–8 Mon.–Thurs., 10–5 Fri., 10–4 Sat. Once a 17th-century colonial jail, this unusual octagon-shaped building today only holds prisoner its troves of books and other national Bahamian treasures.

✒ **Pirates of Nassau** (242-356-3759; www.pirates-of-nassau.com), King and George Sts., downtown Nassau. Open 9–5:30 Mon.–Sat., 9–12:30 Sun. $12 adults, $6 ages 4–17. The premise of this interactive museum whisks you back to the year 1716, when the Golden Age of Piracy rages. The ship *Revenge* is moored in the Caribbean while the crew celebrates. At first light it set sails for Nassau. Vignettes, sights, and sounds expose the fact and fiction behind Nassau's celebrated piratical past, and a final exhibit displays pirates' booty and other artifacts. Lightly educational, the 30- to 45-minute self-tour is entertaining for families and anyone with a fascination for this chapter of island history.

♻ **Pompey Museum of Slavery & Emancipation** (242-356-0495), Bay St., Nassau. Open 9:30–4:30 Mon.–Sat., 9:30–1 Thurs. (closed Sun.). $3 adults, $2 seniors, $1 children under age 14. Known as the Vendue House in colonial times, circa 1760, its French name describes the selling that went on in this erstwhile open-air slave auction marketplace. With sophisticated displays and signage, the museum enshrines that dark era of Bahamian history and celebrates the emancipation that followed. The theme is "Lest We Forget: The Triumph Over Slavery." Besides interpretative signage, grim period artifacts such as shackles, a slave collar, documents, a ball-and-chain, slave-made dolls, and a branding iron subtly remember the horror. A mural by local artist John Beadle portrays the Bay Street waterfront during the slave era.

PIRATES OF NASSAU RECALLS NEW PROVIDENCE ISLAND'S DERRING-DO DAYS.

CULTURAL & HISTORIC SITES ❂ **Clifton Heritage National Park** (242-362-5360), Western Rd., Clifton Point, New Providence Island. Museum open 9–5 Mon.–Fri. Self-tour $2; guided tour $3 adults, $2 children ages 10 and younger. Preserved as a natural beach, the remains of a prehistoric Lucayan Indian village, and the ruins of several 18th- and 19th-century plantations, this 156-acre rural side of Nassau provides a pleasant respite from cruise ship mobs and bustling traffic. At the core of the 156-acre site, a museum tells the site's history, where sugar, indigo, rice, corn, and cotton supported the plantation system. Trails take visitors past slave hut ruins and to the pirate steps leading to the sea. Once a major colonial seaport, it still functions as an industrial pier for adjacent Esso. The ruins of the manor house are visible from the road. Shuttles take visitors to Jaw Beach, a natural stretch where great blue herons and sooty terns live. In addition to its historical sights, it preserves a natural environment of coppice, shoreline, wetlands, forest, and offshore seagrass beds.

Dundas Centre for the Performing Arts (242-393-3728), Mackey St., Nassau. Box office open 10–4 Mon.–Sat. Bahamian and international plays, musicals, ballets, and concerts take the stage year-round. Each spring, the Bahamas National Youth Choir performs.

Fort Charlotte (242-325-9186), Marcus Bethel Way, off W. Bay St., Nassau. Open Mon.–Sat. 10–4:30, Sun. 10–4; daily tours 8–4. $5 adults, $3 seniors, $2 children under age 14. Governor Lord Dunmore built this fort in the late 1780s, when war was raging in France and the Bahamas wanted to protect itself against Napoleon. It was Nassau's third, built on a hill overlooking the harbor across the street from Arawak Cay. It consisted of three forts and 42 cannons, which were never fired in battle. You can do a self-guided walking tour of the premises, where exhibits interpret the fort's history. Look closely to read deep etchings in the walls engraved by sentries 200 years ago, including names, dates, pictures of ships and flags, and other symbols. There's a gift shop in the fort and a straw market convenes outside its gates.

❂ **Fort Fincastle & Queen's Staircase** (242-356-9085), off Shirley St. at Elizabeth Ave., Nassau. Daily tours 8–4. One of four forts that protected early Nassau from foreign and pirate invasion, Fort Fincastle sits at the top of Bennett's Hill, the island's highest point, and affords a sweeping view of the waterfront and port. It was built in 1793, the second of four, and is a

WALK THE 65 STEPS OF HISTORIC QUEEN'S STAIRCASE.

popular spot for cruise ship bus tours. Tour guides relate the fort's history in booming voices to be heard over other guides, the bustle of the crafts market outside, and the occasional impromptu Junkanoo band drumming and bell-ringing. Slaves carved the staircase's original 66 steps (now only 65) and the road out of the limestone hillside in the 18th century to create an escape route from the fort above. Named for Queen Victoria, its limestone arcade leads to steps splashed by waterfalls and lush with foliage—a great photo op.

Fort Montagu (242-323-1925), off E. Bay St., Nassau. Currently closed to the public. Built in 1742, Fort Montagu can be seen overlooking Nassau Harbor and is the oldest of the town's four fortifications. A Revolutionary American War party led by John Paul Jones attacked and captured the fort in 1776, allowing the U.S. its only, if brief, possession of the Bahamas.

Government House (242-322-3622 or 242-323-1853 for tea party), Blue Hill Rd., Nassau. Open during changing of guard and teas. Watch the changing of the guard at 11 AM on the second and last Saturday of each month. On the last Friday of the month from January through August, the People To People program hosts a free tea party for visitors. The imposing pink-and-white, neoclassical house, home to every governor general since 1801, makes an impressive hilltop statement with its Columbus monument at its doorstep. Originally the queen's ambassador, the governor today is appointed by the Bahamian prime minister.

Graycliff Cigar Factory (242-302-9150 or 800-476-0446; www.graycliff.com), West Hill St., Nassau. Open 9–7 Mon.–Sat. The Garzaroli family added a genuine cigar factory to its famously historic inn and restaurant in 1997. Like everything else they touch, this enterprise turned to top quality, employing only master rollers from Cuba. Tours take in 12 stations where they hand-roll about 30 different limited-edition cigar styles, turning out 90 to 180 each day. It's a two-year process from leaf to lip, and visitors can see the two-level aging process whereby the cigars emit their ammonia-scented impurities and absorb the flavor of the Spanish cedar. The tobacco is a blend of Nicaraguan, Costa Rican, Guatemalan, and Dominican Republic. A smoking room and Brazilian churrascaria restaurant expand the experience for those stirred by the aura of it all. Graycliff also arranges cigar and rum tastings for cruise ship and other groups, and of course sells its cigars, which are legal for Americans to take home (as opposed to the Cubans one finds in local shops and at Graycliff). Staff will also provide cigar-rolling lessons upon request.

Gregory's Arch/Grant's Town, Market and Duke Sts., Nassau. Near the Government House, it marks the entrance to Grant's Town, a community built by former slaves post-emancipation.

National Centre for the Performing Arts (242-393-2884), Shirley St., Nassau. In addition to the National Dance Company, it hosts other theatrical performances.

National Dance Company of the Bahamas (242-328-7588; www.ndcbahamas .com), National Centre for the Performing Arts, Shirley St., Nassau. Tickets $15–$25. Established in 1992 to celebrate the quincentennial of Columbus's

landing in the Bahamas, the troupe travels internationally. In Nassau, it performs
six times between April and August and at other guest performances.

✪ ✎ **Nettie's Different of Nassau** (242-327-8153; www.nettiesplace.com,
changing to www.nettiesdifferentofnassau.com), W. Bay St., Nassau. Tours at 11,
noon, and 1 daily except Tues. $15 adults, $5 children. Step into the world of
Out Island yesteryear in the Bahamian Heritage Centre at this native hotel complex operated by 75-year-old Nettie Symonette, a veteran Bahamian hotelier and
mother of seven. A museum displays rare and antique artifacts from Nettie's
granny's era and before. In honor of her ancestor, she has re-created Granny's
Bedroom in the museum and Granny's Kitchen across the street in a parklike
setting that includes native plants and bush medicines, an old rock oven, land
crab habitat, storytelling around an old bus, a maypole, corn-grinding, and the
Lil Ole Chapel. Nettie's vibrant paintings fill the walls of her gallery, inn rooms,
and all available surfaces. Sit with Nettie for a cup of hot fever grass tea or
"switcher" (Eleutheran limeade). The café prepares local specialties by reservation only. This is, as the Bahamians would say, a "true true" Bahamian cultural
experience.

Supreme Court (242-322-3315), Bank Ln., off Bay St., Nassau. Open 10–5:30
Mon.–Fri. The public is invited to watch the justices and counsel in wigs and
long gowns, British-style, in session. The dress code is casual, but no shorts
allowed. The ceremonial opening in January includes a performance by the
Royal Bahamas Police Force Band and an inspection of the force by the chief
justice.

PARKS & GARDENS ✎ **Ardastra Gardens, Zoo & Conservation Center**
(242-323-5806; www.ardastra.com), off W. Bay St., Nassau (look for signs). Open:
9–5 daily (last admission 4:30). $15 adults, $7.50 ages 4–12. The highlight of this
experience? A couple dozen flamingos parading military-fashion during shows
three times (10:30, 2:10, 4:10) throughout the day. Many of the graceful, usually

FLAMINGOS HEADLINE THE ZOOLOGICAL ATTRACTIONS AT ARDASTRA GARDENS.

extremely shy birds walk freely around the grounds honking daylong and are accustomed enough to people that you can get quite close to take their pictures. The other great photo op happens at 11, 1:30, and 3:30, when zoo staff members take you into the lorikeet cage to feed the pretty little singers bits of apple. They land on your head and arms in their excitement. The rest of the grounds' 5½ acres holds birds, monkeys, snakes, and iguanas from around the tropics, organized in no particular pattern.

♂ **Versailles Gardens** (www.oneandonlyresorts.com), Behind One&Only Ocean Club Resort, Paradise Island. Huntington Hartford II once owned Paradise Island. Today what's left of his fantastic vision for a world-class resort serves as the foundation of the island's most exclusive resort, and the terraced gardens he fashioned after France's Versailles gardens are one of its loveliest, most-photographed spots. Many of those photos have a bride and groom in them. Greek columns mark the garden's entrance and a 12th-century life-sized statue of Hercules graces the lily pond. Statues of two of Hartford's heroes, Franklin Roosevelt and David Livingstone, flank Hercules.

CHURCHES & RELIGIOUS SITES Christ Church Cathedral (242-322-4186), King and George Sts., Nassau. One of Nassau's oldest buildings, circa 1670, this Anglican/Episcopalian, neo-Gothic church holds an important role in history. When it became a cathedral in 1861, Queen Victoria first granted Nassau its city status.

St. Francis Xavier Cathedral (242-322-8528; www.stfrancisxaviercathedral .com), West and W. Hill Sts., Nassau. Near the National Art Gallery, it is the island's oldest Catholic Church, built in 1886.

St. Matthew's Anglican Church (242-323-8220), Shirley and Church Sts., Nassau. In addition to holding an 1802 pedigree, its cemetery contains the remains of two national heroes: Sir Milo Butler, the first Bahamian governor general, and Sir Cecil Wallace Whitfield, former leader of the Free National Movement political party.

GALLERIES & STUDIOS Anthaya Art Gallery (242-327-1045; www.anthaya art.com), W. Bay St., Cable Beach. Locally made art from paintings to fine straw bags to jewelry.

○ **Doongalik Studios** (242-363-1313; www.doongalik.com), Marina Village, Atlantis, Paradise Island. Named for the telltale sounds of Junkanoo, this gallery owned by premier Bahamian artist Jackson Burnside III sells gifts and art on commission, from $15 Christmas ornaments crafted from conch shells to four-figure works by Amos Ferguson, Brent Malone, Max Taylor, Burnside, and his brother Stanley. A location at 18 Village Rd. in Nassau is Burnside's original studio; call 242-394-1886 to visit.

Nassau Glass Art Gallery (242-393-8165; nassauglass.com/art-gallery.htm), Mackey St., Nassau. This gallery carries the top names in Bahamian art: Amos Ferguson, Max Taylor, Eddie Minnis, Antonius Roberts, Rolfe Harris, Alvin Moss, and more, plus master woodworks and international artists.

✪ The National Art Gallery of the Bahamas (242-328-5800; www.nagb .org.bs), West and W. Hill Sts., Nassau. Open 10–4 Tues.–Sat. $5, $3 students and seniors. Opened in 2003, the gallery hosts three annual changing exhibits of local artists in a beautifully restored 19th-century Great House with balconies, balusters, and other gracious architectural charms. Inside, the space flows through the two floors with works attractively arranged to showcase the artist's thoughts and creativity. The gift shop sells local art and crafts. It's easily reachable on foot from the downtown waterfront, near the Graycliff complex.

MUSIC & NIGHTLIFE Atlantis Casino (242-363-6000; www.atlantis .com), Atlantis, Paradise Island. Nightlife and daylife happen here at this 24-hour casino. Unlike other dark, cavernous casinos, this one has

THE NATIONAL ART GALLERY OF THE BAHAMAS HOSTS CHANGING EXHIBITS OF LOCAL WORKS IN A COLONIAL SETTING.

an ocean view. At 60,000 square feet, it claims to be the biggest in the Caribbean, with 1,100 games and tables. Its Pegasus Race & Sports Book takes bets on all major sporting events. Two food-and-beverage outlets mean you can spend hours without leaving—or until your cash runs out.

Aura (242-363-3000, Ext. 29), Atlantis Casino, Paradise Island. A 9,000-square-foot, state-of-the-art, posh nightclub with models for waiters, a sunken, illuminated dance floor, and VIP sections.

Club Land'Or (242-363-2400), Paradise Island. Oasis Lounge hosts live music 7–12 nightly with happy hour specials and free hors d'oeuvres 5–7 Mon.–Sat.

Compass Point (242-327-4500), W. Bay St., Gambier Village. Local bands entertain Thurs.–Sun., and its two bars offer happy hour drink specials starting at 9 AM.

Crystal Palace Casino (242-327-6200; crystalpalacevacations.com), Wyndham Nassau Resort, W. Bay St., Cable Beach. Nassau's only casino, its 30,000 square feet hold more than 400 slot and video poker machines, plus 40 game tables, a sports book, and the Junkanoo Bar. Restaurants and a nightclub are conveniently located on the second floor above it. The casino is open to the public 24 hours.

Travellers' Rest (242-327-7633), W. Bay St., Gambier Village. Weekend live entertainment ranging from calypso to blues courtesy of Tabatha & Gernie and the Caribbean Express Band. Free food and happy hour drink specials 6–8 Fri.

✳ To Do

BEST BEACHES ☉ **Cabbage Beach,** Paradise Island. This is one of the destination's most well-loved beaches, and deservedly so. Its easternmost end around the One&Only Club is the most secluded. At its western extreme, it fronts Atlantis (the resort refers to it as Atlantis Beach), which of course makes it more crowded. Palms, sea grapes, and Australian pines line the 1-mile stretch of white sand and tame, aquamarine waters.

Caves Beach, The Caves, New Providence Island. The closest beach to the airport, it gets its name from the Lucayan caves found in this area. The area itself is known as The Caves. The beach is a slight, coved strip with no development or facilities, but restaurants and shops are nearby.

Jaws Beach, West End, New Providence Island at Clifton Heritage National Park. Despite its daunting name, this lovely, natural beach is part of Clifton Heritage Site on the island's west end. It's popular with locals and nature-lovers. Australian pines shade the narrow strip, and trails lead through habitat to the site's historic ruins and slave's staircase.

Long Wharf Beach, W. Bay St., Nassau. Also known as "Spring Breakers Beach" for obvious reason, it's close to downtown and equipped with restrooms and other facilities to accommodate the party crowd. Arawak Cay is a short walk away for casual dining and drinking options and often outdoor concerts.

FISHING Although such Out Islands as Bimini, Andros, Abaco, and the Berry Islands are more renowned for their fishing, Nassau-Paradise Island is no slouch. The destination may lack the bonefishing allure, but reef and deep-sea fishing? Spectacular, but often eclipsed by the destination's more glitzy, manufactured attractions.

Charter: **Chubasco Charters** (242-324-3474; www.chubascocharters.com), Bayshore Marina, E. Bay St. Fish aboard a 36- to 48-foot fishing-outfitted boat offshore. Capt. Mike Russell guarantees fish or the excursion is free.

GOLF Cable Beach Golf Club (242-677-4175; www.crystalpalacevacations .com/golf), Wyndham Nassau Resort, Cable Beach. The Bahamas' oldest golf course, it's open to the public along with its clubhouse and pro shop. Fred M. Settle redesigned the 18-hole, 6,453-yard course in 2002, creating new sand traps and water hazards. The complex includes a driving range with free use of clubs, lessons, and a snack bar.

Ocean Club (242-363-6682), One&Only Ocean Club, Paradise Island. Open only to resort and resort affiliate guests (including Atlantis), this beautiful, ocean-view course includes a putting green, driving range, pro shop, and clubhouse. Tom Weiskopf designed the 18-hole course. It's the site of the annual Michael Jordan Celebrity Invitational Golf Tournament.

HORSEBACK RIDING Happy Trails Stables (242-362-1820; www.bahama horse.com), Coral Harbour. Closed Sun. $150 per person, includes hotel pickup. Ride along the beach on either of two morning rides lasting 90 minutes. Riders

Atlantis

ATLANTIS'S SERPENT SLIDE WHISKS YOU
SAFELY THROUGH A SCHOOL OF SHARKS.

must be older than 11 and weigh less than 200 pounds.

KID STUFF Atlantis (242-363-6950 or 800-ATLANTIS; www.atlantis .com), Paradise Island. $35–$110 for adult one-day admission; $25–$80 for kids ages 4–12. You don't have to be a guest to take advantage of all the fun Atlantis has to offer. You do have to have deep pockets, however. The $110 wristband buys you admission to all of the water amenities and kids programs. Two other levels of admission allow limited access. For an extra charge, parents also can drop off their charges, ages 3 to 12, for anywhere from an hour to a full day of supervision. But most likely you'll want to experience the complex with your kids. The activities are nearly endless. Each pool has something different to offer, such as a lazy and a not-so-lazy (wavy) river, fountains, zero-entry, slides, a Mayan temple, a tube plunge through swimming sharks, and sand beaches. Dolphin and sea lion encounters let families interact with the creatures (extra charge). There are three levels of dolphin interaction—a shallow-water experience, a deepwater swim involving a self-propelled scooter you hang onto, and trainer for a day. These are, by the way, animals rescued from Mississippi after Hurricane Katrina. There's also a Walk with the Sharks snuba experience and a Sea Keepers Adventure where you feed stingrays and snorkel with manta rays. Don't miss the underwater tunnel (Coral Tower) or "The Dig" (Royal Tower), where the aquarium experience imagines an archaeological excavation of the Lost City of Atlantis. Climber's Rush offers 11 rock-climbing surfaces and lessons.

SPAS Mandara Spa (242-363-3000; www.atlantis.com), Atlantis Resort, Paradise Island. This expert in spa design at Atlantis combines elements of Balinese and European therapies with Bahamian tradition. Its comprehensive menu offers all manner of massages, facials, body treatments, and beauty services.

✪ **Natural Mystic Spa** (242-702-2800; www.marleyresort.com), Marley Resort, W. Bay St., Cable Beach. Named, as is everything at this resort, for a Bob Marley song, this intimate,

BAHAMA TALK
Got no brought-upsy: Said of children with bad manners.

three-room spa features an outdoor foot-washing area, steam room, Japaneselike deep plunge pool, African nuances in the three treatment rooms, all-Caribbean natural products, and treatments such as One Cup of Coffee Rub, Island Mint Tea Scrub, and Sabai Fusion Touch massage.

WATER SPORTS *Anchorages:* **Atlantis Marina** (242-363-3000), Atlantis, Paradise Island. Holds 66 vessels up to 206 feet. Harborside Village time share and Marina Village retail center border the marina.

Charters: **Barefoot Sailing Cruises** (242-393-0820 or 242-393-5817; www.bare footsailingcruises.com) Half-day sail and snorkel cruises, six-hour barbecue lunch cruise, and sunset champagne sails.

Booze & Cruise (242-393-2973 or 242-393-3722; www.boozecruisebahamas .com), hotel pickups. The quintessential Bahamas party experience, this one sails on four-hour cruises that include snorkeling, lunch, beaching, and unlimited cocktails. Also sunset cruises with dinner, live entertainment, and of course limbo.

Dolphin Encounters (242-363-1003; www.dolphinencounters.com) Swim and interact with the dolphins at Blue Lagoon Island, where guests can also enjoy volleyball, snorkeling, swimming, kayaking, games, exploring historic sites, or snoozing in a hammock.

Flying Cloud (242-363-4430; www.flyingcloud.info), Paradise Island Ferry Terminal) A 57-foot sailing catamaran does two daily 3½-hour cruises, one five-hour tour on Sunday. Snorkeling and beaching on Rose Island. The cruise includes a complimentary rum punch or soda and a cash bar.

Island World Adventures (242-363-3333; www.islandworldadventures.com), Paradise Island Ferry Terminal. Fast-boat excursions take you to the Exuma Cays for beaching, snorkeling, and picnicking.

Powerboat Adventures (242-363-1466; www.powerboatadventures.com), Paradise Island Ferry Terminal, #1 Marina Dr., Paradise Island. Regularly scheduled full-day speedboat (1,000 hp) excursions include an iguana encounter on Allen's Cay in the Exumas, a nature walk, drift snorkeling, and stingray feeding. Also overnight and charter excursions.

Stingray Adventure (242-322-8446; www.stingrayadventure.com) If you've never felt the silky underbelly of stingray, you're missing out. This excursion departs from the cruise ship wharf in a 65-foot catamaran, which takes you to a private setup on Blackbeard's Cay. Here, passengers not only feed and learn about the rays, they can play volleyball and basketball, go kayaking, and dine at the grill.

Sub Bahamas (242-362-4171; www.sub-bahamas.com) Your personal SUB (scenic underwater bubble) submerges you 15 feet for a safe 40-minute diving experience with no certification necessary.

Day Water Sports Excursions: Even around relatively urban Nassau, the waters remain pristine—an amalgam of blues where the waters are shallow, and the deepest and purest marine blue where they drop off. So don't be lured by landside attractions, because what's truly special lies beneath the surface. Consider all the underwater movies and TV shows filmed here, including *Thunderball, Into the Blue,* and Lloyd Bridges episodes—and you'll get an idea how gorgeous the down-below landscape truly is.

Snorkeling & Diving: Underwater sightseeing reefs and wrecks abound. One of the most famous, **Elkhorn Gardens,** was the shoot location for *20,000 Leagues Under the Sea.*

Less famous but equally awesome sites include **Barracuda Shoals** (shallow with three reefs and lots of fish), **Fish Hotel** (in 10 to 30 feet with juvenile grunts and lots of sea fans), *De La Salle* **wreck** (upright in 70 feet), and **Shipyard** (four wrecks including a wooden-hulled cargo ship).

Recommended Charter: ✪ **Stuart Cove's Snorkel Bahamas** (242-362-4171; www.stuartcove.com), hotel pickups. "Get in the water without splashing, no kicking, and do not panic or thrash around," the tour operators told us as we prepared for our third snorkel site. Why all the stealth? That had something to do with the 30-some reef sharks that were schooled some 30 feet below us. Sure, they were distracted by the cage of chum the guides had dropped to the ocean's floor, but there was that one that kept rising close to the rope where the eight of us clung for dear life. "Don't panic if one comes near you," our guide had told us. "They can sense panic and that will get them all agitated." Hmmm, wonder if they were sensing that I was now questioning my sanity. I had been tempted to sit out the third dive, but I knew I'd regret that too. As it worked out, it was as awesome as they promised, watching the finned creatures up to 10 feet long circling below. And it made great Facebook fodder. The first two dives at **Southwest Reef** (where I also spotted one nurse shark on the bottom) and **Schoolhouse Reef** (named for its abundant juvenile fish, but I saw some gorgeous adult queen angelfish too) were spectacular before the third upstaged it with all the drama. Known as **Runway Wall,** it is also the site of the *Bahama Mama* **wreck** and filming for *Into the Blue.* Stuart Cove's is the first and last name for underwater adventure in Nassau. Students and divers from Sean Connery to Princess Di have been previous customers. Discovery Channel's *Shark Week* regularly features the operation, named for its owner. It picks up customers at their hotels and transports them to its facility on the island's west end for scuba and personal submarine excursions (www.sub-bahamas.com) in addition to the snorkeling.

WILDLIFE SPOTTING Bahamas National Trust Ornithology Group (242-362-1574) Call for accredited birding tour guides. Cost for adults is $65.

✳ Lodging

The Nassau/Paradise Island hotel scene constantly fluctuates. Last year's Radisson is a Sheraton, Marriotts become Hiltons, and Holiday Inn becomes privately owned, but basically the properties have kept their place for the many decades the islands have drawn sun-and-fun seekers.

Crystal Palace Resort (now a Wyndham) was the islands' first megaresort when Carnival Cruise Lines opened its 600 rooms in 1990. Atlantis on Paradise Island changed the course of local hoteling when Sun International began work a couple of years later on Phase I of a playground the likes of which the Bahamas had never seen. Later known as Kerzner International, it completed its second two phases by 2007, and has, it's rumored, more plans up its sleeves, perhaps to turn the old Club Med property it purchased into a theme park.

On Nassau's Cable Beach, Starwood Hotels makes plans for Baha Mar, with five luxury resorts including the already-existing Sheraton plus a St. Regis, W., and Westin. Its 1,000-plus acres, according to plans, will also include a Jack Nicklaus golf course, casino, spa, and water features. A Chinese firm will reputedly be backing the development, but islanders are skeptical, and only time will tell.

Price Codes

Inexpensive	Up to $100
Moderate	$100 to $200
Expensive	$200 to $300
Very Expensive	$300 and up

(An asterisk after the pricing designation indicates that the rate includes at least a continental breakfast in the cost of lodging and possibly more extensive meal service as noted in the listing.)

ACCOMMODATIONS

Cable Beach

✪ ☙ **Breezes Bahamas** (242-327-5356 or 800-GO-SUPER, 954-925-0925 (U.S); www.superclubs.com), W. Bay St. Two separate wings comprise this sprawling complex on Cable Beach, which has been open since 1996 and is part of Jamaican-owned SuperClubs. The east wing has four floors, the west wing eight—adding up to 400 rooms along a wide beach and spread of four swimming pools, one with a swim-up bar. This is the kind of place you'd never have to leave during your entire stay in Nassau. All meals and most activities are included in the room rate, and the activities are exhaustive—from live shows, sumo wrestling, and aerobic classes to a climbing wall, flying trapeze, and piano bar. The one thing it doesn't have is Wi-Fi access, but there is a guest computer. Rooms are decorated in standard-issue tropical florals, with a flat-screen TV, fridge, and vessel sink in the bath. Besides the buffet dining room, guests can choose from the romantic Garden of Eden 'neath the shade of an enormous silk cotton tree or Pastafari for dinner. The Pool Grill serves drinks and snacks throughout the day, while cavelike Club Hurricane provides a lively disco scene in the after-dark hours. Very Expensive.°

✪ "ᵼ" **Marley Resort & Spa** (242-702-2800 or 866-737-1766; www.marleyresort.com), W. Bay St. I could feel the positive vibrations the moment I stepped in the door, but then I'm a huge Bob Marley fan. Stopping first in the library, I could see video of Bob on stage, sparking memories of the one time I saw him live, along with displays of his platinum albums, family photos, and other memorabilia. The famed, prophetic reggae star escaped here with his family back in the days when his life was in danger. They probably lived in the spartan manner of his Rastafarian tenets in those days, but his surviving children have turned the site into a top-class, beautifully decorated boutique hotel with beachfront and all the trappings of a full-service resort, Jamaican style. Each of the 16 rooms is named for a Marley hit, such as One Love, the stunning honeymoon suite with his-and-her showers, a Jacuzzi, and a patio overlooking the property's two pools. Every detail in every room and throughout the property has received careful thought and tasteful selection, from the door carvings and African-inspired furnishings to the natural rock pool with lounge chairs shaped like palm fronds. The bar, Stir It Up; restaurant, Simmer Down; and spa, Natural Mystic, also demonstrate distinct character. Very Expensive.

Nettie's Different of Nassau

(242-327-7921; www.nettiesplace .com, changing to www.netties differentofnassau.com), W. Bay St. Bahamas hotel matriarch Nettie Symonette began work on this latest project well into her 70s after turning over her Different of Abaco property in the Out Islands. In Nassau, she tries to re-create that environmental and cultural climate on her spread of land with a village, tours, and demonstrations re-creating old Bahamian ways. Currently, 15 rooms decorated in wood furnishings and equipped with TVs accommodate guests. Another 24 are on the slate along with a swimming pool and private beach. Guests have access to the facilities on both sides of West Bay Street, which include games, storytelling, a cooking studio, bush tea tastings, a café, a fountain courtyard, and a gallery. The name promises something unusual, and this truly is for Nassau—more like what you would find in the Out Islands even today. Moderate.

Sheraton Nassau Beach Resort

(242-327-6000 or 800-627-9114; www .sheraton.com/cablebeach), W. Bay St. This property shares a Crystal Palace casino with Wyndham Nassau Resort, located on the east side of the casino. Guests at both have charging privileges at the other, and one of these years, if all goes according to plan, both will be part of the Baha Mar development and resort, along with a Westin, W, and St. Regis hotel and a water park. For the time being, the resort received a recent dramatic $95 million facelift that makes it feel shiny new—from its 694 rooms and suites to its free-form, waterfalls pool with swim-up bar. Recreation and dining options are diverse. Work out in the fitness center, golf across the street, kayak, sail, wind surf, or snorkel. Send the kids to half- or full-day supervised programs. Grab coffee and breakfast at Caribe Café, lunch at Bimini Market's buffet, or do drinks indoors at sophisticated Telegraph Bar or outside at Edgewater Bar. Amici, A Trattorio specializes in original ambiance and Italian creations come dinner, after which you can head to the casino, then lay your head on the comfy Sheraton Sweet Sleeper bed. Sky blues, Androsia batik fabric (made on nearby Andros Island), classic leather luggagelike accents, a stainless bathroom vanity, designer lamps, and basket weave-motif carpeting comprise the rooms' distinctive décor. Moderate to Very Expensive.

SIGN ALERT
The restroom sign at Nettie's: "Terlets Dem."

ISLAND CHARACTER: NETTIE SYMONETTE

"Three years ago, I wanted to create more than a hotel," said Nettie Symonette, age 75. "I wanted to create something as close to nature as I could in an urban atmosphere."

You can take the lady out of the Out Islands, but you can't take the Out Islands out of the lady.

So Nettie, an Eleuthera native and longtime Abaco resident, brought the Out Islands to Nassau—old traditions, plants, cooking, bush teas, and all.

"I'm here but I'm not here," she admits. Her Cable Beach acreage lets guests and tourists peek into the nature and culture of the Out Islands. They can learn about native vegetation and which leaf is good for high blood pressure, a strong back, and strong, well, other body parts. Her yard designates places for storytelling, playing dominoes, and even making coal.

On the other side of West Bay, Nettie serves traditional Bahamian food in her café and teaches lessons in Bahamian cooking. A museum contains a recreation of her granny's house and showcases other aspects of old Bahamia. Another building is devoted to Nettie's latest passion—painting. She started painting in 2003 in Abaco. "I painted everything!" she remembers.

Her brightly painted canvases, buckets, fabrics, and even old-fashioned chamber pots cover not only the walls and floor of the gallery, but guest rooms and every available space. In the courtyard hangs "The Journey," her four-piece painting that will hang in the new airport when completed in 2011.

"I wanna do something that's totally different," says Nettie, whose goal is to preserve the Bahamian culture and environment. "When I go, I want my legacy to be that I made a difference."

NETTIE SYMONETTE FOUND HER INNER ARTIST LATE IN LIFE; ONCE SHE LET IT OUT, SHE PAINTED EVERYTHING IN SIGHT.

WYNDHAM'S BACKYARD IS ALL ABOUT WATER AND BEACH.

⁰ᵀ⁰ Wyndham Nassau Resort & Crystal Palace Casino (242-327-6200 or 800-WYNDHAM; www.wyndhamnassauresort.com), W. Bay St. This property dates back to Carnival Cruise Line's Crystal Resort of the 1990s, and although it has a retro cruise ship structural appearance, a recent massive makeover has it looking like a modern upscale complex worthy of the Wyndham brand. The Crystal Palace Casino retains its original identity and is the only casino on New Providence Island. But unlike the back-then days, guests are more likely to haunt the beach or the fun-for-all pool and its gently coiled slide built into a rocklike waterfall structure topped with a band stage, its Tiki Hut swim-up bar, and its grill. A boardwalk loops around the beach, pool with gazebos, and Da Daq Shack waterfront bar, which blends up fruity daiquiris. Its two signature restaurants draw deserved attention: MOSO does Asian fusion with a strong Chinese influence, while Black Angus Grille, as you might suspect, specializes in steaks but also excels at seafood. A breakfast buffet, beach bar and grill, and coffee-deli shop complete the dining options. The nightlife hot spot, 22 Above, overlooks casino action with a cool vibe and live music that defies categorization (from Lynyrd Skynyrd to Bob Marley to Earth, Wind & Fire). The three hotel towers house 559 guest rooms and suites, yet the property doesn't feel crowded even when full. The rooms are appointed in the most modern manner, with some elements that date them such as the sliding glass door to the balcony, porthole windows, and radius-corner walls. For golfers, the Cable Beach Golf Club is across the street. Expensive to Very Expensive.

Coral Harbour

⁰ᵀ⁰ Coral Harbour Beach House & Villas (242-362-2875; www.bahamas-mon.com/hotels/harbour), Coral Harbour Rd. On New Providence Island's south side, the waters are shallow and calm, which for some reason has kept it lightly populated and developed. This place has the feel of the Out Islands with its Sand Bar Beach Restaurant, hammocks strung between casuarinas, and neighborhood atmosphere. Fourteen rooms and a two-bedroom beach house (Very Expensive) come complete with kitchens ($5 per night cookware rental fee), TVs, and either a private sitting room or balcony. You'll feel like you've left Nassau, yet the drive downtown takes less than a half-hour, depending on traffic. The narrow beach runs for a nice walkable distance, and kayak rentals and other on-site activities may lure you out of the breeze-rocked hammock. Moderate.

Gambier Village

✪ ⁿⁱⁿ **Compass Point** (242-327-4500; www.compasspointbeachresort.com), W. Bay St. It looks like a crayon factory exploded across the Bahamian-shack-inspired cottages of this exclusive resort away from the tourism scene of Nassau. Its 18 one- and two-story cottages come conveniently equipped with a refrigerator, coffeemaker, microwave, toaster oven, stereo, DVD player, iPod dock, and sundecks overlooking the water—in as many shades, but more subtle. Built by reggae music mogul Chris Blackwell, it manages sophistication and barefoot abandon in one sweep of way-white beach. The resort's popular restaurant overlooks the pool and beach, and room and spa service are available. Very Expensive.

Nassau

♂ ⁿⁱⁿ **British Colonial Hilton** (242-302-9001; www.hiltoncaribbean.com/nassau), 1 Bay St. A longtime fixture on Nassau's harborfront, this property recently got a makeover that elevated the grande dame to her rightful throne. Built on the grounds of a historic fort in 1923, its red barrel-tile roof and stucco facade ape colonial style. Some random ruins from the colonial era can be seen on the grounds, but in more ways than

not the "colonial" in the name is a stretch. That doesn't detract from the newfound grandeur it expresses, though. A dramatic entrance takes you through a marble-tiled atrium lobby hall with faux cabbage palms as sentinels. A sweeping staircase to the mezzanine understandably appears in many a wedding album. Historic photographs decorate hallway walls. Its 280 rooms vary in size, each furnished with granite tile baths, leather-padded headboards, refrigerators, flat-screen TVs, and a feeling of revitalization. The pool and its bar sit on the resort's private beach. Bullion Lounge, with its appropriately chunky furnishings and dark wood, is a hot spot for hip nightlifers looking for fashionable and classic house-made drinks. The new Aqua Restaurant specializes, as its name suggests, in seafood. Moderate to Very Expensive.

♂ ⁿⁱⁿ ✪ **Graycliff Hotel** (242-302-9150; www.graycliff.com), W. Hill St. Forgotten grace and delicious decay: That describes the patina of this circa-1776 gem, a National Register of Historic Places landmark. During its lifetime, the property has served as home to pirate Captain John Howard Graysmith, an Anglican Church (which the Spanish destroyed but for spare ruins still noticeable on property), headquarters and garrison for the American Navy after the 1776 rebuilding, one of the earliest plantations worked by freed slaves, an inn, a Civil War mess hall, a private home, and finally, in 1973, today's incarnation. Always a leader in good taste, it became equally famous for its dining and world-class wine cellar as its lodging. In 1997, the family added a cigar factory and other expansions that have brought it to 20 individually decorated guest rooms, two pools, two restaurants, and a spa and fitness center. Future plans call for renovating six historic buildings across the street that the family has purchased or leased for a chocolate factory, artists' galleria, retail space, coffee-roasting facility, culinary school, and other upscale attractions that would draw cruise ship passengers above the Bay Street line. In the meantime, the house wears its age like a grande dame—some signs of aging here and there, but with a near haughtiness that stays true to its Old World finesse and faithful guests, even while seeking ways to win over new clientele. Each room has its own personality, generally heavy on the brocade, thick tasseled cords, antiques, and period trinkets. In summer, its drafty or flung-open windows can mean a little less cool comfort than some might prefer in the season's humidity, but Graycliff isn't for everyone—especially the budget-minded—and doesn't try or need to be. Its ultimate strength lies in its meticulous service, which trickles down from hands-on family management. Very Expensive.

🦈 **Land Shark Divers Hotel** (305-515-8408 or 866-572-4876; www .landsharkdivers.com), W. Bay St. Poised between downtown Nassau and Cable Beach, the Land Shark can afford to offer reasonable prices. Its two-story, hot pink stucco building accommodates divers' basic needs with an open-air, vaulted-ceilinged restaurant serving all meals and beverages. Some of its 40 rooms have showers between two rooms that must be shared, while others have tubs in a private bathroom. Nine are designed for underwater photographers, with large sinks and counter

space. There's a TV, fridge, and paddle fans in each room, but no telephone. Tank-filling and a swimming pool further serve diver needs; excursions go through Stuart Cove's, and packages are available. It keeps earth-friendly in small measures, such as providing a complimentary mug and bar of soap to use during your stay to minimize disposables. Inexpensive to Moderate.

Paradise Island

✦ "T" **Atlantis** (242-363-3000; www .atlantis.com), 1 Casino Dr. Clearly the most recognized property in the Bahamas, Atlantis rivals Orlando and Las Vegas for sheer drama and glitz. Opened in 1994 with two lodging towers, known today as the Beach and Coral towers, plus the start of its ever-expanding water park and aquarium, today it encompasses 171 acres and is still growing. Phase II entailed relocating its casino (the largest in the Caribbean, they say) to a new building that connects to the Royal Towers. An administrator compared property accommodations thusly: Beach and Coral are coach, Royal Towers are business class, The Cove is first class. The last was, with The Reef condo-hotel, part of the latest phase, which departed from the resort's Lost City theme with an Asian, oh-so-Zen flair. In the meantime, so many amenities and attractions have cropped up that it takes at least a week to enjoy them all. Besides shops and restaurants in each of the towers, Marina Village re-creates the feel of a Bahamian settlement with Bahamian-New England-style cottages holding 20-some shops and restaurants. Family entertainment goes well beyond the resort's 12 theme pools. Take for instance the Atlantis Speedway, where

EXQUISITE ARCHITECTURAL DETAIL EVOKES A MYTHICAL LOST UNDERWATER KINGDOM AT ATLANTIS.

you can build and race your own car or monster truck; or Club Rush, just for tweens and teens; or free movies in the theater. Its dolphin interaction programs go one step beyond others with the Deep Water Swim, where participants have use of a motorized, handheld water scooter to swim and dive with the animals. For adults, the casino, a spa, a golf course, and three nightclubs entertain. The Cove is most suited to couples, with its own adults-only Cain at the Cove pool exclusively for its guests, complete with poolside blackjack and craps tables, cabanas, and a bar. Besides all these amenities, guests can hop a shuttle to the One and Only Ocean Club, the resort's upscale sister property (to complete the analogy, described as a private jet) minutes away. Both offer beach access and snorkeling. With 38 restaurants and lounges, you could stay a couple of weeks and still have new experiences—if your credit card doesn't have a meltdown first. Expensive to Very Expensive.

ⁱⁱ **Club Land'or** (804-346-8200 or 800-552-2839; www.clublandor.com),

Paradise Beach Dr. Tucked into a corner of Paradise Island that Atlantis hasn't yet claimed, Club Land'or reflects the aura of an era before. Its one-bedroom villas with porches or balconies occupy low-rise two- or three-story buildings on the backside of Atlantis Marina and overlook the fountain in the courtyard. White wicker, tile, and floral patterns characterize the décor of the time-share units, which are rentable by the week and can comfortably accommodate four. Fully stocked kitchens include appliances down to flatware. Wireless Internet access is available for a fee. A pool and pool bar plus scheduled activities keep guests occupied when they're not off exploring Atlantis, Paradise Island's easily accessible shopping, and Nassau. (The ferry to Nassau is a five-minute walk away.) The resort's Blue Lagoon restaurant (see *Dining*) is acclaimed for its classic Continental fare and Bahamian breakfasts. Oasis Lounge hosts live entertainment six nights a week. Beverage, activities, and meal-inclusive plans are available. Expensive.

ⁱⁱ **Comfort Suites** (242-363-3680 or

800-517-4000; www.comfortsuitespi
.com), Paradise Island Dr. This comfortable, well-rounded place to stay is
one way to enjoy nearby Atlantis without quite the sticker shock. Guests
have complimentary access to
Atlantis's beach, water parks, kids
camp, and more, plus charging privileges and a convenient walkway to the
casino. The property—pretty with
Bahamian-inspired architecture, but
slightly chipped—has its own nice, little, vegetation-hidden pool with a
swim-up bar, a restaurant for complimentary continental breakfast (lunch
is also available), and a guest laundry.
Its 228 junior suites have a sitting
area with a sofa bed and a refrigerator. Expensive to Very Expensive.

♂ "1" **One&Only Ocean Club**
(242-363-2501 or 800-321-3000; www
.oneandonlyresorts.com), 1 Casino Dr.
If Atlantis isn't rich enough for your
blood—or if it's just plain too big—
opt for this sister property, long a Paradise Island showpiece. It dates back
to 1962 and A&P heir Huntington
Hartford II, who once owned most of
the island. His original resort holds
roughly 50 of the property's 105
rooms and suites (plus three villas).
The rest occupy the newer, circa-2000
Crescent Wing overlooking a wide
spread of green lawn, hammocks
strung on palms, and Cabbage Beach.
Everything here is over-top-of-the-
line, including a fresh bowl of fruit in
the room (red wine and complimentary laptop use in the suites), 19-inch
TVs and oval Jacuzzis framed with
mosaic arches in the bathrooms,
shower and steam rooms, bidets, rain-
forest showers, complimentary DVD
and Wi-Fi use, and designer plantation-style décor with hardwood floors.
Thick, gorgeous gardens line pathways between the buildings, yoga
deck, and rolling golden sand beach
with roped-off swim area. The highlight of the grounds, the Versailles
Garden and Cloisters terrace, are the
scene of many a wedding. The Tech-
no-gym features a groundbreaking
system of customized workouts. The
spa has an Asian temperament with
villa treatment rooms; staff members
first serve tea to you on a daybed in
the outer room, and you can enjoy the
Jacuzzi tub before your treatment.
The Versailles pool (must be 15 or
older) and zero-entry family pool plus
two other restaurants complete this
picture of secluded privilege. KidsOn-
ly activities cater to 4- to 12-year-olds.
Guests can also enjoy Atlantis by hopping aboard the free shuttle. Very
Expensive.

✳ Where to Eat

Cost categories are based on the
range of dinner entrée prices or, if
dinner is not served, on lunch
entrées.Reservations are accepted
only where indicated.

Price Codes
Inexpensive	Up to $15
Moderate	$15 to $25
Expensive	$25 to $35
Very Expensive	$35 or more

Cable Beach
Amici, A Trattoria (242-327-6000 or
800-627-9114; www.sheraton.com/
cablebeach), at Sheraton Resort. I
need an Italian fix no matter where I
vacation, and this is Nassau's best
choice as far as I'm concerned. It's
classic enough to satisfy my comfort
food urges, yet experimental enough
to excite my culinary sense of adventure. You get that feeling the minute
you walk in. The airy space has a ceil-

ing that reaches to the lobby one floor up. Oversized lanterns and strung light bulbs keep it bright while peach-colored, sail-like cloths soften the effect to create an atmosphere at once ultrastylish and casual. For the utmost casual, ask for a patio table with a view of the sea and beach. Start with something off the antipasti menu, such as the excellent yin-yang, crispy cream *cuscinetti vegetarani* (roasted vegetables in lightly fried pasta pockets with tasty plum tomato coulis), or the chilled calamari with radicchio slaw and hot cherry pepper vinaigrette. Like any good Italian menu, it's divided among pasta (seafood risotto, spaghetti and meat-balls), meat (balsamic-glazed grilled lamb loin, roasted pork chop stuffed with prosciutto and fontina), and fish (pan-seared salmon with honey citrus thyme glaze, lobster tail with tomato basil cream, and lobster ravioli). Expensive. Reservations accepted.

& **Androsia Steak & Seafood** (242-327-7805), at Shoppers Haven Plaza. A bit of Andros Island influence, a bit of *français,* and a good deal of creativity went into the making of this corner strip mall gem. Its signature peppersteak au Paris, classic with peppercorn brandy cream, comes from a Les Halles restaurant recipe. For breakfast, you can sample all the traditional souses and stewed dishes in addition to pancakes and omelets. Andros is famous for its land crab harvests, so it's no surprise to find "Andros buttons"—crab cakes—on the menu. Conch and sweet potato fritters, however, are a pleasant discovery. For dinner entrées, in addition to standard Bahamian fare, you'll find garlic shrimp, fruit-stuffed pork chops, papas Androsia (twice-baked

potatoes with lobster conch chowder), and the Sun, Sand & Sea—grilled honey garlic chicken breast, beef strips, and pan-seared grouper. Moderate to Expensive. Reservations accepted. No breakfast served Sunday or Tuesday.

& ○ **Black Angus Grille** (242-327-6200 or 800-WYNDHAM; www.wyndhamnassauresort.com), Wyndham Nassau Resort. The name obviously refers to the moo on the menu, but doesn't give a true picture of its breadth. Take for instance, its unusual blackened conch appetizer, an impeccable and entertaining tableside Caesar salad performance, seared scallop gnocchi tossed with roasted pumpkin lemon sage cream sauce, THE best lobster mac and cheese side dish (enough for many), and a strawberry shortcake that defies description. The signature dish is roasted garlic filet with gorgonzola sauce. Steaks arrive precisely as ordered with a choice of sauces such as truffle herb butter or brandy peppercorn, and service is over-the-top. The wine list showcases mostly California vintages in a nice variety. Located on the floor above Wyndham's Crystal Palace Casino, it feels like a touch of class after trailing through casino lights-and-smoke flashiness. White tablecloths and heavy leather chairs nod to classic steakhouse style. Expensive to Very Expensive. Reservations accepted. Closed Sunday and Monday.

& **Simmer Down** (242-702-2800; www.marleyresort.com), Marley Resort & Spa, W. Bay St. Like its adjacent Stir It Up bar, the restaurant is named for songs by the late reggae kingpin Bob Marley, who once vacationed in the home that has become this resort. Some of his favorite dishes

DINE ALFRESCO OR IN A COZY INDOOR ROOM AT MARLEY RESORT'S SIMMER DOWN.

show up on the menu, including pan-fried catch with sweet potato polenta. Other specialties are rooted in Jamaica and the Bahamas: Ital (Rasta vegetarian) pepper pot soup, lobster and coconut froth, seafood and cheese terrine, jerk chicken roulade with rice croquette, Bahamian lobster duo (fried and broiled) with Jamaican vegetable rundown and homemade mango chutney, and Junkanoo consommé—fresh tropical fruit in a chilled ginger vanilla consommé with mango sorbet, a pineapple wonton, and sesame brittle. Of course there's Blue Mountain coffee and soothing views of the sea or the restaurant's fountain. Very Expensive. Reservations accepted.

Gambier Village

&. **Compass Point** (242-327-4500; www.compasspointbeachresort.com), W. Bay St. Opening onto Love Beach and its sparkling ocean surf, this place has held onto the endearing aspects of old-island dining while adding a modern-day, trendy touch that draws locals and visitors from downtown to this resort getaway, especially for Sunday brunch ($25.95 for adults, $12.95 for kids 11 and younger). Lunch is popular too, with fusion selections such as conch wrap, fish burger, and jerk-grilled chicken Caesar wrap. Extensive for such a small place, its dinner menu goes from Bahamian staples such as cracked conch and roasted chicken with barbecued ribs and fried plantains to seafood pot pie, grilled tuna, and chicken Parmesan. For dessert, go native with the guava duff or fusion with the coconut crème brûlée. Moderate to Expensive. Reservations accepted.

✪ **Travellers' Rest** (242-327-7633; www.bahamastravellersrest.com), W. Bay St. A perfect way to decompress after a day of flying, Travellers' Rest is near the airport but even nearer to the sea. From its casual porch, all the colors of Bahamian gem-waters shimmer. You could choose to sit inside with the luxury of tablecloths (Androsia batik—this restaurant is owned by the family who started that industry on Andros Island), but there's no air-conditioning and it cuts down on the view. Lunch and dinner menus are the same, except you don't get a choice of two sides—yard salad, peas 'n' rice, or french fries—with lunch. Specialties include barbecued ribs, minced crawfish (lobster) with onions and peppers in tomato sauce, surf and turf (with grilled or minced crawfish), fried snapper, and seafood platter of fish fingers, cracked conch, and breaded shrimp. Don't miss: conch chowder with johnnycake, smudder fish (fried grouper steamed in tomato sauce), and guava cake. On weekends, there's conch salad and fritters. Moderate.

Nassau

& **Bullion** (242-302-9001; www .bullionnassau.com), 1 Bay St. Mainly designed for sipping, it's also an affordable spot to drink fashionably while mingling and noshing on small-plate specialties such as coconut and sweet potato soup, cranberry-pome-granate salad, skewered meatball with red and yellow pepper coulis, honey-sesame shrimp, mini Angus burgers, vegetable wraps, jerk chicken bruschetta, and the like. The food is good, but the cocktails are truly gour-met, mixed with all house-made syrups and resurrecting old classics such as the Manhattan and Sazarac. The Rumbullion, the old-school name for rum, uses fresh lime and pineap-ple juice with a homemade ginger infusion to sweeten its dark rum. The signature quaff, named Quackenboss, blends bourbon and passion fruit with a mint-lime sugar rim. Bullion also has a select menu of wines and cham-pagnes, all served in stylish glassware to go with the overall art deco feel. Sit at the burnished copper bar or upon one of the chunky couches and chairs in shades of orange, plum, and lime. Inexpensive.

♣ & **Café Skan's** (242-322-2486), Bay St. When a Bahamian puts his or her name on a restaurant, you can be sure there's pride in the food and home cooking in the kitchen. Skan's serves classic island dishes—chicken souse, stew fish, crack (deep-fried) lobster, pan-fried conch, steamed snapper—as well as American favorites such as omelets, croissand-wiches, grilled pork chop sandwiches, and burgers. You'll also find Greek specialties such as Greek salad, gyros, and grilled octopus. Nightly specials range from beef liver to wahoo. A diner-style joint with an open kitchen right smack on otherwise overpriced Bay Street, it's a favorite with locals and value-seekers. Inexpensive to Moderate.

& **Conch Fritters** (242-323-8778), Marlborough St. A popular downtown spot that tends to be a little too crowded and a little too warm inside after you've been traipsing downtown, Conch Fritters is equally popular with visitors and locals for its wide variety of Bahamian food. Many come for the $10 daily lunch special, such as lamb chops, fried snapper, baked chicken, or lasagna. Otherwise, there's every-thing from burgers and barbecued chicken to T-bone steak, grilled salmon, and a $50 seafood sampler. Friday's Bahama Buffet is $19.95. Moderate to Expensive.

❖ **Graycliff Restaurant** (242-302-9150; www.graycliff.com), W. Hill St. It's rare these days to find in the U.S. the classic tableside manners inspired by French culinary standards. The Bahamas have held on longer in places such as Graycliff, and how refreshing it feels. You begin this defining Nassau dining experience in the parlor, where couches, paddle fans, a baby grand, and shelves full of the finest liquors, wines, and liqueurs induce relaxation. You may start with the signature aperitif of champagne, Chambord, Calvados, Grand Marnier, and a slice of orange and cherry in a flute—Sangria elevated. Or one of a dozen fine Caribbean rums or cognac on the rocks. Or a sip from one of the 275,000 bottles the wine cellar underneath the lobby holds—the world's third largest. Dorothy, I don't think we're in the Bahamas anymore. Not true, really: This is the Bahamas of the wealthy in colonial days, the European flip side to the African that makes such an intriguing yin-yang Bahamas whole. Back to the food: You make your decision in the lobby and once you've ordered you're seated at a table in one of a half-dozen venues—the windowed Gallery Room, the most popular. It can be a multicourse affair, but doesn't have to be. The night I dined I noticed some dropped standards on dress and decorum. Courses came at a leisurely pace; service was overattentive. Between my signature house salad—greens with a peppercorn-studded vinaigrette—and coconut flake-flavored slices of bread, I slurped a spoonful of raspberry sorbet. My *coeur de filet quatre poivres* was flawless in degree of doneness and execution of the four-peppercorn and brandy sauce. One of the white-jacketed members of my service team presented the grand finale—guava soufflé—by topping it tableside with a creamy hard sauce inspired by the islands' popular guava duff dessert. The macho way to end the experience is with a cigar freshly rolled in the lobby by one of the hotel's cigar factory rollers. Wine-lovers can attend wine luncheons complete with a tour of the wine cellar, where American Navy soldiers garrisoned in the 1770s.

You can also commission its private dining room if you dig dungeons and the presence of 3,800 different vintages, including what they claim to be the world's oldest bottle of wine: a $200,000 1727 German white. Very Expensive. Reservations highly recommended.

🦐 ♿ **New Briland Big Ten Lounge, Restaurant & Bar** (242-326-3395), W. Bay St., Arawak Cay. Known for its fresh conch stands, the huddle of colorful eateries at Arawak Cay (a.k.a. Fish Fry) also provides a variety of sit-down restaurants specializing in native cuisine. The restaurants cater to Bahamians in business suits and tourists in sunburns, and sidewalk hawkers vie vigorously for the latter's business. (The locals already have their favorites.) I chose this one because on a hot September day, it promised air-conditioning on its second floor, where there's also a balcony for alfresco dining with a view of Fort Charlotte on yonder hill. Its name hints at a Harbour Island (Eleuthera) connection—islanders there call themselves Brilanders. Downstairs has more of a bar atmosphere, sans AC. The all-day menu specializes in steamed snapper, Creole-style grouper or lobster and dumpling (a doughy, hockey-puck-like starch), grilled conch, and fried grouper. The extensive menu also offers stir-fry lobster, shrimp, or conch; steak; and grilled lobster. Pick your choice of two sides: peas 'n' rice, potato salad, baked macaroni and cheese, or fried plantain. Other recommended restaurants in the complex include Twin Brothers and Goldie's. Inexpensive to Moderate. Reservations accepted.

🦐 ♿ **Pepperpot Grill** (242-323-8177), King and Market Sts. Tucked off the typical cruise ship passengers' beaten path, this small family-run eatery offers a taste of a different West Indian island, where jerk chicken was invented and ackee and saltfish is the national dish. Yah, Jamaica, mon. Heaping plates of oxtail, curry or jerk chicken, escovitch (fried and pickled) fish, curried mutton, and pan-seared, grilled, or steamed grouper come to plain tables. In the Jamaican Ital (health food) tradition, the restaurant owners juice fresh soursop, mangoes, carrots, and more according to season. Here's a good place to escape the throngs for something genuinely island. Inexpensive. Closed after 5 and on Sunday. Credit cards not accepted.

♿ **The Poop Deck** (242-393-8175; www.thepoopdeckrestaurants.com), E. Bay St. One of the destination's most oft-mentioned favorites, The Poop Deck's harbor setting and fresh seafood combine for an inimitable experience. Trays of fresh fish greet you as you enter, and you can choose which will become your dinner or lunch. Whole hogfish or red snapper are the specialty (market price). Other seafood choices include grilled grouper, stone crab claws (in season), grilled lobster tail (market price), and combo platters. In addition to Bahamian specialties at lunch, the menu offers a choice of burgers (try the peppercorn-crusted version) and other hot and cold sandwiches and salads (grilled mahi Caesar, for example). Moderate to Expensive. Reservations accepted.

Paradise Island
♿ **Anthony's Grill** (242-363-3152; www.anthonysgrillparadiseisland.com), Paradise Village Shopping Center. To escape the sticker shock at Atlantis, take a short walk to this brightly decorated place with a page-after-page menu designed to please all hankerings. Breakfast is American-style with a few offbeat offerings such as oatmeal with cinnamon and nutmeg, smoked salmon platter, and sirloin and eggs. Lunch and dinner menus list some typical Bahamian conch-fish selections that make them palatable to American tastes, but also pizza, pasta, conch cakes, steaks, and a full assortment of rum blender drinks. Gold-yellow walls, fanciful fish, and striped booths make the big dining room inviting. Moderate to Expensive.

♿ **Bimini Road** (242-363-3000, Ext. 29; www.atlantis.com), Marina Village, Atlantis. With all the color and flavor you expect from the Bahamas, Bimini Road's contemporized setting and menu present one of Atlantis's most affordable and authentic options. The name comes from underwater ruins found offshore of Bimini, which have led the fanciful to conjure a road that once led to the Lost City of Atlantis. Take a seat on the porch, around the bar, or in a booth around the display kitchen—framed to look like the front of a traditional Bahamian home—and its seafood showcase. A bright Junkanoo mural and masks also decorate the inside space. The bar/lunch menu is limited. For dinner, take a culinary sail around the Caribbean with such starters as seven-bean soup with smoked pork, fried tostones with barbecue pulled pork and melted cheese, and key lime Caesar. In addition to burgers, Cuban sandwiches, crab wraps, and shrimp rolls, there are Kalik-battered cracked conch, tamarind-glazed St. Louis ribs, lobster tail, fire-grilled rib eye with stewed

Kalik onions, guava duff, and chocolate-mango rum cake with tamarind syrup. Moderate to Expensive.

Blue Lagoon Seafood Restaurant (242-363-2400; www.clublandor.com), Club Land'or Resort. Because I'm a huge fan of Bahamian traditional breakfast, I come here whenever I'm on the island for stew fish, souse, or whatever else they have available that day. Last time it was steamed tuna and grits, the fish minced with onions, bell pepper, and tomato sauce. Expect to wait 30 minutes for its famous stew fish when available. Its breakfast menu also offers American favorites plus a Friday breakfast buffet. At dinner, seafood takes a Continental turn with grouper amandine, lobster thermidor, seafood en brochette, scampi with mushrooms, and roasted rack of spring lamb or chateaubriand for two. The restaurant perches above the lobby like a crow's nest, and its bar, decorated with nautical brass and stained glass, overlooks the resort's courtyard through a wall of windows. It holds onto an era of Bahamian dining where tableside service and classic French cuisine held sway. Indulge in the crêpes suzette a l'orange for two or go native with guava pudding. Expensive to Very Expensive. Reservations accepted.

& **Chopstix** (242-363-3000, Ext. 29; www.atlantis.com), Coral Tower, Atlantis. Low lighting gives this sweeping dining room an intimate feel, warmed by the limestone rock wall in the bar. Like most of Atlantis's restaurants, it gives Chinese cuisine an upscale boost, serving everything from noodle dishes to dim sum to grilled New York strip steak. Dim sum comes in flavors such as scallion rolls, chicken potstickers, and lobster

shu mei. There's something for everyone on the entrées bill of fare—vegetable and tofu dishes, caramelized hoisin beef, wok-seared grouper with garlic sauce, red curry shrimp, or grilled chicken breast or grouper with your choice of sauce or rub. Moderate to Very Expensive. Reservations accepted.

& **Dune** (242-363-2501; www.oneandonlyresorts.com), One&Only Ocean Club. Would you prefer spicy or rosemary oil with your salty bread, a cross between ciabatta and johnnycake? Still or sparkling water? So begins your decision-making at the inimitable Dune, named for its eyeful of sand and water right outside the window. The restaurant serves all meals, with bar and snack service at the outdoor white clapboard beach bar in between. Traditional classic Bahamian and American breakfasts offer nice variety. Big eaters can pay $34 for a spread of French toast with mango, potato galette with smoked salmon, and eggs Benedict. Lunch prices in the $20 range get you a burger, black truffle and fontina pizza, grilled chicken club with avocado, and other generous if costly specialties. Dinner's tasting menu costs $98, or you can opt for à la carte fusion masterpieces such as sushi, grilled shrimp with avocado and soy-garlic vinaigrette, roasted grouper with herb mashed potatoes, lobster with baby bok and fried plantains, Parmesancrusted organic chicken, or stir-fry of asparagus, lotus root, and shiitake mushrooms. Splurge on the crème fraîche chocolate cake with fresh berry compote. Besides the beach, which is all the atmosphere one needs, the restaurant's interior soothes with Asian design, a vaulted ceiling, and a display kitchen. Very Expensive. Reservations highly recommended.

&. ☺ **Mesa Grill** (242-363-6900; www.mesagrill.com or www.atlantis.com), The Cove at Atlantis. Food Channel celeb Bobby Flay's third venture transplants his brand of Southwest U.S. fare to tropical climes in a fairly seamless manner. Most of this menu sticks close to the same culinary tenets he practices at his New York and Vegas restaurants, but with some small bows to Bahamia such as the spiced chicken skewers with mango vinaigrette and crispy conch appetizers or the pan-roasted grouper with coconut curry on the entrée list. Closer to Flay's specialty, you'll find complex inventions such as the multidimensional blue pancake and barbecued duck appetizer; ancho chile-honey glazed salmon with spicy black bean sauce and roasted jalapeño crema; cornmeal-crusted chile relleno filled with roasted eggplant, manchego cheese, and red pepper sauce; and chipotle-glazed rib eye with red and green chili sauce. Have a cactus pear margarita at the red terrazzo-style bar and count the number of tequilas—more than 35—and single-village mescals. Totally hip in design, practically every table in the lofty space, divided only by open shelving filled with huge apothecary jars of orchids, overlooks the sea. Guests must be 12 years or older. Expensive to Very Expensive. Reservations crucial.

&. **Nobu** (242-363-3000, Ext. 29; www.atlantis.com), Atlantis Casino. Chef Nobuyuki Matsuhisa creates his aura of Asian peace and umami at this ultracool, ultraexpensive marina-side space. Elemental in design with rocks

strung from the ceiling at the entrance, raw wood, and bamboo, it brought Atlantis dining to its peak when opened in 1998. A backlit marble bar centerpieces the sexy lounge and the sushi bar. A private sake room affords a tasting experience, including the chain's own Nobu sake, for at least six diners paying $260 each. Don't gasp—special multicourse meals are $150 each; washu beef goes for $22 an ounce. You can eat more frugally by choosing sushi, ceviche, and tempura nibbles with soup or noodles. Hot dishes such as oysters in filo with vegetable sauce, squid pasta, and Arctic char won't break the bank. One specialty of the house is wood-oven-grilled (kushi-yaki) dishes such as organic chicken, tenderloin, and Bahamian or Maine lobster. Make your reservations as far ahead as possible because, despite the price tags, this place fills up. Very Expensive. Reservations crucial.

Mount Pleasant
&. **Goodfellow Farms** (242-377-5000; www.goodfellowfarms.com), Nelson Rd., West End. Especially pleasant during the cool winter and spring months, Goodfellow Farms sets tables among its gardens and features whatever is in season on its ever-changing menu. Walk through the shop where you can ogle and buy its fresh, organic fruits and vegetables, then check in outside to place your order from the dry-erase board offering a dozen or so choices that might include smoked turkey and couscous salad on greens, pastrami panini, or shrimp and pasta salad on greens. Then pick your beverage—juice, soda, or beer—from the cooler on the way to your alfresco table. Everything tastes fresh and you just

feel healthy sitting among the blossoms and hummingbirds. The farm supplies a lot of local restaurants and is something of a secret. It's out west near Lyford Cay—best to call ahead for directions. Moderate.

BAKERIES Tortuga Rum Cake Bakery (242-363-3000, Ext. 29; Marina Village, Atlantis, Paradise Island) This Cayman Islands product has expanded across the islands with flavors such as banana, chocolate, coconut, key lime, and pineapple in addition to the original rum cake. Also sells coffees.

HEALTH FOODS Jamba Juice (242-363-3000, Ext. 29; Marina Village, Atlantis, Paradise Island) Fresh fruit and vegetable smoothies and juices, including wheat grass juice. Also salads and sandwiches.

ICE CREAM & CANDY Bahama Sol (242-326-8678; www.sundrop creations.com; Paradise Shopping Plaza, Paradise Island) It carries Bernie's Bahamian-made ice cream by the taster, cone, pint, or quart. Flavors such as mango, guava, soursop, and rum raisin are mildly sweet, natural, and very tasty.

Oh Sugar (242-363-3000, Ext. 29; Marina Village, Atlantis, Paradise Island) Bulk candy; gummies in dozens of shapes and flavors, from sand sharks to cola bottles; jelly beans; and much more.

ISLAND MARKETS Farmer's Market (New Providence Community Center, near the airport) Held every Saturday.

Goodfellow Farms (242-377-5000; www.goodfellowfarms.com; Nelson

THE SEAFOOD VENDORS OF POTTER'S CAY COLLECT UNDER THE BRIDGE TO PARADISE ISLAND.

Road, Mount Pleasant, New Providence) Homegrown produce, quality meats, seafood, cheeses, and other gourmet items. Serves lunch in the gardens daily.

SEAFOOD ✪ **Potter's Cay** (under the Paradise Island Bridge) Vendors sell fresh fish and produce straight off the boats. Try McKenzie's (242-455-3582) for the best conch salad and other fresh Bahamian seafood.

✳ Selective Shopping

Nassau is a buyer's market. Bay Street and Woodes Rogers Walk are lined with duty-free shops, jewelry stores, T-shirt and souvenir shops, and the Nassau straw market—so you can find something in every price range. Many of Nassau's stores also have satellite branches at Atlantis. The Crystal Court near the casino holds the high-end shops such as Bulgari, John Bull, Versace, Gucci, David Yurman, et al. Marina Village feels more genuinely Bahamian in its outdoor setting with craft kiosks and a Junkanoo or steel band playing in the evenings.

Atlantis Kids (242-363-3000, Ext. 29), Coral Tower, Atlantis, Paradise Island. Besides its gratuitous logo wear, it carries T-shirts, swimwear, and other clothing for girls, plus stuffed sea-themed toys and other kid stuff.

Bahama Craft Centre, Paradise Island near Atlantis. A typical straw market with dozens of vendors selling straw bags, knockoff designer handbags, hats, T-shirts, jewelry, and wood carvings.

Bahama Sol (242-326-8678; www .sundropcreations.com), Paradise Shopping Plaza, Paradise Island. A nice sampling of Bahamian-made gifts such as Androsia batik, jams, hot sauces, soy candles, soaps, and Christmas ornaments.

✪ **Bob Marley Boutique** (242-327-4391), Marley Resort, W. Bay St., Cable Beach. Clothing designed by members of the Marley family, Rasta sandals and T-shirts, Marley posters, reggae CDs, Jamaican-made jewelry, and other Caribbean and African arts and crafts.

Coin of the Realm (242-322-4862; www.coinrealm.net), Charlotte St. off Bay St., Nassau. Housed in a circa-1700 gunpowder magazine, it explodes with treasures such as a pink flamingo broach of conch pearl and diamonds, other jewelry, treasure coins, and stamps. It specializes in conch "pearls." The only Bahamian native gem, it forms inside the queen conch.

Cole's of Nassau (242-363-3000, Ext. 29), Crystal Court, Atlantis, Paradise Island. Women's apparel from board shorts to dressy frocks, sandals, bags, and pumps.

Festival, Wharf, Nassau. Geared to grab cruise ship passengers' dollars,

CONCH SOUVENIRS
Bahamians and their visitors eat tons of conch every month, and the leftover shells don't get wasted. Stands along West Bay Street sell the shells whole. In recent years, craftsmen have begun to fashion lovely, porcelainlike works from their pretty-in-pink interiors. You'll find bowls, implements, Christmas ornaments, jewelry, and other souvenirs in the finer gift shops and galleries.

its jaunty, indoor, air-conditioned collection of stands made to look like Bahamian homes sells books, straw items, rum cake, and other souvenirs. Down the street at the straw market, you can get the same stuff for half the price. A pseudo Junkanoo band grabs guests to play along and take pictures.

The Island Shop & Island Book Shop (242-322-4183 or 242-322-1011 for bookstore), Bay St. Nassau. Up front, it's tourist stuff. Head to the back of the store to find the best selection of Bahamian and West Indian literature and books.

Park Lane Jewelers (242-363-1234), Marina Village, Atlantis, Paradise Island. Among all the chain duty-frees at Atlantis, this one stands out with exclusive collections such as Roberto Coin, DiModolo, Krieger Swiss Watches, Kabana, and Gento.

✪ **The Plait Lady** (242-363-1416), Marina Village, Atlantis, Paradise Island. If you're looking for authentic straw works made by Bahamian hands, skip the straw markets, pay more, and get quality baskets, hats, mats, and other items made on Andros and Long Island. It also carries unique gifts such as beautiful dish-and-spoon sets carved from conch shells, Bahama Mama dolls, and Christmas ornaments.

Royal Palm Boutique (242-363-3000, Ext. 29), Coral Tower, Atlantis, Paradise Island. Roxy T-shirts and Tommy Bahama shirts to dressy fashions for women.

✪ **Sea Grape Gift Shop** (242-327-1308), W. Bay St., Gambier Village. Next to the popular Travellers' Rest seaside restaurant, it sells Androsia batik clothing, jewelry, and other nice Bahamian souvenirs.

Tommy Bahama (242-363-3000, Ext. 29), Coral Tower, Atlantis, Paradise Island. Tropical-style clothing, shoes, watches, sunglasses, and other accessories for men only.

✳ Special Events

In the Bahamas, **Cricket Season** runs March through November at the Haynes Oval Nassau Cricket Club, across the street from Arawak Cay. Matches take place every Saturday and Sunday throughout the season. A restaurant and bar at the Cricket Club looks out on the oval.

Rugby Season (242-328-7888) starts the end of September and continues through April at Winton Rugby Field off Prince Charles Drive.

March: **Nassau Race Week** (242-393-5132; www.miaminassaurace week.com), Montagu Bay, Nassau. Three days of sailing and partying, including a Miami to Nassau race.

June: **Junkanoo Summer Festival** (Arawak Cay, Nassau). Every Saturday in June, experience a taste of this holiday parade tradition from 1 to 10 PM.

August: **Emancipation Day** (Fox Hill Village, Nassau). Bahamians celebrate their freedom from slavery on Aug. 3 with Junkanoo, religious services, games, music, and the "climbing the greasy pole" competition.

October: **Regatta World Championship** (Nassau Yacht Club). Ten days starting midmonth.

November: **Christmas Jollification** (242-393-1317), The Retreat, Village Road, Nassau. Three days late in the month. You've got to love the name! Get jolly on holiday food and music and Bahamian arts and crafts.

December: **Bahamas International Film Festival** (242-356-5939; www .bintlfilmfest.com). One week midmonth. Films from the world over, workshops, and awards. **Beat Retreat** (Rawson Square, Nassau). One day midmonth. The Royal Bahamas Police Force Band presents its drill display to traditional and Bahamian Christmas music. **Junkanoo** (throughout Nassau and Paradise Island). Around the holidays. It begins with Junior Junkanoo and National Junkanoo Competition Finals along Bay Street and in Rawson Square, and reaches fever pitch on Boxing Day (Dec. 26) and New Year's Day.

Grand Bahama Island

LUCAYA

FREEPORT

WEST END

EAST END

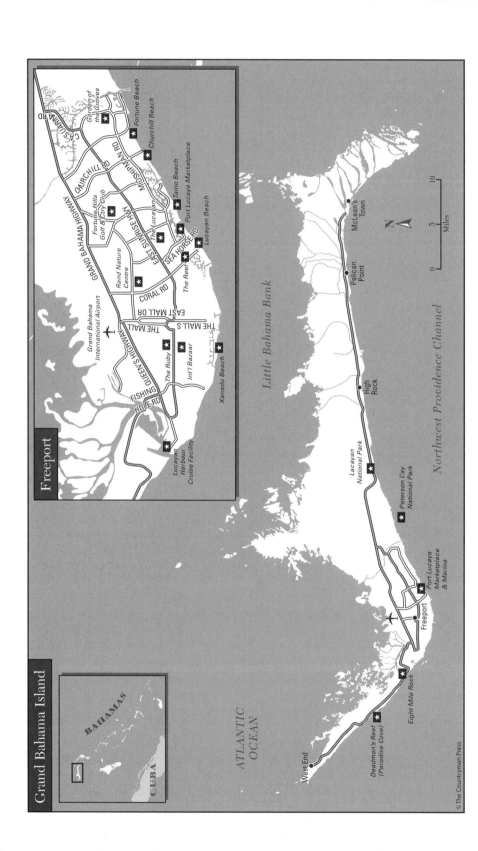

Grand Bahama Island

Freeport

BAHAMAS

CUBA

ATLANTIC OCEAN

West End

Deadman's Reef
(Paradise Cove)

Eight Mile Rock

Freeport

Port Lucaya
Marketplace
& Marina

Peterson Cay
National Park

Lacayan
National Park

High
Rock

Pelican
Point

McLean's
Town

Little Bahama Bank

Northwest Providence Channel

N

0   5   10
Miles

© The Countryman Press

Garden of
the Groves

Fortune Beach

Churchill Beach

Taino Beach

Port Lucaya Marketplace

Lucayan Beach

CASUARINA RD

CHURCHILL RD

MIDSHIPMAN RD

GRAND BAHAMA HIGHWAY

Fortune Hills
Golf & Cr'y Club

The Lucayan

EAST SUNRISE HWY

SEA HORSE RD

Rand Nature
Centre

The Reef

CORAL RD

Grand Bahama
International Airport

EAST MALL DR

THE MALL

THE MALL S

The Ruby

Int'l Bazaar

Xanadu Beach

FISHING
HOLE RD

QUEEN'S HIGHWAY

Lucayan
Harbour
Cruise Facility

GRAND BAHAMA ISLAND

CITY MOUSE, COUNTRY MOUSE

I t's 8 AM and I am obviously the first visitor of the day to the trails that plumb the bowels of the earth and cross a mangrove forest that you actually look down upon. The caves are deathly still—like the remains of the Lucayan aboriginals that have been discovered here.

But on the boardwalk crossing the tidal creek and its stunted, leather-leaved mangroves, I flush startled and squawking small birds and one majestic great blue heron, Seusslike in its deliberate but graceful ascent into the December morning's cool.

Lucayan National Park: When Freeport first blipped across travelers' radar in the '60s, no one paid much attention to "the bush," as locals call its outback. Tourists were too busy discovering the exotic lure of a resort, casino, and shopping center that whisked their whims off on an Arabian Night's magic carpet.

I discovered Grand Bahama Island back when it was simply known as **Freeport,** back in the days when the onion-domed Princess Resort with its two golf courses, International Bazaar, and casino was the epicenter and *raison d'etre*. Who realized it tied but a small knot in the 96-mile-long island's composition?

The blackjack tables have turned. Today Freeport's big resort lies fallow, while its neighboring **Lucaya** upholds the island's resort/casino/duty-free shopping reputation. Port Lucaya Marketplace and Our Lucaya Beach and Golf Resort have upstaged Freeport's erstwhile act, helped by 2004's hurricane decimation of the Royal Oasis resort that had ascended Princess's throne.

In a way, it's a strange kind of karma. Freeport had dealt the same blow to **West End** in the '60s. The island's capital and one-time hot spot, West End and its Jack Tar Village embraced rumrunners to name-brand vacationers looking for escape.

When American financier Wallace Groves conceived Freeport, 25 miles to the east, as a tax-free haven for shipping and resorts, thriving West End deflated. Today, with the American economic situation upon which the Bahamas are so dependent, Grand Bahama Island continues a struggle to regain the glory of its early West End and later Freeport days.

In the meantime, the emphasis has turned to ecotourism. That ground had been laid in the late '60s, when a Lucaya-based diving operation named UNEX-SO (Underwater Explorers Society) focused on the island's marine treasures. About the same time, the Bahamas National Trust gave the world Lucayan National Park, some 30 miles east of Lucaya. Its 40 acres encompass the doorway to one of the world's longest mapped underground cave systems, home to nesting bats in summer and a new species of crustacean discovered there. The caves led to the preservation of the unspoiled acreage, which spreads through a variety of ecosystems before reaching its beach and marine habitats.

Much of GBI's early and existing reputation has been based on golf—the best, most varied golfing in the Bahamas with four 18-hole courses and one nine-hole course functioning and another at the Royal Oasis property waiting to reopen. An Irish firm has purchased the property's 2,500 acres and has back-burnered the project, officials say, until the American economy improves. The same is true of Ginn sur Mer, an American-owned development that has stalled at West End. Plans, however, are moving forward on a new cruise ship facility in **William's Town,** a now-quiet little beach settlement near Freeport lined with funky restaurants and bars.

Other small settlements spread on either side of the Freeport-Lucaya area to provide an Out Island, outback experience that balances the island's metro, resort side. Headed toward the East End, one encounters **Smith's Point,** famous for its Wednesday Fish Fry parties. Out past Lucayan National Park, **High Rock** boasts a beautiful, usually secluded beach with a couple of lodges

A STRIP OF SHACKS PAINTED IN JUNKANOO COLORS AND KNOWN AS SUNSET VILLAGE SERVES HOME-COOKED EATS IN THE SEASIDE SETTLEMENT OF EIGHT MILE ROCK.

and beach shack restaurants and a lighthouse replica. The road east ends at **McLean's Point,** home of the annual Conch Cracking Contest. A short ferry ride takes you to the time-stilled settlement of **Sweeting's Cay,** where the yeasty scent of fresh-baked bread sweetens the morning air.

West of Freeport, **Eight Mile Rock** hugs the beach with its historic church, Boiling Hole, and Sunset Village, a cluster of seafood shacks newly rebuilt after Hurricane Wilma in 2005. **Deadman's Reef** is home to Paradise Cove, a resort and snorkeling operation on a beach within short swimming distance to its eponymous reef.

At West End, conch shacks appear along the quiet, mostly deserted waterfront road leading to Old Bahama Bay at Ginn sur Mer, a gated resort. Like the rest of Grand Bahama Island, there's a sense of waiting. It seems a bit ironic that the island boasts the best roads, signage, and tourism infrastructure where the economic picture has been glum and on pause for so long. On the other hand, it's a sign of hope, a hope that has been kept alive since talk about building Our Lucaya first began some 15 years ago. A hope that doesn't falter despite Nassau competition, construction delays, hurricanes, and American recession. A hope that keeps alive this island that somehow combines the best of the Bahamas' urban vibes and Out Island spirit.

DON'T MISS
- Diving or dolphin encounter with UNEXSO.
- Sunning and funning on gorgeous Taino Beach.
- Grilled conch at Billy Joe's on Lucaya Beach.
- Snorkeling at Paradise Cove.
- Kayaking to Lucayan National Park.

SUGGESTED READING Inside Grand Bahama, by Dan Buettner. A dated (1990) guidebook, but with good background information.

✳ To See

CULTURE TOURS East End Charm Tour (242-727-2368; www.jcspecialty tours.com). This six-hour journey to old-island treasures begins in small settlements en route to Lucayan National Park. After exploring the park, tourists experience a conch-shucking demonstration, lunch in a native restaurant, and beach time. Groups can add on kayaking and reef snorkeling for an extra fee.

MUSIC & NIGHTLIFE Club Amnesia (242-351-2582), E. Mall Dr., Freeport; across from International Bazaar. Live entertainment and dancing weekend nights; sports bar open daily.

Outriggers Beach Club (242-373-4811), Smith's Point. Outriggers hosts a Bonfire Party every Tuesday and Thursday night with native foods and unlimited Bahama Mamas. Experience Bahamian entertainment at its finest—fire dancing, crab races, and a conch-shucking demonstration. Wednesday night is Fish Fry, another purely local form of party.

Prop Club Sports Bar & Dance Club (242-373-1333), Sea Horse Rd. at Our Lucaya Beach and Golf Resort, Lucaya. By day, the club rolls up its

> **SIGN ALERT:**
> Littering is Stupid. Don't Do It.

doors to become a beach bar with casual eats. By night, the dance floor comes alive on certain nights, depending on the season. There's also karaoke nights and sports-TV Sundays.

Treasure Bay Casino (242-350-2000 or 888-687-4753), Sea Horse Rd. at Our Lucaya Beach and Golf Resort, Lucaya. Grand Bahama Island was once THE gambling destination of the Bahamas, but with the closing of Freeport's casino due to storm damage in 2004, this remains to bolster the reputation for the time being. Elegant and tropically appointed, it belies the never-see-daylight profile of the erstwhile gambler. Its 320 slot machines are open 24 hours on weekends, and the 33 tables open at 10 am and stay open until as late as 3 am some nights. Games include poker, Caribbean stud, mini-baccarat, craps, blackjack, and roulette. The Cove restaurant replenishes die-hard gamblers, plus there's live entertainment in the evening.

✷ To Do

BEST BEACHES Gold Rock Beach, Lucayan National Park, Old Freetown. Accessible from a quarter-mile trail or by kayak, its rugged good looks attract a breed of nature-lovers over fun-loving beach buffs. Some picnic tables are the only concession to humans. Australian pines line the beach but are toppling as it erodes. Strong swimmers or kayakers can make their way 1½ miles offshore to snorkel the reef around Peterson Cay National Park. This is a remote, sun-baked area, so be sure to bring along plenty of water, sunscreen, and other supplies.

✪ **Paradise Cove** (www.deadmansreef.com), Deadman's Reef. On the way to West End, take a sun and snorkel break at the best swim-to reef on Grand Bahama Island. Pay your guest fee at the Red Bar, where you can rent snorkel equipment, kayaks, and other beach toys. Snorkeling tours are also available. The long, white-sand beach can be deserted at times, but the two-cottage resort often picks up guests at Freeport-Lucaya resorts to enjoy the property (call 242-349-2677 to arrange a pickup; packages available for snorkeling and kayaking), and so it can get more crowded at times. The Red Bar also sells drinks and snacks, so it's a good place to spend an entire beach day. Admission: $3 per guest.

✪ **Taino Beach,** W. Beach Rd., Lucaya. Arguably one of the prettiest beaches in the Bahamas, miraculously it is also lightly developed at its east end. Its long coved shape starts at a grouping of resorts on Jolly Drive. It continues eastward, edging the neighborhood known as Millionaire's Row, where the island's nicest homes reside. Off West Beach Road, you come to the main public access, with lots of parking, a nicely shaded playground, and a hilltop royal-palm-flanked memorial. A number of restaurants and water sports concessions once catered to beachgoers here. Now it's down to a beach club called Junkanoo, whose list of drinks is thrice as long as its food menu, and Tony Macaroni's Conch Experi-

VOLLEYBALL, WATER SPORTS, AND SPARKLY WATERS ATTRACT BEACH-LOVERS TO TAINO, ONE OF GRAND BAHAMA'S LOVELIEST STRETCHES OF SAND.

ence, a beach shack in the finest tradition where roasted conch, Gully Wash cocktails, and volleyball happen. A short walk takes you to Smith's Point, home of a Wednesday night Fish Fry and a scattering of native restaurants.

Xanadu Beach, Sunken Treasure Dr., Freeport. In addition to the adjacent time-share resort's guests, some of the local no-beach resorts shuttle their guests here, but it's wide and long enough to comfortably accommodate a lot of people on its powdery white sands. This is a lively beach where an alfresco grill serves up burgers and cold Kaliks.

BIKING Flat as can be and boasting stretches of roads with little traffic, Grand Bahama Island makes an ideal biking destination. Some of the major roads designate a bike path. Some resorts have bike rentals available, and a few tour operators incorporate biking.

Calabash Eco Adventures (242-727-1974) Its West End tour combines 10 miles of biking with snorkeling for a 6½-hour adventure.

Grand Bahama Nature Tours (242-373-2485 or 866-440-4542; www.gbntours .com) The five-hour biking tour takes you shopping, to lunch, and to Taino Beach.

FISHING Inshore catches include snapper, jacks, and porgies. Out in deep water, anglers pull in mahimahi, wahoo, tuna, blue marlin, and sailfish. If you're looking for bonefishing, your best bet is to head to the West or East End.

Charters: Expect to pay $300 for four for a half day and $350 for a full day for charter fishing. Party boat fishing runs about $60 per person.

Bonefish Folley & Sons (242-346-6500), West End. Bonefish Folley is legendary in these parts, but at age 90 he has relegated his reputation for catching the elusive bonefish to his two sons.

Reef Tours Ltd. (242-373-5880 or 242-373-5891; www.bahamasvacationguide .com/reeftours), Port Lucaya Marketplace, Lucaya. A party boat excursion of more than three hours, Reef Tours will take you bottom and reef fishing with light tackle. Smaller boats take up to six deep-sea fishing for about four hours.

GOLFING If you love to golf, Grand Bahama Island is your best choice in the Bahamas. It has several challenging choices. The newest golf course at Ginn sur Mer is not currently open to the public.

✪ **Our Lucaya Beach and Golf Resort Lucayan Course** (242-373-2002; www.ourlucayan.com), Balao Rd., Lucaya. Dick Wilson designed this 6,824-yard, par-72, 18-hole course with its famed dramatic stone structure and double lakes at the 18th hole. The new clubhouse overlooks the final hole, where you will also find a practice putting green and covered areas for golf instruction.

Our Lucaya Beach and Golf Resort Reef Course (242-373-2002; www .ourlucayan.com), Sea Horse Rd. at Our Lucaya Beach and Golf Resort, Lucaya. Lots of water and a tricky dogleg left on the 18th hole characterize this 6,930-yard, par-72, 18-hole course designed by Robert Trent Jones Jr.

Ruby Golf Course (242-352-1851; www.rubygolfclub.com), W. Sunrise Hwy. and Wentworth Ave., Freeport. Once part of Freeport's grand megaresort, it reopened in late 2008 after repairs were made to its 18 holes. The par-72 course is long with lots of sand traps.

WATER SPORTS *Anchorages:* **Grand Bahama Yacht Club at Lucayan Marina Village** (242-373-8888; www.lucayanmarina.com), Midshipman Rd.,

THE SUN SETS ON OUR LUCAYA'S REEF COURSE.

Our Lucaya Beach and Golf Resort

Lucaya. It has 125 slips for boats up to 175 feet. Besides its clubhouse, bar and grill, and swimming pools, it shuttles guests to Port Lucaya Marketplace for more options and Customs and Immigration.

Old Bahama Bay Marina (242-350-6500 or 800-444-9469; www.oldbahama bay.com), Old Bahama Bay Resort, West End. Has 72 slips for boats up to 120 feet long; customs and immigration office, fuel, electric, cable, water, and laundry facilities.

Port Lucaya Marina (242-373-9090; www.portlucayamarina.com), Port Lucaya Marketplace, Lucaya. It accommodates 106 vessels of up to 190 feet with full-service facilities in addition to all of the shops, restaurants, and bars available at the marketplace. Customs and Immigration officials are on-site full time.

Day Cruising Recommended Charter: ✪ **Bahama Mama Cruises** (242-373-7863; www.superiorwatersports.com), Port Lucaya Marketplace, Port Lucaya. No one does a booze cruise like the Bahamas; it's quite possibly the country that invented them. This company, named for the popular rum punch it serves, does a variety of cruises, from strictly sunset cocktailing to a surf-and-turf dinner cruise with live entertainers. Don't be surprised if you end up doing the limbo, either. The sunset and evening "booze" cruises are adults-only and just plain fun.

Other Day Cruising Charters: **Bahamas EcoVentures** (242-352-9323 or 242-375-1491; www.bahamasecoventures.com) This zippy airboat tour takes in local wildlife, blue holes, history, and culture. The four-hour tour includes complimentary transportation and lunch.

Reef Tours Ltd. (242-373-5880 or 242-373-5891; www.bahamasvacationguide .com/reeftours), Port Lucaya Marketplace, Lucaya. Glass-bottom boat tours aboard the 60-foot *Ocean Wonder* visit a wreck near Treasure Reef. The 48-foot sailing catamaran *Fan-Ta-Sea* does daily snorkel and evening sails.

Seaworld Explorer (242-373-7863; www.superiorwatersports.com), Port Lucaya Marketplace, Lucaya. A specially designed deep-hulled pontoon with windows in the floor allows passengers to stay dry while watching the marine life at Treasure Reef. Or you can don snorkel equipment and swim with the fishes. A diver feeds the fish right outside the windows, so photo opportunities are rife during the two-hour excursion.

Paddling & Ecotours: **Grand Bahama Nature Tours** (242-373-2485 or 866-440-4542; www.gbntours.com) It offers two different kayak tours. The six-hour excursion leads into Lucayan National Park for a guided nature walk, beaching, and lunch. The five-hour tour combines kayaking with snorkeling at Peterson Cay National Park. Transportation is included.

Powerboat Rentals: **Reef Tours Ltd.** (242-373-5880 or 242-373-5891; www .bahamasvacationguide.com/reeftours), Port Lucaya Marketplace, Lucaya. Experienced boaters can rent 17- or 25-footers for three or six hours.

Snorkeling & Diving Recommended Charter: ✪ **UNEXSO** (242-373-1244 or 800-992-3483; www.unexso.com), Port Lucaya Marketplace, Port Lucaya. When we last dived with UNEXSO (Underwater Explorers Society), they videotaped us. I'm thinking they spliced the tape, because when we watched it, a shark was following close behind us. That might convince some to buy it, but I was a little suspicious. UNEXSO is pretty well known for pioneering shark diving, but this was just a regular old dive to the West End Site Reef, about 60 feet down. I did, however, see my first shark underwater on that dive—a mere three-footer, but still! Something for the log book. Other than the video sleight of hand I suspected, UNEXSO runs a tight ship and tip-top operation, known world over for being pioneers in the field of dolphin encounters and specialty diving such as exploring GBI's extensive cave system. I've also done its dolphin encounter, and although I'm not a fan of such programs, this one does allow the dolphins to come and go out of Sanctuary Bay as they please. A boat transports guests to the bay about two miles from its facility. Here you can get into the water with the creatures or stay on the deck to interact as the dolphins approach. There's also a scuba dolphin encounter experience available. Other dives include a one-day Discover Scuba Reef Diving course, where you take a short class in the 17-foot-deep training pool, then dive in open water with an instructor by your side. Full certification courses are also available, as are rentals and a nice shop that sells everything from gear to clothing and toys.

Other Snorkeling & Diving Charters: **Caribbean Divers** (242-373-9111; www .bellchannelinn.com), Kings Rd. at Bell Channel Inn, Lucaya. Hardcore divers stay at the inexpensive, slightly run-down Bell Channel Inn and dive every day with this on-site operation. Nonguests, too, can take advantage of their years of experience, choosing from resort courses, one- or two-tank dives, shark dives, and full certification courses. A daily schedule takes in the island's best sites, only a five-minute boat ride from the dock: Taino Beach Reef, Treasure Reef, Theo's Wreck, Orson Well Wreck, and others. The inn and dive shop offer packages.

Reef Tours Ltd. (242-373-5880 or 242-373-5891; www.bahamasvacationguide .com/reeftours), Port Lucaya Marketplace, Lucaya. Go snorkeling by powerboat or sailboat. Refreshments, equipment, and instruction are included.

WILDLIFE SPOTTING *Nature Preserves & Eco-Attractions:* ♂ ✪ **Garden of the Groves** (242-374-7778), Midshipman Rd. and Magellan Dr., about 5 miles east of Lucaya. Open. 9–5 daily. $15 adults, $10 children. Reopened in 2008 after post-hurricane renovations, this national treasure shines brighter than ever. Before the hurricanes, a Miami parrot attraction operation had run it for several years. The parrots are gone, but the original gardens, first opened in 1973, remain with some new additions. Its signature chapel, modeled after one in the town of Pine Ridge before it was erased to create Freeport, still looks down upon the gardens. A sprawling outdoor café with multiple decks and a charming shopping village are new, as is the labyrinth, a walking meditation path that follows the design of Chartres' cathedral in France. The garden's 12 acres showcase Bahamian flora such as lignum vitae (the national tree), powderpuff trees, silver trumpet trees, royal poincianas, mahogany, black olives, and more. Signage throughout identifies butterflies and birds visitors might see: Bahama swallowtails, monarchs, zebra wings; stripe-headed tanager, hairy woodpecker, moorhens, gray catbirds, bananaquits, and Cuban emerald hummingbirds. Guided tours take place at 11 and 2 daily.

ON THE BOARDWALK AT LUCAYAN NATIONAL PARK, YOU CROSS A TIDAL MANGROVE CREEK EN ROUTE TO THE BEACH.

✪ **Lucayan National Park** (242-352-5438), Grand Bahama Hwy., Old Freetown. Open 9–5 daily. $3 adults, children younger than 12 admitted free. Amid these 40 acres you can explore a microcosm of 96-mile-long Grand Bahama's ecology. Perhaps the most fascinating are the limestone caves, one of the most extensive underwater cave systems (more than 6 miles long) explored to this day. A trail from the parking lot leads to two openings. The first, Ben's Cave, is an important bat-breeding cave that closes in June and July on their behalf. Farther along, the Burial Mound Cave is the resting place of ancient Lucayan tribesmen. Archaeologist have discovered remains and artifacts in the cave. At both, you climb down stairs into the dark depths (you may want to bring a flashlight) to observation platforms, where you can peer into the clear depths where a rare breed of crustacean was first discovered. Across the road, the loop path takes you through mangroves, a tidal creek, hardwood forest, and pine forest before it reaches Gold Rock Beach. Much eroded and slim-to-nothing at low tide, it's a desolate stretch lined with Australian pines. Tours come here to kayak and snorkel out to Peterson Cay National Park, a small island and reef about a 1½ miles from shore. Up the road about 3 miles, kayakers can also put in at Gold Beach Creek to kayak downstream to the park. The creek access also happens to be the site for a special apparatus used in the *Pirates of the Caribbean* filmings to make the ship appear to be tossing. Birds are the most gregarious wildlife in and around the park—look for great blue herons, green herons, hummingbirds, belted kingfishers, and the Bahama yellowthroat. Morning and winter are the best time for sightings. In summer, you'll see orchids and other native shrubs in bloom. This is the easiest way to access the "bush," as locals call it, without the assistance of a native guide.

Rand Nature Centre (242-352-5438; www.bnt.bs), E. Settlers Way, Freeport. Open 9–4 weekdays. $5 adults, $3 children ages 5–12. In the midst of city bustle but away from the tourist scene, this 100-acre plot operated by the Bahamas National Trust is worth seeking out to get your bearings about Bahamian fauna and flora. For the best introduction, show up at 10:30 AM on Tuesday or Thursday for a guided tour, included in admission. The first fauna you'll see is a one-eyed Bahama parrot the center has adopted and caged and an indigenous Bahamian boa—neither of which are found today on Grand Bahama Island. Even on self-guided tours, you'll learn the name of local plants such as strongback, Bahamian maiden bush, guavaberry, weeping fig, poor man's orchid, chicken toe, frangipani, and mahogany. Caribbean yellow pine and palmetto make up most of the forested land. In the wilds along the half-mile loop trail, you may spy a Cuban emerald hummingbird or red-tailed hawk. Displays outside and inside the visitors center acquaint guests with the local environment.

Nature Tours: **Grand Bahama Nature Tours** (242-373-2485 or 866-440-4542; www.gbntours.com) Certified Bahama birding guides lead a birding tour of the island tailored to your interests.

✳ Lodging

With the opening of Princess Resort in the 1960s, Grand Bahama Island became the nation's leader in the megaresort concept. Long before that, there was Jack Tar on West End, a precursor to the all-inclusive movement. Then, on the tails of Nassau's Crystal Palace and Paradise Island's Atlantis, Our Lucaya Resort arose from the rubble of imploded resort buildings. Like Atlantis, it offers a spread of water park attractions and restaurants.

In the meantime, Princess underwent different identities, first as Bahamia, then a Holiday Inn product, later as Royal Oasis, which reconfigured not only its property but Freeport's street layout to build its own water park while capitalizing upon its casino and International Bazaar shopping mecca. Unfortunately, a few years later, hurricane damage closed the property, which still awaits the right climate to re-emerge under its new ownership.

In the interim, the historic Xanadu Hotel, known for its Howard Hughes penthouse, has discontinued its resort aspect, functioning wholly as a time-share resort.

Still, many vital options to stay on Grand Bahama Island survive, ranging from simple hotel rooms to a lavish, private, five-bedroom home.

Price Codes

Inexpensive	Up to $100
Moderate	$100 to $200
Expensive	$200 to $300
Very Expensive	$300 and up

(An asterisk after the pricing designation indicates that the rate includes at least a continental breakfast in the cost of lodging and possibly more extensive meal service as noted in the listing.)

ACCOMMODATIONS

Fortune Beach
⁰ℸ⁰ Viva Wyndham Fortuna Beach (242-373-4000 or 800-996-3426, Wyndham reservations; www.vivaresorts .com), Doubloon Rd. and Churchill Dr. In the neighborhood of Millionaire's Row, this all-inclusive resort sequesters guests on one of the island's whitest, widest, and most gor-

geous beaches. Its 276 rooms are small but brightly decorated, and many have views of the beach from the porch or balcony. They are scattered among low-rise, colonial-style buildings. The all-inclusive rate includes meals and drinks in any of the resort's three restaurants, airport transportation, use of bicycles and nonmotorized water sports equipment and lessons, Kid's Club, and professional performances and interactive lessons on the property's circus trapeze. Scuba diving, massages, and island excursions are extra. Dining options include buffet-style breakfast, lunch, and dinner at colorful, open-air Junkanoo, Asian dinner at Bamboo, or Italian dinner at La Trattoria. For nighttime entertainment, there's a disco and theater featuring live performances nightly. Expensive.°

Freeport

°¶° **Castaways Resort and Suites** (242-352-6682 or 800-528-1234; www.castaways-resort.com), E. Mall Dr. next to International Bazaar. Once valued for its proximity to International Bazaar and Freeport's pre-hurricane casino, it still is a convenient location to the airport. Beach shuttles, a restaurant, and an on-site pool add to the convenience. Nicely decorated with rattan and floral and earth tones, its coral-rock-walled lobby and rooms are kept tidy, and its staff is exceedingly friendly and helpful. Guest amenities include a small gym, free wireless Internet access, and refrigerators in all the rooms. Moderate.

High Rock

Bishop's Bonefish Resort (242-353-5485) The settlement of High Rock lies off the main highway about 45 miles east of Lucaya, skirting along a lonely stretch of beach—a handful of homes, a cemetery, church, and faux lighthouse. At the western end of the town's one road, Ruben "Bishop" Roberts has been serving home-cooked meals for as long as I've been visiting, which was before there was electricity to this part of the island and when the roads were impossible. Today, the roads are paved, there's power, and Bishop has added a seven-room strip motel and beach club to his operation. Folks looking for an Out Island experience will be happy here. Although there's "bonefish" in the name, you won't find any of the sport nearby, but Bishop can arrange excursions to the East End, where you will. The rooms are simple with tile floors and refrigerators. Moderate.

Lucaya

✦ °¶° **Our Lucaya Beach and Golf Resort** (242-373-1333 or 866-870-7148; www.ourlucaya.com), Sea Horse Road. Grand Bahama Island's top destination resort claims a nice patch of beach across the street from the dining, entertainment, shopping, and marina at Port Lucaya Marketplace. Guests, however, needn't even leave the property to find a variety of dining and recreational opportunities in addition to a few shops and the island's only casino, Treasure Bay, with more than 350 machines and tables. The resort's 372 acres offer several accommodations options. Reef Village, the most affordable and family-friendly, is a tower of 478 rooms near the resort's sugar-mill-themed water slide and its kids club. In the Radisson-branded part of the resort, Breakers Cay, a 10-story high-rise, gives the impression of an art deco cruise ship with curvilinear profile and room design. This is the heart of

BEACH AND POOL FEATURES FOCUS OUR LUCAYA RESORT ON ALL THINGS SPLASHY.

the action, with its infinity pool, lap pool, swim-up bar, and restaurants. Cruise ship shore excursions drop passengers here for the day, so it can get quite hectic. To avoid the crowds and jostling, you can upgrade to a suite at Lighthouse Point or Lanai Suites, built and grandly decorated in the style of old island plantation manors. The warm, comfortable lobby area takes its cues from that era too. Here you can hook into Wi-Fi surrounded by faux palm trees, join friends in the cigar bar, or dine at elegant Churchill's Chophouse. In all, the resort encompasses nearly 1,300 rooms and suites, 13 restaurants from Caribbean to Asian, a number of beach bars, a spa and fitness center, and water sports concessions. The tennis center boasts four lighted courts, each with a different surface—grass, rebound, French red clay, and deco-turf. Two 18-hole golf courses provide plenty of challenges. One, the Reef Course, flanks the resort, while the Lucayan Course is a short drive away. All-inclusive meal and drink packages are available. Moderate to Expensive.

✪ ⁶ᴵ⁹ **Pelican Bay** (242-373-9550 or 800-600-9192; www.pelicanbayhotel .com), Sea Horse Rd. at Port Lucaya Marketplace Wharf. It's worth the extra dollars to stay in the suites here, which are decorated with imported furnishings and accessories, have espresso machines and rain showers, and are outfitted with a special door box into which staff delivers pastries each morning. You can also enjoy free continental breakfast waterside. For lunch and dinner, its Sabor restaurant is one of the island's best. Although the property isn't on a beach, Lucaya Beach is minutes away by foot and a ferry transports guests to Taino Beach at no added charge. The regular rooms are also spacious and nicely decorated, dispersed through attractively painted and gingerbread-trimmed buildings that spread between UNEXSO and the harbor. For families, there's an infinity-edged pool on the water, two other pools, and a playground. In early 2010, the resort opened a new conference center, which shifted its focus to corporate rather than leisure, but meeting attendees have their own check-in and are typically gone by the week-end, so the impact on vacationers is light. Moderate.

Taino Beach

🦩 ⁰🍴⁰ **Flamingo Bay Hotel & Marina at Taino Beach** (242-3373-5640 or 800-824-6623; www.tainobeach .com), Jolly Roger Dr. One of the island's best values, here you can stay for little while taking advantage of the high-budget amenities at sister time-share property Taino Beach Resort next door on the beach. The pleasant little three-story harborside Flamingo Bay offers complete services includ-ing water sports, family activities, and an hourly shuttle to Port Lucaya Mar-ketplace from 8 AM to 11 PM. Pretty in pastels, the 65 rooms have a mini-fridge, microwave, toaster, and cof-feemaker. Sliding glass doors open onto the marina. Next door, guests can use the pool and restaurants as well as the beach, one of the island's most breathtaking. Moderate.

West End

⁰🍴⁰ ✪ **Old Bahama Bay at Ginn Sur Mer** (242-350-6500 or 800-444-9469; www.oldbahamabay.com), West-ern tip of West End. Once upon a time, West End blazed as Grand Bahama Island's hot spot. Jack Tar Village accommodated wealthy yacht-in guests in those days, before Freeport was born to steal West End's vitality. Old Bahama Bay has since risen from Jack Tar's derelict ruins to become one of the island's nicest bou-tique resorts. Because it lies far from the shops, restaurants, and other con-veniences of Freeport, it provides an amazing array of facilities for its rela-tively small 73-unit size: a full-service marina with customs and immigra-tion, two restaurants, a small spa and fitness center, a private airstrip, and

private, 18-hole Arnold Palmer golf course. The latter two developments came about after Ginn, a U.S resort development firm, purchased the property in 2008. It revitalized the airstrip built back in the day and began selling residential lots. Its long-run plans are to expand the resort with more marina space, accommoda-tions, and a larger spa, but they are on hold as all of GBI awaits U.S. eco-nomic recovery. For now, guests can enjoy the beach and its nonmotorized water sports equipment on a compli-mentary basis. The rooms were fur-nished with an eye for masculine good looks and practicality. All come with wet bars, bathrobes, kitchen utensils, and DVD/CD players. This is a place to go to get away from it all and be pampered. Very Expensive.

✪ **Paradise Cove** (242-349-2677; www.deadmansreef.com), Deadman's Reef. A few dozen fin flips from shore, the two-system Deadman's Reef is the best amenity here. That and isolation, so if you're looking for resort action, this should not be your first choice. A 15-minute drive from the airport in the middle of nowhere, this is as close to an Out Island expe-rience you can find—with the fortu-nate exception that the long driveway off the main road is less torturous than the potholed ones you find on some smaller, less populated islands. Rebuilt after the years of the hurri-canes, 2004 and 2005, two new, mod-ern, stilted cottages offer the option of one- or two-bedroom accommoda-tions with a full kitchen, dining and living area, and balcony with a sea view. This is the kind of place where it's best to rent a car, stock the kitchen, and cook most meals in because the only on-site dining is a snack concession that feeds guests, snorkelers, and kayakers who come for the day. It rents equipment to explore the reef and its barracudas, angelfish, and sea turtles. The owners run a bus to pick up day-trippers at local resorts, so the beach scene can get a little busy at certain times. But by evening, the natural beach belongs to the few overnighters and the Bahamian family that operates the place. Moderate to Expensive.

William's Town

"1" **Island Seas Resort** (242-373-1271 or 800-801-6884 for reservations; www.islandseas.com), 123 Silver Point Dr. Though technically a time-share property, Island Seas does not restrict minimum stays or check-in/checkout dates. It's off the beaten path, but a few resorts shuttle their guests here, so the beach, its water sports, and restaurant-bar, CoCoNuts Grog & Grub, can get a little crowded around lunchtime. A newer restaurant, Seagrape Grille, serves breakfast and dinner, plus there's a courtesy shuttle to Port Lucaya if you'd like to catch a meal there instead. Within walking distance you'll find a number of beach shacks where you can find everything from conch to jerk chicken. Not all of the property's 195 one- and two-bedroom units are on the rental program, but they are all decorated alike in perky, tropical fashion. Guests also can enjoy shuffleboard and tennis courts, a small gym, and a massage room. Expensive to Very Expensive.

HOME & CONDO RENTALS

There's no one agency devoted to Grand Bahama Island vacation rentals, but if you search it on the Web, you will find listings with several agencies that cover a multitude of destinations.

✳ Where to Eat

Diverse as Grand Bahama Island itself, its restaurants run the gamut from Out Island cuisine to sophisticated renditions of Asian, Italian, and Mediterranean cuisines. From conch shacks to steakhouses, there's something for every appetite.

Price Codes

Inexpensive	Up to $15
Moderate	$15 to $25
Expensive	$25 to $35
Very Expensive	$35 or more

Cost categories are based on the range of dinner entrée prices or, if dinner is not served, on lunch entrées.

Resort and other major restaurants take reservations. For small restaurants outside of Freeport-Lucaya, it's a good idea to call ahead to make sure they're open. Often they require that you order your dinner ahead of time from the two or three selections they may offer that evening.

Freeport

🍴 ♿ **Becky's Bahamian Restaurant & Lounge** (242-352-5247), E. Sunrise Hwy. and E. Beach Dr. Becky's serves a mean breakfast, and you can get it all day long. No matter whether you prefer traditional Bahamian specialties such as chicken souse, corned beef and grits, or even pig feet souse, or you're the all-American type with a preference for steak and eggs, chocolate pancakes, or a mushroom omelet, you'll find it on the menu. I'm partial to her lime-spiced boil' fish. Lunch, too, caters to many appetites with curried mutton, baked chicken, sandwiches, salads, hot dogs, and burgers.

Dinner (served until 8 PM) offers mostly Bahamian dishes such as lobster, pan-fried grouper, cracked conch, and barbecue ribs all served up with peas 'n' rice, plantain, and coleslaw or potato salad. The tidy booth-lined dining room completes this picture of authentic Bahamia. Inexpensive to Moderate.

🦞 ♿ ☉ **Geneva's Place** (242-352-5085), E. Mall Dr. and Kipling Ln. Here is where I discovered Bahamian cuisine many years ago, and Geneva keeps me coming back. I will never forget my first taste of guava duff at her hand, but you don't have to wait for dessert to get the full flavor of local specialties. You can start at breakfast with rich and delicious stew conch or boil' fish with a hot bird pepper on the side. The lunch menu lists salads and sandwiches, but I go for the flakiest cracked conch I've found. For lunch and dinner you can order full meals such as steamed grouper or broiled pork chops with peas 'n' rice or gooey mac and cheese straight out of the oven. The cheerful yellow walls brighten an otherwise plain dining room where the emphasis is on good home cooking. Inexpensive to Moderate.

Pier One (242-352-6674), Freeport Harbour. It drew crowds for its fine cuisine and three-times-nightly shark feedings for many years until the frail wooden structure blew away in 2004's hurricanes. It reopened a few years ago in a sturdier concrete building still decorated with glass buoys and other nautical paraphernalia, but also colorful Junkanoo-painted fish hanging from the vaulted ceiling in the main dining room. Most prefer to sit outdoors on the balcony at long wooden tables, where the breeze

cools and the view of the shark feedings at 7, 8, and 9 PM are best. Have your own shark feeding frenzy by ordering one of the shark specialties from the menu: smoked shark salad, blackened lemon shark filet, shark curry with banana, or pan-fried lemon shark. The extensive dinner menu includes steak, lobster sautéed with shallots and mushrooms, coconut shrimp, and a seafood sampler. At lunch, there's mussels, cracked conch, a mushroom omelet, chicken curry, sandwiches, burgers, and lobster salad. Save room for key lime pie or chocolate mousse cake, or repair to the roomy bar for a Bahama Lullaby—coconut rum, light rum, dark rum, simple syrup, and pineapple and lime juice. Night night. Moderate to Expensive.

♿ **Ruby Swiss European Restaurant** (242-352-8507), W. Sunrise Hwy. In its glory during Freeport's heyday, late-night gamblers could come in during the wee hours for a snack or full dinner. The popular restaurant continues to hold on with its extensive European menus and affordable prices. Windows line the walls of the large, rather formal dining room with its faux palms, flowers, and white linens topped with paper placemats. Its menu is a throwback to old-island days when tableside service and heavy continental dining were the norm. Specialties such as Wiener schnitzel, tableside flamed steak Diana, lobster Alfredo, and pasta dishes still fill the menu, along with burgers, fried chicken, seafood, and steak. A shorter but still complete menu kicks in at 10:30 PM, serving everything from chicken souse to Indian curry. Many patrons at that hour gather around the ample bar

99

GRAND BAHAMA ISLAND

decorated with flags from around the world and its TV sets. Moderate to Expensive.

High Rock

🦞 ♿ **Bishop's Beach Club & Bar** (242-353-5485), off Grand Bahama Hwy. on the west end of town. A good place to head for a fill-up after a morning at Lucayan National Park, about 8 miles away, Bishop's Beach gives you the choice of beaching it or dining in air-conditioned comfort while watching TV around the circular bar. Breakfast is a simple choice of ham or bacon with your eggs and toast. Lunch and dinner present more typically Bahamian options: cracked conch, barbecued ribs, burgers, sandwiches, and broiled lobster. The dining room is plain but cheerful. You're as likely to find religion on the TV as sports. The beach bar opens according to seasonal demands (tour buses to the park sometimes stop here), and overlooks a deserted stretch of lovely beach. Both eateries are part of a small, locally run resort. Bishop himself is often on hand to greet and chat up guests. Inexpensive to Moderate. $30 minimum for credit cards.

Lucaya

🦞 **Billy Joe's on the Beach** (242-373-1333, Ext. 5803), on the beach at Our Lucaya Beach and Golf Resort. Through the many incarnations of the property now known as Our Lucaya Beach Resort, Billy Joe has been a fixture. The colorful beach shack is not owned by the resort, but is embraced by it and its guests as a genuine piece of old Bahamia. Since 1971, Billy Joe has served up his specialty grilled conch—wrapped in foil with onions, green peppers, lime juice, garlic, and butter—along with made-before-your-eyes conch salad, fried lobster,

cracked conch, cheeseburgers, hot dogs, wings, and Bahama Mamas—classic Bahamian beach fare. Listen to local music on the box and the swish of ocean waves from the porch as you watch the guys at the grill or chopping block and the ladies in the kitchen. Inexpensive to Moderate. Credit cards not accepted.

♿ **China Beach** (242-373-1333; www.ourlucaya.com), Sea Horse Rd. at Our Lucaya Beach and Golf Resort. The menu at this chic waterside dining room visits several regions of China as well as Thailand, Japan, and the Bahamas. Go at sunset for a predinner cocktail on the porch, then move into the grand dining space with its display kitchen, curtains, vaulted ceiling, tasteful parasol chandeliers, red tablecloths, and lashed bamboo accents. Under the bamboo menu cover you'll find all your Eastern favorites and then some. Start with sushi or Japanese dumplings. Conch is well-represented both on the sushi rolls menu and among the entrées, where you'll find conch fried rice (tasty and hearty, but could use a bit of spice) and stir-fried conch. All the major Asian food groups are listed, from noodles, curry, and teriyaki to crispy roast duck with plum sauce and green-tea-glazed cheesecake. Dishes are served family-style, so have fun trying several. Moderate to Expensive.

♿ **Churchill's Chophouse & Bar** (242-373-1333; www.ourlucaya.com), Sea Horse Rd. at Our Lucaya Beach and Golf Resort. Our Lucaya's tip-top restaurant in price point and cuisine specializes in beef, but manages to successfully supplement its menu with seafood and creativity. Its lovely setting features tall columns, French

ISLAND CHARACTER: BILLY JOE, THE CONCH MAN

The logic of Bahamian nicknaming is often elusive. Take John Gilbert. His father's name was Joseph, and so when the song "Ode to Billy Joe" came out, friends started calling him Ode to Billy Joe. Later, when he moved from Nassau to Grand Bahama, it got shortened to Billy Joe.

Today the name is synonymous with fresh conch eats on the beach, particularly grilled conch, which Billy Joe claims to have introduced here after learning it from a Chinese man. Since his move to Lucaya Beach in 1971, he has pretty much worked the restaurant every day, despite bouts of gout and his 75 years, along with his wife, Blossom, a sweet Jamaican lady.

When he first went into business, he was paying 50 cents per conch. Today, it's $2.50. On a busy day, he uses 70 to 80 conch a day. "There is no secret," the Cat Island native says of his recipes and long-running success. "People just love conch. Every day it's conch."

"CONCH MAN" BILLY JOE HAS PERFECTED HIS GRILLED CONCH AT HIS LONG-STANDING BEACH SHACK.

windows looking out onto the resort's green lawn with a sea backdrop, and an elevated ceiling decorated with chandeliers and murals depicting Bahamian life. A flashback to plantation days' grandeur, its menu focuses on aged cuts of prime beef, but also prepares braised lamb, lobster and asparagus risotto, surf and turf, grilled wild king salmon with grilled figs, and dishes of equal aplomb. When the resort is busy, a pianist tickles the ivories for dinner guests' entertainment. Expensive to Very Expensive. Closed certain nights in the off-season; call ahead.

East (242-374-2773; www.east restaurantbahamas.com), Port Lucaya Marketplace. This new star on the Port Lucaya horizon is making waves with its top-shelf sushi and cuisine that fuses flavors from Indonesia, Malaysia, Vietnam, Japan, and China. Good-looking in a minimalist Asian vein, with sleek blond wood and bamboo overlooking boats bobbing in the harbor, it's possibly the best thing in the shopping center since Luciano's. Most of the dishes are taster size, so you can sample different nori rolls and hot and cold dishes. The Bahama Mama roll is signature, with tempura conch, avocado, mango, and chili-lime mayo. Other tempting selections: foie gras on pear, tempura nori-wrapped tuna, Szechuan peppercorn beef carpaccio with jalapeño ponzu, and vanilla-poached lobster salad. Ask your server for wine or sake pairing recommendations, or order your favorite cocktail from the full bar selection. Moderate to Expensive. Reservations recommended. Closed Wednesday.

Island Java Coffeehouse & Desserterie (242-352-5282; www .islandjavabs.com), Port Lucaya Marketplace. Opened in 2007, Island Java gave a jolt to the dining scene at Port Lucaya Marketplace with a new, modern vibe. Stop in for a cup of joe, imported and flavored coffee (including organic), espresso, or smoothie. Maybe a guava muffin or croissant to go with that? Or go for full breakfast such as johnnycake and sausage gravy, banana pancakes, coconut French toast, boil' fish, or overstuffed breakfast panini. For the health-conscious, there's fruit, cereal, yogurt, Eggbeaters, and turkey sausage. For lunch, you can order panini, meat pies, salads, and soup. The mixing and matching is practically endless here. You can even make a meal out of the delicious baked goods. Inexpensive to Moderate.

✪ **Luciano's** (242-373-9100; www .thebahamasguide.com/lucianos), Port Lucaya Marketplace. A name that's been around for ages, this one carries a French accent and a formal, romantic setting of linens and candlelight overlooking the harbor at Port Lucaya Marketplace. Staff serves Continental cuisine with timeless finesse; servers wear black ties and execute tableside Caesar salads, shrimp scampi, and crêpes suzette. The menu touches everyone's palate and a wide range of budgets. Begin with tasty coquilles St. Jacques florentine (on a bed of spinach with hollandaise), authentic French onion soup, or a $130 helping of caviar. Go for *filet au poivre vert*, scallops in tomato wine sauce, Dover sole, stuffed quail, chateaubriand, veal sautéed with shrimp and lobster, rack of lamb, and other classics. Linger long over candlelight and sparkly views in the company of the yachtsmen in the harbor and other longtime fans. Expensive to Very Expensive.

Prop Club (242-373-1333; www .ourlucaya.com), Sea Horse Rd. at Our Lucaya Beach and Golf Resort. Youthful and beachside, this is one of Our Lucaya's most affordable and casual dining options. When weather allows, its giant, glass-paned garage doors go up for an alfresco effect. The all-day menu feeds the all-American appetite with pizza, sandwiches, burgers, and ribs. Concessions to what's local include a tasty conch chowder and sour orange-glazed grouper. In the evening, the focus segues into nightclub mode with karaoke or live entertainment many nights, but food is still available. Moderate.

& ✪ **Sabor Restaurant & Bar** (242-373-5588; www.sabor-bahamas.com), Sea Horse Way at Pelican Bay Hotel. Opened in 2008 and still hot, Sabor serves up creative fare alfresco at the marina. The lunch-dinner menu spans the distance between burgers and grilled garlic lobster with such starters as escargot, shrimp wonton, and ginger-fried calamari; and entrées that include Kalik beer cracked conch, broiled hog snapper (a local deepwater fish), mushroom-stuffed chicken, and pepper steak with béarnaise. In lobster season, it has an entire menu of entrées devoted to the sweet shellfish. Guava cheesecake with bourbon whipped cream tops off the meal in inimitable reinvented Bahamian style. The chef-owner's Scandinavian roots show at Saturday and Sunday brunch with the Icelandic eggs Benedict, which swaps smoked salmon for Canadian bacon. An extensive listing of martinis, mojitos, margaritas, and other potables keep the bar lively, especially during two-fer happy hours from 5 to 7 and weekends when live bands mix it up. Moderate.

Smith's Point

🐚 & **Outriggers Native Restaurant & Beach Club** (242-373-4811), off W. Beach Rd. east of Taino Beach. Settlements outside the Freeport tax-free zone are often referred to as "generation lands," property that families have occupied for generations and therefore have free title to. Smith's Point is one such, known for its gently coved white beach within easy walking distance of Taino Beach. Here Miss Gretchen Wilson has run her restaurant out of her home for years, serving typical Bahamian spe-

cialties such as cracked conch, fried grouper, barbecue chicken, and lobster, when in season. Across the street, the family's beach club is the central site of the settlement's Wednesday Fish Fry shebang, which draws locals and visitors in droves for fresh snapper, grouper, lobster, chicken, macaroni and cheese, puddinglike sweet potato bread, conch salad, peas 'n' rice, Bahama Mamas, and live music. Tuesday and Thursday nights it hosts beach bonfire parties, and in season it opens for light lunch. Inexpensive to Moderate. Credit cards not accepted.

West End

Teasers Bar & Grill (242-350-6500; www.oldbahamabay.com), at Old Bahama Bay Resort. Come for breakfast or lunch and spend the day beachside at this replica of traditional Bahamian beach bars where guests come to anchor their day in the sun. Also known as the Straw Bar, its former name, it's as casual as a beach bar should be, with open-air dining, a drink called Seaweed, island music on the box, and a sign over the bar that reads "Life's Too Short to Dance with Ugly Men." Breakfast goes until 10:30 AM and sweeps the range of American

---

BAHAMA TALK

Fish Fry: Anytime there is a gathering of cook shacks chopping up conch salad or frying up local favorites, you have a fish fry, whether it occurs daily or only weekly. The Smith's Point affair is a Wednesday weekly event. Sunset Village in Eight Mile Rock opens daily, but throws its biggest to-do on Thursday evenings.

and Bahamian specialties, including yummy coconut French toast. Lunch, from 11 to 5, consists of a small menu with all the usuals—conch fritters, burgers, sandwiches, cracked conch, and blackened or grilled fresh fish. What's in a Seaweed, you're wondering? Blue Curacao, rum, Galliano, and pineapple and orange juice. If that's a little stiff, ask for a local Sands beer, equally fitting for a beach bar. Inexpensive to Moderate.

William's Town

🦞 ♿ ¶¹ **Bikini Bottom Bar & Grill** (242-373-7951; www.thebikinibottom .biz), E. Beach Dr. One among a line-up of casual beach bars in William's Town, this one is most dependably tasty and lively. Sit out on the porch amid bright, multicolored picnic tables, swings at the outdoor bar, and within eyeshot of turquoise waters. Inside is spacious and cool, with a big bar, darts, and a pool table. Order a draft Kalik or Sands and select from the succinct lunch menu. Judging from the excellent spicy wings, the menu doesn't lie about preparing food to order. So sit back and enjoy the view or take advantage of the free Wi-Fi, because food can take awhile. No big surprises on the lunch menu, but the well-executed selections include conch fritters, fried shrimp, Caesar salad, foot-long beef hot dogs, BLTs, burgers, cracked conch, chicken, and fish fingers. At dinner, try barbecued ribs or chicken with all the fixins. Inexpensive. No dinner Monday through Wednesday. $20 minimum for credit cards.

BAKERIES ✪ **Island Java Coffee-house & Desserterie** (242-374-5282), Port Lucaya Marketplace, Port Lucaya. From cookies and muffins to wedding cakes and Bahamian special-ty desserts such as guava cake and

FRESH AND COLORFUL: THE FISH SHACKS ALONG FISHING HOLE ROAD.

minted tango tarts, this place is guaranteed to satisfy your sweet tooth.

COFFEE ○ Island Java Coffeehouse & Desserterie (242-374-5282), Port Lucaya Marketplace, Port Lucaya. Import coffees from the world over, organic coffee, flavored coffees, espresso, coffee drinks, and smoothies plus pastries, ice cream, and other goodies.

TAKE-OUT ○ The best places for fresh conch salad and fresh seafood are the shacks along the waterfront on **Fishing Hole Road** and on the way to West End. **Sunset Village** in Eight Mile Rock has a row of cook shacks where you can get fried chicken, cracked conch, grouper sandwich, or whatever else is cooking that day.

✳ Selective Shopping

Havana Trading Company (242-351-5685), Sea Horse Rd. at Our Lucaya Beach and Golf Resort, Lucaya. Watch Cuban cigar-rollers at work as you browse the selection of smokes and liquor.

International Bazaar, E. Mall Dr. and E. Sunrise Hwy., Freeport. Once a vibrant center of import and duty-free shopping with a global theme, it has suffered from hurricane and economic swipes in the past six years. Its 35-foot, red torii gateway still stands as a major landmark, and straw market vendors sell their wares. But most of the shops are closed and await renovation by the new owner, and the place has an overall ghost-town feel.

○ Perfume Factory (242-352-9391; www.perfumefactory.com), behind International Bazaar. Part attraction, part shop, come here to buy the signature line of products made from local ingredients, or mix up and bottle your own scent. Staff will give you a free tour of the factory, housed in a pretty Loyalist-style Bahamian building. You can purchase perfumes, colognes, and lotions from the Fragrance of the Bahamas line. Pink Pearl, which contains a conch pearl in each bottle, and, for men, Sands, decorated with a bit of Bahamian shoreline, are the big sellers. To mix and name your own scent costs $30 for an ounce of perfume, $15 for 1½ ounces of body lotion.

○ Port Lucaya Marketplace (242-373-8446), Sea Horse Rd., Lucaya. This shopping center righted two wrongs committed by International Bazaar. First, it was modeled after Bahamian architecture instead of Moroccan and other exotic locales. Second, it's near the beach. The gingerbread-trimmed shops hold duty-free, clothing, and artisan shops, and two straw markets bookend the harborside spread. Some of the island's best eateries also live here, plus marina facilities and the UNEXSO dive and dolphin operation. It's across from the Our Lucaya resort, guaranteeing better vitality than Freeport is currently experiencing. Live bands often perform in its Count Basie Square at the center's heart and on the water.

BAHAMA TALK

Gully Wash: Not as well known as Bahama Mama and Goombay Smash, this is a local indulgence consisting of green coconut water, sweetened condensed milk, and gin—a specialty at Tony Macaroni's.

✳ Special Events

March: **Bacardi Rum Billfish Tournament** (242-373-9090; www.port lucaya.com), Port Lucaya Marina, Lucaya. Six days midmonth. Big game is the name of this game, with festivities at Port Lucaya Marketplace. **Coconut Festival,** Pelican Point. Late March/early April. Sample coconut dishes, watch a coconut tree climbing competition, and enjoy the spirit of this small settlement.

June: **Grand Bahama Sailing Regatta,** Taino Beach. Three days midmonth. Part of the country's regatta circuit, it brings sailing sloops from throughout the Bahamas to compete. Onshore activities include music, dancing, food, and Junkanoo rush-out.

October: **McLean's Town Conch Cracking Contest,** McLean's Town. Twenty days in October. Awards go to the best conch cracker in several categories, including "visitor." Also conch-

---

BAHAMA TALK

Rush-out: This is the old-island term for the informal flooding of the streets with revelers during Junkanoo, but you still hear it used to describe Junkanoo music-playing and festivities in general.

---

eating contests, cook-offs, the Konkathalon, other contests, Junkanoo rush-out, and boat tours.

November: **Conchman Triathlon** (242-727-5886; www.conchman.com), Lucaya. First Saturday. Competition includes a 1K swim, 25K bike, and 5K run; also an Iron Kids contest.

December: **Festival Noel** (242-352-5438), Rand Nature Center, E. Settlers Way, Freeport. Early December. Music, food, wine tasting, and a crafts fair.

Abaco 3

MARSH HARBOUR/GREAT ABACO
ISLAND

ELBOW CAY

GREEN TURTLE CAY

OTHER CAYS

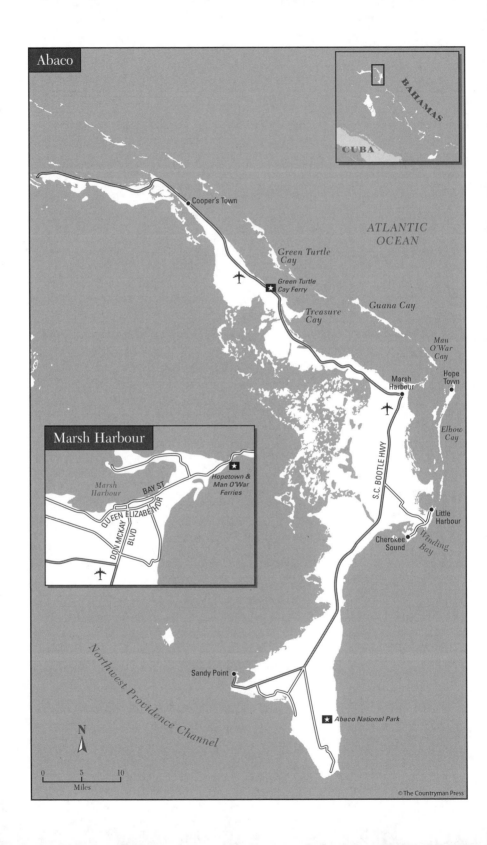

Abaco

BAHAMAS

CUBA

Cooper's Town

ATLANTIC
OCEAN

Green Turtle
Cay

Green Turtle
Cay Ferry

Treasure
Cay

Guana Cay

Man
O'War
Cay

Marsh
Harbour

Hope
Town

S.C. BOOTLE HWY

Elbow
Cay

Little
Harbour

Cherokee
Sound

Winding
Bay

Marsh Harbour

Marsh
Harbour

BAY ST

QUEEN ELIZABETH DR

DON MCKAY BLVD

Hopetown &
Man O'War
Ferries

Northwest Providence Channel

Sandy Point

Abaco National Park

N

0   5   10
Miles

© The Countryman Press

ABACO

BOATER'S WET DREAM

"I am amazed by the brilliance of the sunshine, the quality of the air which seems to have actual body and substance . . ."

—*Randolph W. Johnston, Jan. 17, 1951, in* Artist on His Island:
A Study in Self-Reliance

Marsh Harbour, Abaco's "big city," is proud of its one stoplight. It's the only one in the Bahamas outside of Nassau and Freeport. And, its islanders will further boast, they have another one coming. How long that's been coming, and when it will actually be functional, they can't say. They also brag about their ATM. These are signs of progress in the somewhat renegade, time-mired chain of islands known as Abaco, but don't look for a movie theater or big-box store here.

Made up of about 10 inhabited islands and who knows how many others, the Abaco Islands' chain of cays (say "keys") offers opportunity to explore from relatively populated and rambunctious Marsh Harbour to quiet, teetotaling outposts such as Man-O-War Cay, and various stages in between.

Ever since the Loyalists fled post-war ire in the 1770s to settle here, Abaco has embraced escapees. Its tangle of islands makes a perfect hideaway, and its variety keeps it ever-fresh. "Renegade" has always been in Abaco blood. The Loyalists came largely from Carolina plantations, having brought with them their slaves and farming know-how. They found the islands uninhabited; the native Lucayans who lived there back in Christopher Columbus's day were long gone.

Pineapple was among the earliest crops, particularly on **Green Turtle Cay,** the chain's second most populated island and home to the picket-fence, New England-style village of **New Plymouth.** After less than sterling success at farming the islands' rocky foundation, settlers turned to the sea and the noble professions of fishing and boat-building, and sometimes ignoble trade of wreck-salvaging. (It's said that the unscrupulous often flashed lights to lure ships into certain wreckage upon the reefs.) In the early 1900s, the islands' natural, indigenous crop of yellow pine brought a massive logging and lumber operation known as Wilson City to the main island, including a railroad.

DESERTED BEACHES SUCH AS MUNJACK ISLAND BECKON THE INNER ROBINSON CRUSOE.

Today, islanders on **Great Abaco Island**—the chain's largest (the Bahamas' second largest at 150 miles long) and home to **Marsh Harbour**—farm neem trees for natural health products. Abaconians, however, still largely depend upon the sea for their income—whether boatbuilding, fishing, or guiding tourists. Marsh Harbour, the third largest town in the Bahamas, casts its map star on the Sea of Abaco, pretty much dead center on the island. Part business, part pleasure, its commercial enterprises—KFC, Ace Hardware, Butler & Sands Liquor, the post office, and all the necessary stores, including one named Bed Bath & Between—line the road from the airport. Bay Street leads to the pleasure part, known as the Tourist Strip. A few resorts, a number of restaurants, and plenty of shops are all within walking distance. Other settlements on Great Abaco include **Treasure Cay,** a prime resort area known for its award-winning beach; **Little Harbour,** home to an art mecca; **Winding Bay,** and, at the southern extreme, **Sandy Point.** White limestone bluffs give the island elevation in the south around **Cherokee Sound,** a slowly developing area with deserted beaches.

Across the sea from Marsh Harbour, you can spot one of the Bahamas' most recognizable landmarks, the lighthouse on **Elbow Cay.** Here, **Hope Town** (also written Hopetown, population 260) presents another delightful village that feels like a movie set or a Disney creation, where the lighthouse looks like a candy cane and the houses seem cut from gingerbread. Because if its New England architectural influence, people often refer to it as the "Nantucket of the Bahamas." The island is known as a haven for artists. A ferryboat from Marsh Harbour delivers visitors into Hope Town's harbor, where the first rule is posted on a piling "SLOW DOWN you're in HOPE TOWN." The use of cars and other motor vehicles is prohibited in town except by those who procure special permits.

If you must slow down for Hope Town, then you've gotta practically stand still once you get to tiny 2.5-mile-long **Man-O-War Cay** (population less than 300) and **Great Guana Cay,** the longest of Abaco's offshore cays at 7 miles (but no more than 100 full-timers). The first is known for its boatbuilding and "dry" status (no alcohol sold or served); the latter, quite the opposite, has built a party reputation based on its beach bars, favorites of the boating crowd.

Even more than "renegade," the Abaco Islands have "boating" thick in its blood. Boatbuilding dates back to Abaco's colonial days, when the Abaco dinghy served commercial purposes for the fishermen. Eventually it evolved for sporting pursuits. Boatyards on every cay continue the tradition of boatbuilding, restoration, storage, and repair.

Many yachters have second homes in the Abacos, which has made it one of the Bahamas' most prosperous destinations. Between winter's snowbird population and summertime regatta season, the waters around Abaco stay lively with boat traffic year-round.

The remainder of Abaco's 100-something cays are mostly uninhabited. Some hold a single home or serve as destinations for recreational boat tours. **Black Sound Cay, Pelican Cays,** and **Tilloo Cay** and surrounding waters are designated national wildlife reserves. The dice-toss of islands makes the merriest sort of island-hopping adventure. Ferryboats, charters, and rentals let you explore at your leisure this throwback to pure and simple island living.

DON'T MISS

- Island-hopping to cay settlements or a private beach all your own.
- Dinner at Curly Tails in Marsh Harbour.
- Snorkeling or diving—anywhere, anytime!
- Feeding stingrays with your toes on one of Brendal's Tours' excursions from Green Turtle Cay.
- A climb to the top of Elbow Cay Lighthouse.

SUGGESTED READING *Abaco: The History of an Out Island and its Cays,* by Steve Dodge, White Sound Press.

The Abaco Guide Including Grand Bahama Island and Bight of Abaco, by Stephen J. Pavlidis, Seaworthy Publications, Inc. A cruising guide.

Abaco Journal (www.abacojournal.com) A tourist rag with useful visitor info. A general, comprehensive treatment with a boatbuilding appendix. $19.95.

Abaco Life **magazine** (www.abacolife.com) This fine, long-published quarterly covers Abaco news, people, and lifestyle in depth.

The Abaconian (www.abaconian.com) The islands' true newspaper since 1993.

Artist on His Island: A Study in Self-Reliance, by Randolph W. Johnston. The journal of sculptor Johnston, who moved his family to Little Harbour in Abaco, then only accessible by boat, in the 1950s to escape what he termed "the megamachine."

The Cruising Guide to Abaco, by Steve Dodge. Updated annually, it's a must for boaters and divers, complete with charts and GPS points. $24.95.

A Guide & History of Hope Town, by Steve and Marjorie Dodge and Vernon and Barbara Malone. A walking tour of the town with a brief history, available for purchase locally for $5.95.

✴ To See

A curious blend of British, African, American, and mariner culture combine to give Abaco a flavor that's heavy on the salt and spice. As far as its arts scene, Abaco has always quietly maintained an artist vibe, beginning with Winslow Homer, who often painted here. Later, renowned sculptor Randolph W. Johnston and native Bahamian Alton Lowe furthered that reputation. Hope Town is an art center, where students visit to learn plein-air painting and other techniques from the local artist community.

ARCHITECTURE Known as Loyalist architecture, cracker-box homes—particularly in New Plymouth and Hope Town—show the charm of New England style with pastels, picket fences, gingerbread, gables, and porches.

GALLERIES & STUDIOS For information about other Abaco artists and outlets, visit the Abaco Art Guild Web site at abacoart.org.

Alton Lowe Studio (242-365-4264), New Plymouth, Green Turtle Cay. Visit by appointment to view the vibrant paintings of Abaco's most famous and prolific artist.

Joe's Studio (242-365-6082; www.joesstudioabaco.com), Man-O-War Cay. Find exquisite wooden boat models crafted by Joe Albury himself, plus other paintings and crafts by local artists.

✪ Pete's Pub & Gallery (242-366-3503; www.petespubandgallery.com), Little Harbour. The foundry and studio here were built by Randolph W. Johnston and his family. Johnston is most famous locally for the bronze *Bahamian Woman* sculpture at Nassau Harbor. He wrote a book, *Artist on His Island: A Study in Self-Reliance,* about his family's adventures settling this land, then only accessible by sea. Son Peter J. Johnston continues his father's work, predominantly in gold but also in bronze like his father. He also sells fine works of other island artists. His Swiss Family Robinson-style pub is a popular spot to gather for Kaliks and seafood.

✪ Vertram Lowe (242-365-4170), Bay St. at Gully Alley, New Plymouth, Green Turtle Cay. Son of Albert Lowe (see *Museums & Historic Sites,* below), Vertram took up the model-shipbuilding craft when his father died some 20 years ago, leaving his son to complete a presold, three-masted model commissioned by a Bahamian hotel. Now he's top-dog in the field. Visit his studio by prior appointment.

MUSEUMS & HISTORIC SITES ✪ Albert Lowe Museum (242-365-4094), New Plymouth, Green Turtle Cay. Open 9–11:45 and 1–4 Mon.–Sat. $5. A prime example of early Bahamian-New Englandesque architecture, this was the home of boatbuilder Albert Lowe, a well-known artistic surname in these parts, starting in 1825. Albert himself was an artist, but his son Alton, who still lives on the island, is even more famous for his paintings and postage stamp designs. Albert's brother, Vertram, still builds exquisitely detailed boat models in his studio down the street. Today the home, a museum since 1976, holds Lucayan artifacts; period furnishings, some made out of the mahogany that once grew on the

THE ALBERT LOWE MUSEUM RESIDES IN ONE OF GREEN TURTLE CAY'S HISTORIC LOYALIST HOMES.

islands; and historic pictures of pineapple farming, shark fishing, turpentine producing, hurricanes, and more. One of its amusing highlights is the collection of booze bottles excavated from the privy out back. Owner Alton Lowe conjectures that the women of the house hid their stash there to enjoy while their husbands were out at sea.

ELBOW CAY LIGHTHOUSE LENDS WHIMSY AND HISTORY TO THE LOCAL HARBOR LANDSCAPE.

✪ **Elbow Cay Lighthouse,** Hope Town, Elbow Cay. Open 9:30–6 daily. Donations requested. Climb its 101 steps—89 feet high, 120 feet above sea level—for a breezy view. Originally built in 1864, the landmark candy-cane-striped tower was rebuilt in 1934. It's an easy climb with OMG views from every landing and an over-the-top view of the harbor and town from the open-air apex. One of three kerosene-powered lights in the world (the other two are also in the Bahamas), it was built to assist wreckers back in the day.

Loyalist Memorial Sculpture Garden, New Plymouth, Green Turtle Cay. Built in memory of Green Turtle Cay's founders, it is a quiet oasis in an already quiet Out Island town. Its sculptures depict the Loyalists landing in Abaco with their slaves as well as busts of their descendants. A bronze plaque tells the story of the various historical figures.

ISLAND CHARACTER: ALTON LOWE

He lives in a gingerbread, gabled house that looks like one of his paintings. For more than 30 years, Alton Lowe, the unofficial artist laureate of the Bahamas, has been selling his realistic portraits of island scenes, people, flora, and fauna.

Inspiration comes right from his little house with its lush gardens of orchids, rare roses, and views of the sea from two directions.

As an artist, Lowe got his big start in Miami Beach under the patronage of a couple of Lincoln Road studio owners/artists. His first one-man show in Nassau, "to get it out of his system," sold 22 of 24 paintings in one day, he says as he tosses bits of bread to marauding hermit crabs.

His paintings hang in the Royal Family's Windsor Palace. Some of his most recognizable works grace highly collectible Bahamian postage stamps, including a recent "potcakes" series. Besides his high artist profile, his civic-minded roles in the community have resulted in the Albert Lowe Museum, the nation's first museum, and Loyalist Memorial Garden. His vast body of work has immortalized old-island character and buildings, some of which no longer exist.

○ **Wyannie Malone Historical Museum** (242-366-0293; www.hopetown museum.com), Hope Town, Elbow Cay. Open Nov.–July, Mon.–Sat. Adults $3, students and children age 13 and younger $1. Duck into this typically charming Hope Town home and step into eras bygone in Abaco history. Named for Hope Town's plucky founder, a Loyalist defector from Charleston, South Carolina, it scans a history fraught with Lucayan Indians, pirates, rumrunners, wreckers, Loyalist refugees, shipbuilders, hurricanes, and torpedo freighters. Period furnishings, tools, utensils, artifacts, and photos bring the past to the forefront at this 19th-century way-stop.

MUSIC & NIGHTLIFE Watch for wherever the **Gully Roosters**, a favorite local band, is playing, and you're sure to find a good time.

Abaco Beach Resort (242-367-2158, Ext. 6021; www.abacobeachresort.com), Bay St., Marsh Harbour. It bills itself as "Entertainment Capital of the Abacos." Hear everything from gospel and rake 'n' scrape to karaoke and local talent shows.

Curly Tails Restaurant (242-367-4444; www.abacocurlytails.com), Bay St. at Conch Hotel, Marsh Harbour. Upstairs with an elevated view of the harbor, it features live music on weekends, a great wine list, and potent Goombay Smashes.

○ **Miss Emily's Blue Bee Bar** (242-365-4181), New Plymouth, Green Turtle Cay. The epitome of a good-time Bahamian bar, this is home of the Goombay Smash, a rum concoction that does pretty much what its name suggests. It may be the reason for all the T-shirts hanging on the walls and ceilings, too. Visit with

PIÑA COLADAS MAKE THE
ENTERTAINMENT AT ABACO BEACH
RESORT GO DOWN EVEN BETTER.

Violet Smith, daughter of the late Miss Emily. Violet doesn't drink, but she does like to talk. She will not, however, divulge her secret recipe no matter how long you chat her up.

Pineapples Bar & Grill (242-365-4039), Green Turtle Cay. On the water, it's most spirited with live music on Friday nights.

✪ **Snappas Grill & Chill** (242-367-2278; www.snappasbar.com), Bay St., Marsh Harbour. The entertainment often has more to do with watching the yachtie crowd than the live band. It shuts down on the early side due to complaints from residents.

✳ To Do

BEST BEACHES You can find beaches away from the main settlements where you can stay the day and never see another person. Most beaches are undeveloped stretches, with the notable exception at Treasure Cay on Great Abaco Island.

Bita Beach, Green Turtle Cay. If you love Miami Beach, you're going to hate it here, where there's nothing but quiet, rocks, sands, and washed-up seaweed. Ask locals for directions, stock a cooler, squeeze on the sunscreen, and prepare to be lulled.

Elbow Cay, east side of the island. Pinkish sands stretch for 2 miles along a reef only 30 feet offshore, making it popular with snorkelers. Surfers like Garbanzo Beach, where the reef ends and allows waves to wash ashore—Abaco's best surfing. Sea Spray Resort's Garbanzo Reef Bar is handy for nourishment.

Great Guana Cay Beach. This 5-mile stretch of white powder is not only beautiful to look at, it's a short swim away from the Great Abaco Barrier Reef—equally beautiful to see. Beach bars provide the convenience of food and drink. Plan to spend an entire day. (The ferry from Marsh Harbour makes the 30-minute trip back and forth five times daily.)

✪ **Treasure Cay,** Treasure Cay Resort, Great Abaco Island. Part of a resort but open to the public, it's not only the most beautiful beach on the main island, it's the most happening. Its ultrafine white sand has won it best beach awards from *Caribbean*

> **BAHAMA TALK**
> Potcake: This somewhat endearing, somewhat derisive term for a Bahamian mixed-breed dog comes from their help with after-dinner cleanup by eating the caked rice off the bottom of the pan.

TREASURE CAY BEACH TAKES THE PRIZE FOR SOFT SAND AND A FUN-TIME ATMOSPHERE.

Travel & Life and *National Geographic* magazines. Coco Beach Bar keeps things lively, along with beach volleyball, banana boating, Hobie Cat sailing, and more.

BIKING By bike is a good way to get around the small cays where cars are scarce.
Rental Shops: **Brendal's Dive Center** (242-365-4411; www.brendal.com), White Sound, Green Turtle Cay. Rents adult bicycles by the day and week.
Dive Guana (242-365-5178; www.diveguana.com), Great Guana Cay. Rents bikes by the day.

FISHING The easily spooked, elusive bonefish are the tricky catch of the islands. At home in the grass flats, they are well-suited for fly-fishing. The marls off Great Abaco's western shore are a favorite spot to find them. Out in open water, barracuda, yellowtail snapper, and grunts are common. Also a signature of the islands, grouper in various varieties haunt deep waters, as do dolphin and wahoo.
Charters: The going rate for charter fishing is $350 to $550 for a half day and $800 to $850 for a full day. Any number of native islanders are ready to take you to their sweet spots.
Capt. Will Key (242-366-0059), Hope Town. This 60-something native islander and third-generation guide hauls up to six fishermen aboard his 20-foot *Day's Catch* for open-water fishing.
Robert Lowe (242-366-0266), Hope Town. Excursions aboard his 32-foot boat go to open water for dolphin, wahoo, and billfish.
Capt. Rick Sawyer (242-365-4261; www.abacoflyfish.com), Green Turtle Cay. He comes highly recommended for bonefishing around Green Turtle Cay and offshore fishing.

WATER SPORTS *Anchorages:* For day anchorages, you will find mooring buoys at many of the most popular reef sites. They mark voluntary no-take zones, meaning you should not feed, spearfish, or collect any marine life at these sites. For overnighting, Abaco boasts nearly 20 full-service marinas.

Abaco Beach Resort & Boat Harbour Marina (242-367-2158), Marsh Harbour. Full-service with 198 slips, a restaurant and bars, groceries, laundry, and a full complement of services.

"♈" **Conch Inn Hotel & Marina** (242-367-4000), Marsh Harbour. Its 80 slips accommodate vessels up to 200 feet in length with 10-foot drafts. Cable TV, electricity, Internet service, fuel, a swimming pool, a dive shop, showers, and restrooms are available.

ABACO FERRYTALES: ISLAND-HOPPING ON A BUDGET

Tidily uniformed school kids climbed aboard as the crew loaded sacks of flour, a boxed microwave, some spare luggage, and various other unidentifiable bundles onto the ferryboat. Despite the early hour, everyone was cheerful, nodding "good morning" to fellow passengers whether they knew them or not. The captain crawled through the window, gunned the engine, and we were on our way through the morning sea air from Treasure Cay on Great Abaco Island to Green Turtle Cay.

Other seafarers that day were piloting million-dollar yachts that were costing them a small fortune in anchorage fees to travel around the Abaco Islands, the Bahamas' boating capital. Us? We were paying $17 round-trip to hop out to Green Turtle Cay.

It's my favorite pastime in the Abacos, day-hopping to its scattering of small islands or overnighting to soak up as much of each island's character as possible.

Elbow Cay is the most popular excursion because the ferry leaves from the Marsh Harbour municipal dock to take you to the fairy-tale Hope Town.

Sailors-in-the-know know Great Guana Cay for Nippers Beach Bar & Grill, one of the most famous yachtie bars in the tropics—especially come Sunday, when it throws one heck of a wild boar roast. Drink something rum here, grab a Guana Grabber at Grabbers Bar & Grill, and you'll understand the rhythm of this island.

The antithesis of Great Guana Cay's revolving happy hour, Man-O-War Cay sells or serves no booze. So why go there, you may wonder? As the boatbuilding capital of the Bahamas, it's an interesting place to watch craftsmen making boats, repairing them, creating models, and making ditty bags out of sailcloth.

You can rent or charter boats throughout the Abacos. It's one of those places where you MUST get out on the water. But for those who want to do it with the least amount of hassle and ka-ching, the value and pleasures of the local ferryboat system is no fairy tale.

⁰1⁰ Green Turtle Club Resort & Marina (242-365-4271), White Sound, Green Turtle Cay. Guests have access to resort amenities in addition to the 35-slip marina's electricity, water, cable, and wireless access. Boats up to 130 feet allowed.

Lighthouse Marina (242-366-0154; www.htlighthousemarina.com), Hope Town, Elbow Cay. A full-service marina with fuel, hauling, dry storage, and a complete ship's store, including liquor.

Treasure Cay Marina (242-365-8250; www.treasurecay.com), Treasure Cay, Great Abaco Island. Offers 150 slips with laundry and shower facilities and all the rest, including a swimming pool, bar, tennis courts, restaurant, and dive shop. Boat rentals and guides available.

Day Cruising: **Island Gal Charters** (242-577-0284; www.islandgalcharters .com), Marsh Harbour. Half- and full-day sailing cruises include snorkel picnics and sunset-gazing. Sailing lessons included.

Powerboat Rentals: Boat rentals are plentiful throughout the Abaco Islands. Daily rates start at $160 in the off-season, $200 in-season.

Abaco Dorado Boat Rentals (242-367-1035; abacodoradoboatrentals.com), Conch Inn Marina, Bay St., Marsh Harbour. Offers 22- to 26-foot boats equipped with dive ladders, a bimini or T-top, and other necessities.

B&B Boat Rentals (242-367-7368), Marsh Harbour. Fuel-efficient 23- and 26-foot center-console boats with GPS, CD player, and safety equipment. Rent for one, three, or seven days, or long-term.

Island Marine Boat Rentals (242-366-0282; www.islandmarine.com), Parrot Cay, Hope Town. Offers 17- and 21-foot Boston Whalers and locally made boats from 20 to 23 feet.

Reef Rentals (242-365-4145), Green Turtle Cay. Rent 17- to 26-footers to use in the Green Turtle Cay area for a three-day minimum.

Rich's Boat Rentals (242-367-2742), Marsh Harbour. Rents 21- to 26-foot boats by the day, three days, or week. Also fishing and snorkeling gear, bait, and guides.

Sea Horse Boat Rentals (242-367-2513; www.seahorseboatrentals.com), Marsh Harbour at Abaco Beach Resort & Boat Harbour. Locally made and other boats range from 15 to 23 feet.

Paddling & Ecotours: **Brendal's Dive Center** (242-365-4411; www.brendal .com), White Sound, Green Turtle Cay. Rents single and double kayaks by the hour, day, and week.

Dive Guana (242-365-5178; www.diveguana.com), Great Guana Cay. Kayak rentals by the day.

Snorkeling & Diving: Depending upon who's telling it, Abaco's offshore reef is either the third or fourth largest in the world (actually fourth after Australia, Belize, and Andros). Within a short boat ride, Abaco dive masters can find nearly 20 dive sites for divers of all persuasions. **The Pillars** makes for an easy 35-foot dive where pillar coral reaches from bottom to top. At 50 and 60 feet, coral caverns and formations await. **Valley of the Sponges** is a colorful 90-foot dive. At **The Ledge,** 100 feet below, huge grouper swim. For man-made dives, try the wreck of the *Violet Mitchell* in 45 feet or the historic wreck *San Jacinto,* the U.S.'s first steamship, which sank in 1865 and rests at 50 feet. **Fowl Cay Preserve,** a national underwater park, lies off the north end of Man-O-War Cay. For specialty divers, the many **blue holes and extensive cave system** of Abaco present challenge and eerie beauty.

No matter who's telling it, Abaco's waters are among the cleanest, clearest in the islands, mainly because no rivers or trenches flow into the Sea of Abaco.

Recommended Charter: ✪ **Brendal's Dive Center** (242-365-4411; www.brendal .com), White Sound, Green Turtle Cay. THE first name for diving in these parts, Brendal Acklins has raised his operation to the surface on sheer personality and competence. Established in 1985, the business has been featured on CNN Travel and the Discovery Channel. Nondivers can get their feet wet on his snorkel-picnic tour that includes relishing just-caught fish on a private island. Or they can sign up for one of his courses; he's capable of certifying anyone who has begun training, no matter the organization. He can take divers on his original tarpon dive, to historic wrecks, reefs, miniwalls, whatever their pleasure. His dive shop has everything you need to rent or purchase. He teams up with Green Turtle Club Resort & Marina for hotel and dive packages.

Other Charters: **Abaco Beach Resort** (242-367-2158 or 800-468-4799; www .abacobeachresort.com), Marsh Harbour. Custom dive trips, scuba and snorkeling tours, instruction, private charters, island hopping, sunset cruises, rentals, and air fills. Accommodations-dive packages available.

HUGE STINGRAYS ANSWER THE FEEDING CALL ON BRENDAL'S TOURS.

Above & Below Abaco (242-367-0350 or 321-206-9197 (U.S.); www.aboveand belowabaco.com), E. Bay St., Marsh Harbour. Specializing in customized dive trips for eight divers or less; also scuba and snorkeling tours, sunset cruises, equipment rentals, and tank fills.

Dive Abaco (242-367-2787; www.diveabaco.com), at Conch Inn Hotel & Marina, Marsh Harbour. A 30-year operation with snorkeling and diving trips plus instruction, including a day resort course.

Dive Guana (242-365-5178; www.diveguana.com), Great Guana Cay. Diving and snorkeling rentals and tours, including a one-day resort course.

Froggie's Out Island Adventures (242-366-0431 or 888-774-9328; www .froggiesabaco.com), Elbow Cay. Book well in advance for Froggie's snorkel and dive trips, dolphin encounters, and other adventures. Froggie's also offers certification courses, including a sample resort course.

WILDLIFE SPOTTING Nature reserves on Great Abaco Island are home to two unusual species: the green **Abaco Bahama Amazon** (a subspecies of the Cuban Amazon but also known as the **Bahama parrot**) and **wild Barbary horse.** The latter's DNA tests back to the Spanish era. While once it numbered in the 200s, its population is now down to about a half-dozen due to dogs and people killing them off. Biologists further believe they are unable to reproduce anymore. **Wild boars** also wander Great Abaco's wild regions.

As for the green parrot with its pink legs, its numbers are dwindling, too. Once found throughout the Bahamas, it now sticks mostly to Abaco and Great Inagua. Other notable bird species found on the islands include Bahama yellowthroat, pine warbler, Kirkland warbler, red-legged thrush, blue-gray gnat-catcher, olive-capped warbler, loggerhead kingbird, lasagra's flycatcher, greater Antillean bull-fish, striped-headed tanager, Bahama swallow, Cuban emerald hummingbird, Bahama mockingbird, and the West Indian woodpecker.

Nature Preserves & Eco-Attractions: **Abaco National Park** (www.bnt.bs), Sandy Point. Open daily. Established by the Bahamas National Trust (BNT) on 20,500 acres on Great Abaco Island's southwest side, it contains more than 5,000 acres of pine forest, which is the preferred habitat of the Bahama parrot. Fresh water and a number of other bird species make this one of the Bahamas' most important birding sites. Although there are no facilities, hikers and birders are welcome to explore, as long as they bring their own supplies and take them back out with them. The drive to get there, however, is unpaved for quite a distance, and rental companies are not thrilled about their cars going there. Better option: Friends of the Environment (242-367-2414; www.friendsoftheenvironment.org) organizes birding tours and counts.

Also, as part of BNT, there are four aquatic-land preserves offshore, popular diving spots—Pelican Cays Land & Sea Park, and Black Sound Cay, Tilloo, and Walker's Cay National Reserves.

BAHAMA TALK

Peckerwood: You will often hear Bahamians refer to woodpeckers by this colloquialism.

ISLAND CHARACTER:
BRENDAL ACKLINS

"It tastes like a salty gummy bear," he told me, urging me to suck down the piston from a conch he'd just shucked—"just like a noodle." Usually it's the man who gets the piston when Bahamians are shucking conch, because, as in Brendal Acklins's words: "It makes your sticker peck out."

Brendal, of Brendal's Dive Center, is every bit as entertaining as the moray eels, giant lobsters, groupers, snappers, and riotously hued coral one encounters on his snorkeling and diving excursions. As his crew boated us to our snorkel point, he turned live conchs into lime-marinated conch

BRENDAL ACKLINS SHUCKS A CONCH TO MAKE CONCH SALAD FOR HIS SNORKELING TOUR'S BEACH PICNIC.

salad, cracked jokes, and laughed his deep belly chortle like a man who simply enjoys life. And why not? He gets to be out on and in the water daily if he so desires. He is legendary on Green Turtle Cay, where he maintains his full-service shop, everyone seems to know him, and he plays guitar with a band at Pineapples Bar & Grill.

After snorkeling, he and the crew roasted grouper over an open fire on a private island known as Munjack. It turns out even the stingrays know Brendal. Shortly after we docked, they swept in, grazing our bare feet. OK, so it was grouper scrap handouts they were looking for. Actually, "footouts" would be more accurate. We stuck the snippets between our big and second toes for them to nab, their velvety underbellies sensuous. (Warning: Keep toes flat on the sand unless you want one to chomp down on your toe. I know this from experience!)

A tour with Brendal, certified seven ways for dive instruction, is high-energy, with music, rum, and always the jokes. One has to wonder where the guy gets his energy. Especially when one discovers the slim, muscular man is 60-something!

ABACO

✳ Lodging

Resorts are small and personal in this part of the world. Don't think that necessarily means inexpensive, because in general the Bahamas run high for lodging rates, Abaco perhaps more so than others. In addition to the base rate, the government and hoteliers throw another 6 to 12 percent on top of that for taxes and service charges. Accommodations are most expensive in the winter-spring season, Christmas through Easter. Some hotels may close during August, September, and October.

Price Codes

Inexpensive	Up to $100
Moderate	$100 to $200
Expensive	$200 to $300
Very Expensive	$300 and up

(An asterisk after the pricing designation indicates that the rate includes at least a continental breakfast in the cost of lodging and possibly more extensive meal service as noted in the listing.)

ACCOMMODATIONS

Elbow Cay

"I" ✪ **Hope Town Harbour Lodge** (242-366-0095 or 866-611-9791; www.hopetownlodge.com), Hope Town. Set into a flowery hillside with a beach backdrop, this is the perfect place to stay if you want to get into the local Hope Town scene. It's compact with only 20 units, but remarkably self-sufficient, claiming its own dining room, a cocktail lounge, a pool bar and grill, and a quiet beach edged with dunes and coconut palms. Rooms in the three-story lodge's historic building are small, decorated in Tommy Bahama-style, with no bathtub, TV, or phone. Brightly painted

Adirondack chairs decorate the walkway outside. Gingerbread cottages closer to the beach and swimming pool sleep four to six, and have kitchen facilities and white beadboard walls. There are minimum stay requirements in-season. Moderate to Very Expensive.

"I" **Sea Spray Resort & Marina** (242-366-0065; www.seasprayresort.com), White Sound. Stretching between the Atlantic Ocean and Sea of Abaco, its seven modern, Bahamian-style villas in pastel hues range from one to three bedrooms with full kitchens, a private hammock, telephones, wireless Internet, and daily maid service. Its protected, full-service deepwater marina accommodates boaters (guests with boats under 23 feet dock for free), plus there's a freshwater pool, the Boat House Restaurant serving all three meals, and the poolside Garbanzo Reef Bar. The beach, known to have the best surfing waves and wind surfing breezes in the Abacos, lies a short, barefoot walk from the cottages. A complimentary shuttle transports guests to Hope Town. Moderate to Very Expensive.

Great Guana Cay

Oceanfrontier Hideaway (519-389-4846 or 888-541-1616; www.oceanfrontier.com), Great Guana Cay. Along Guana Cay's fabulous five-mile beach, its six air-conditioned, rustic-chic cabins sleep four to six in two bedrooms and a loft with full kitchens, private decks, and CD and DVD players. Nippers restaurant and pool are steps away. Staff can arrange boat or golf cart rentals and any number of snorkeling or boating excursions. A near-shore reef provides easy snorkeling opportunities, but bring your own gear. There's a small extra cleaning charge for stays of less than three nights. Expensive.

Green Turtle Cay

⁰**ı**⁰ ✪ **Green Turtle Club Resort & Marina** (242-365-4271 or 866-528-0539; www.greenturtleclub.com), White Sound, Green Turtle Cay. Wake up in the morning to a view of regal yachts bobbing on water that looks too blue to be true. Who needs coffee? Just in case, there's a coffeepot in each unit, along with a small fridge and DVD player. Thirty-one rooms and villas—all individually decorated—are tucked into a palm-swayed hillside with private patios overlooking beach and harbor. The grandest, Beau Soleil, has four bedrooms in its main and pool house, with a semiprivate pool and private boat dock. Walk five minutes to reach the island's beautiful beach. If you're boating in, tie up in the 35-slip marina. In operation since 1964, this island landmark comes complete with a popular boaters' restaurant and a seasonal bar and grill poolside, where happy hour is actually two hours long. Moderate to Very Expensive.

Man-O-War Cay

Schooner's Landing (242-367-4469 or 242-365-6143 (reservations); www.schoonerslanding.com), Man-O-War Cay. Man-O-War Cay has no traditional hotels or resorts, but there are cottages and condos to be rented, such as the three bluff-set beach houses here, all with balconies overlooking the ocean or pool. The units are fully stocked with kitchen appliances and necessities, TV, laundry facilities, and a telephone. They can accommodate four to six people. Guests have use of a freshwater swimming pool with an inviting deck and

easy access to boat and golf cart rentals. Within walking distance of town, it also provides laundry facilities and use of gas grills. Expensive.

Marsh Harbour

✪ **Abaco Beach Resort & Boat Harbour** (242-367-2158 or 800-468-4799; www.abacobeachresort.com), Marsh Harbour. Abaco's largest resort, this property boasts 80-some rooms, two-bedroom cottages, and condos all overlooking one of the Bahamas' biggest marinas (198 slips) and a homemade beach. The spacious, simply decorated rooms come equipped with a wet bar and tiny fridge, white wicker furniture, porcelain tile floors that housekeeping mops daily, a TV, a phone, a coffeemaker, a comfy bed dressed in a white down comforter and lots of pillows, but alas, a shortage of drawer space. The resort's groundbreaking Bahama Buddies kids program involves local young "ambassadors" who teach their visiting peers how to fish, crack open a coconut, snorkel, and other local lifestyle basics. There's also a full-service dive shop, boat and water sports rentals, boat charters, a fitness center, two tennis courts, a sand volleyball court, a playground, and two pools on-site. Guests, other visitors, and residents alike come for its live entertainment and dinner in Angler's. The resort is in the process of building luxury resident accommodations. Three so far are on the rental program. Very Expensive.

🦞 **Conch Inn Hotel & Marina** (242-367-4000; www.conchinn.com), Marsh Harbour. The small but pleasant rooms here are a sideline to the marina operation, but even non-mariners will appreciate its yachtie amenities: a dive shop, excellent restaurant (Curly Tails; see *Where to Eat*) and bar, pool, and laundry facilities. Each room—decorated with tile, rattan, and colorful bedspreads—has its own refrigerator, TV, and air-conditioning. The marina hosts Moorings and Sunsail yacht-sailing schools and rentals. Convenient to Marsh Harbour's best bars and restaurants, it's a good choice if you like to be in the thick of activity or plan to spend most of your days in and on the water. Moderate.

Island Breezes Motel (242-367-3776), Marsh Harbour. For those looking for pleasant, affordable accommodations within walking distance to Marsh Harbour's shops, marinas, and restaurants, this fits the bill. Nothing fancy, but its eight units are tiled, clean, and uncluttered, furnished with a TV, refrigerator, microwave oven, and a deck with picnic tables. Like many budget Out Island accommodations (and even

some of the high-end ones), it has no phones in the rooms. Moderate.

Treasure Cay
○ **Treasure Cay Hotel Resort & Marina** (954-525-7711 (U.S.) or 800-327-1584; www.treasurecay.com), Marsh Harbour. A full-service resort, Treasure Cay boasts a renowned Dick Wilson 18-hole golf course, 150-slip marina, and club named Coco Beach Bar right on an award-winning, 3½-mile beach. Two other venues also give guests drinking and dining options—the relatively formal Spinnaker and often raucous Tipsy Seagull, poolside. The resort's more than 90 accommodation units—including standard rooms, one- to three-bedroom suites, and a cottage—don't have beach views, but face either the marina or the lush, well-tended gardens. Treehouse Villas, however, do face the beach. In addition to marina amenities—boat rentals, charters, and fishing guides—guests will find a full

THE COCO BEACH BAR AT TREASURE CAY HOTEL RESORT IS A HOT SPOT FOR SUNNING AND FUNNING.

range of water sport rentals on the beach, plus tennis and a dive shop. Many are content to spend their time on the incredibly powdery white sand, playing volleyball, tossing back Kalik beers, or merely soaking up the rays. Moderate to Very Expensive.

HOME & CONDO RENTALS

Abaco Vacation Resorts (978-874-5995 or 800-633-9197; www.abaco vacations.com) More than 70 homes, cottages, private islands, condos, villas, resorts, and inns through the cays.

Hope Town Hideaways (242-366-0224; www.hopetown.com), Hope Town, Elbow Cay. Waterfront and other homes with access to a 12-slip marina and pool

✳ Where to Eat

You'll find the greatest concentration of restaurants along Marsh Harbour's Bay Street, many of them embedded within hotels and resorts. It's a rare experience no matter where you eat in the Abacos to be out of eyeshot of water—whether it's the ocean or a boat harbor. Most restaurants throughout the chain offer the Bahamian standards: cracked conch, fried chicken, Bahamian lobster (in season), grouper, snapper, and mahimahi. Burgers, fish sandwiches, and pork chops are also common finds. Abaco is famous for its boating bars—colorful spots to dock for grog, grub, and good times. You'll also find a few places where creativity and sophistication offer a respite from the typical fried seafood menu.

Price Codes

Inexpensive	Up to $15
Moderate	$15 to $25
Expensive	$25 to $35
Very Expensive	$35 or more

Cost categories are based on the range of dinner entrée prices or, if dinner is not served, on lunch entrées.

Resort and other major restaurants take reservations. For small restaurants outside of Marsh Harbour, it's a good idea to call ahead to make sure they're open. Often they require that you order your dinner ahead of time from the two or three selections they may offer that evening.

Elbow Cay

♿ **Cap'n Jack's Restaurant and Bar** (242-366-0247), Queen's Hwy., Hope Town. One of the local favorites, Cap'n Jack's has a party-down reputation, especially when there's live music happening, but it's also a good place to grab a grouper sandwich, cracked conch, the fresh catch-of-the-day, fried chicken, and lobster when in season. The view of the harbor from the open deck and the key lime pie are bonus reasons to stop for lunch or dinner (also serving breakfast). Moderate to Expensive. Closed Sunday.

"CHICKEN IN DA BAG" STARTED AS A POPULAR TAKE-OUT TRADITION IN THE BAHAMAS. TODAY IT AND THE LESS-COMMON "CONCH IN DA BAG" ARE FAVORITES AT HARBOUR'S EDGE.

&. **Harbour's Edge** (242-366-0087), Queen's Hwy., Hope Town. Plastic chairs and fried chicken in a bag: This place has the proper Bahamas attitude and view. In addition to the usual Bahamian "burgers" and specialties, the erase-board lunch menu offers wraps and other hot and cold sandwiches. The "chicken in da bag" is a classic presentation of fried chicken and preketchuped french fries (tossed also with a little hot sauce). Harbour's Edge also does cracked conch in the bag, which you don't find many places. It's the ultimate Bahamian comfort food. At dinner, sandwiches are still available, plus some more gourmet-style dishes such as duck confit with Grand Marnier sauce or crawfish sautéed with spinach and served over linguine with a white cheese wine sauce. Moderate to Expensive. No reservations.

Great Guana Cay

&. **Grabbers Bar & Grill** (242-365-5133; www.grabbersatsunset.com), harbor side. Its claim to fame is the Guana Grabber, a three-rum drink that dates back to the 1960s, when the Guana Beach Resort occupied the location. Should you want to insulate your stomach against its effects, the beach shack also serves burgers, Philly traditions such as cheese steaks and hoagies, and other sandwiches, plus cracked conch, wings, and other bar bites. For dinner, it does nightly specials such as Wednesday Potluck Night, Thursday Italian Night, and Saturday Rib Night. Try to make it to toast sunset. Inexpensive to Moderate.

Nippers Beach Bar & Grill (242-365-5143; www.nippersbar.com), north side. One of the most famous yachtie bars in the tropics, Nippers serves hardy chow along with views of sand and water from the two-level pool bar that outsparkle precious gemstones. A reef lies just offshore, so snorkeling is often part of the Nippers experience, as is sipping a frozen Nipper Tripper rum cocktail. (Thank the island gods for the Nippermobile to give you a lift back to the public dock.) Lunch is all about beach food—burgers, conch, and lobster salad sandwiches. The dinner menu features coconut conch, a signature fish dish marinated and cooked in foil, local grilled fish, and surf and turf. Enjoy open-air dining amid an explosion of painted wood colors along one of the Bahamas' best beaches. Sunday's wild boar roast buffet begins at noon and brings in up to 1,000 party animals. The all-you-can-eat buffet ($22–$25) includes all the fixings—macaroni and cheese, peas 'n' rice, Cajun coleslaw, potato salad, corn custard, and bread pudding. Inexpensive to Moderate.

Green Turtle Cay

○ **Green Turtle Club** (242-365-4271 or 866-528-0539; www.green turtleclub.com), White Sound. As part of a resort and marina, Green Turtle Club serves mainly guests and boat-in diners in a casual, open-air deck or lattice-trimmed screened porch setting beneath paddle fans. For something cozier, walk through the

BAHAMA TALK

Burger: This can mean a hamburger. But it can also mean any hot sandwich captured within a bun—from fried chicken to cracked conch. The difference between burger and sandwich in local parlance? Sandwiches come on toast.

currency-covered lobby to the formal dining room. Breakfast and lunch stick to the traditional, with pancakes, a seafood omelet, a fine rendition of eggs Benedict, all things conch, a lobster baguette and quesadilla, wraps, burgers, and a nice choice of salads. Dinner showcases local fresh catches in the grouper poached in foil, seafood cake, and seafood Alfredo. The nightly specials offer a divergence of about a dozen creative starters and entrées, from sweet potato bisque and crab ravioli to rum-and-pepper-painted grouper, grilled lamb chops, and roasted Cornish game hen. Call by 5 PM to order your entrée for the 7:30 seating. Wash it down with the bar's signature Tipsy Turtle Rum Punch. Moderate to Expensive.

McIntosh Restaurant & Bakery (242-365-4625), Parliament St., New Plymouth. The real thing when it comes to Bahamian eats, the bakery specials add to the sweetness of the cozy experience. Sandwiches such as fried grouper and cracked conch come on Bahamian bread, sweet and thick. Dinner brings on the overload with mac and cheese, coleslaw, and peas 'n' rice heaping up plates of lobster, fish, shrimp, and pork chops. Then there's fresh-made dessert. Remember the bakery? Try the cake du jour or a wedge of coconut cream pie that tastes fresh off the tree. Inexpensive to Moderate.

Man-O-War Cay

&. **Dock & Dine** (242-365-6139), on the waterfront at Man-O-War Marina, Man-O-War Cay. Not exactly the dining capital of the Bahamas, Man-O-War lacks the funky little watering holes of other islands because of its teetotaling reputation. But that doesn't mean you'll go unfed if you're stopping in. Here's a pleasant harborside spot where you can score some munchies, a quesadilla (with your choice of flour, spinach, or tomato basil tortilla), a cheeseburger, or some chicken wings. The most unusual item on the regular menu is the Docker's Salad—lettuces, tomatoes, grapes, pineapple, walnuts, bacon, and croutons. Dinner brings nightly specials such as ribs, lamb, pork chops, and shrimp skewer. The staff is pleasant and helpful. Moderate to Expensive.

Marsh Harbour

&. **Angler's Restaurant** (242-367-2158; www.abacobeachresort.com), Bay St., at Abaco Beach Resort. The fresh Bahamian lobster and shrimp stuffed with chorizo score high at dinnertime. I became a quick fan of its breakfast menu, which bows to Bahamian tradition with boil' fish and chicken souse, and also American tastes with a nearly religious lobster Benedict (called "eggs Abaco" on the menu). Seating is indoor or out, overlooking the beach and marina. The lunch menu, also served around the pool bar, ranges from individual pizzas to a lobster wrap and a tasty fish taco. The evening entertainment is pure fun, with much of the talent coming from the resort's own staff, including the general manager, who plays the drums. This is one of Abaco's most formal settings, and a good place for casual lunch as well as special-occasion dining. Moderate to Expensive.

&. ✪ **Curly Tails Restaurant** (242-367-4444; www.abacocurlytails.com), Bay St., at Conch Inn Hotel. By far the best restaurant I've experienced in the Abacos, it takes a step away from traditional Bahamian cuisine while keeping one foot firmly planted. In addition to the ubiquitous fried chicken and conch fritters, it excites the taste buds with such creative visions as sweet plantain-crusted grouper with papaya salsa, vodka-flamed mahimahi with roasted potato hash and red Thai coconut curry and shrimp sauce, and grilled rosemary veal rack chops. Don't pass up the fig and prosciutto salad for first course. Dessert poses more of a dilemma: orange raspberry rum cake, wild orange crème caramel, guava rolly polly, or coconut key lime pie? Yes to all. Curly Tails, named for the local salamander-sized lizards with their coiled rear extremities, also serves breakfast and lunch daily, with selections equally varied as the dinner menu: salmon Benedict, stew conch, Mediterranean ciabatta, jerk chicken pizza, and chipotle lobster linguine. The wine list, too, stands out from other local restaurants. Eat outdoors harborside under the soft glow of round, buoylike oil lamps or in the linen-set dining room. Upstairs, the sophisticated bar serves the strongest Goombay Smashes and hosts local musicians. Service here is also uncharacteristically expedient and accommodating. Moderate to Expensive.

& **Mangoes Restaurant** (242-367-2366 or 242-367-4255; www.mangoes marina.com), Bay St. Like other of Marsh Harbour's best restaurants, this one overlooks the yacht-filled harbor with both indoor and outdoor seating. The Bahamian specialties are authentic, but the menu stretches beyond with finger food such as fried yucca with guacamole, chicken quesadillas, burgers, sandwiches, wraps, and salads for lunch. At dinner, the selections are split between From the Sea (mango orange grouper is signature) and From the Farm (Bahamian BBQ ribs, grilled rib eye, and vegetarian

selections). Cap it off with the daunting house Mango Millennium rum concoction. Every Wednesday night is Pasta Night, either by the bowlful or all you can eat. Moderate to Expensive. Closed Sunday.

BAKERIES Miss Lola (no phone) You won't find her, but she'll find you as she drives around her golf cart in Marsh Harbour selling her bread, pastries, and other baked delights.

COFFEE Hope Town Coffee Shop (242-366-0760), near the Lower Public Dock in Hope Town, Elbow Cay. Get your morning wake-up call with a latte, mocha, espresso, and homemade pastries.

Java (242-367-5523), Bay St., Marsh Harbour, Great Abaco Island. An artsy spot for coffee, espresso, frappes, cappuccino, latte, caramel macchiato, and baked goods.

GROCERS Curry's Sunset Grocery (242-365-4171), on the waterfront in New Plymouth, Green Turtle Cay. Dock and shop for all your grocery needs, including homemade bread, fresh fruit and vegetables, and ice.

JAVA BLENDS ART AND CAFFEINE.

ICE CREAM Dips, Sips & Wishes
(242-365-6380), Man-O-War Cay. The
"dips" is ice cream; "sips," Barnie's
coffee and other drinks; "wishes," kids
gifts, electronics, cell phones, and
U.S. imports.

New Plymouth Dock, on the waterfront in New Plymouth, Green Turtle
Cay. The ice cream man doesn't play
a catchy tune here, he lures you via
loudspeaker with the promise of
something sweet and icy as you pull
up to Government Dock. The
coconut flavor is yummy and chunky.
Take a few more steps and you can
pick up some fresh fried conch fritters
to slake your at-sea hunger.

TAKE-OUT Bahamians love their
take-outs, where they stop for breakfast, lunch, and dinner to-go. Some
take-outs are mobile—operated out of
the back end of an SUV or van
stopped alongside the road. Here are
some favorite stationary spots the
locals favor.

Anna's Sweet Pot (no phone), west
of the stoplight in Marsh Harbour.
Look for an old Chevy van, where you
can get lunch that ranges from curried chicken to stuffed pork chops
with fresh bread and salad.

Dis We Style (242-367-4244), Crock-
et Dr. at Forest Dr., Marsh Harbour.
Translation: This is our style. Food:
seafood platters, cracked conch, fried
chicken, and daily specials.

Pop's Place (242-367-3796), Stratton
Dr., downtown Marsh Harbour.
Famous for his rotisserie chicken,
Pop is open for lunch take-out week-
days.

✳ Selective Shopping

The best shopping is found in Marsh
Harbour and Hope Town. There's a

sameness to the shops of Marsh Har-
bour, however; most carry an array
from cheap trinkets to artsy gifts.
Hope Town has a few similar shops.
Man-O-War Cay's smattering of shops
takes a distinctly nautical heading.
Most shops close on Sunday. See also
Galleries in the *To See* section.)

Abaco Gold (242-367-4405), Marsh
Harbour. Beautiful, handcrafted jewelry inspired by the sea and its creatures. Also gemstones, resort wear,
and gifts.

Abaco Neem (242-367-4117; www
.abaconeem.com), Marsh Harbour.
Abaco farms this native Indian tree
known for its medicinal attributes.
Balms, teas, soaps, lotions, and other
products help with high blood pressure, diabetes, inflammation, and bac-
terial infection prevention.

Albury's Designs (no phone), Man-
O-War Cay. Collector-mounted and -
framed three-dimensional boat
models including the Abaco dinghy,
sailboats, and others.

✪ **Albury Sail Shop** (242-365-6014),
Man-O-War Cay. Many folks come to

ALBURY'S SAIL SHOP IS FAMOUS AROUND
THE WORLD FOR ITS DURABLE SAILCLOTH
BAGS.

ISLAND CHARACTER: MISS ANNIE ALBURY

Some pronounce it Allberry, others Albry. In either case, it's a name you'll run into over and over again in Abaco (it fills a complete telephone directory page). Miss Annie is third generation Albury. Her grandfather, Norman, was a sail-maker whose wife, Lina, got the idea of using scraps and other sturdy materials to make ditty bags that last for decades.

"I was in the shop. I grew up in it," says Annie, who started sewing at about age 18. Everything she and her other seamstresses produce at the dockside shop gets sold right on the premises. It's done assembly line-style. She sews the seams and straps, while three others sew in zippers, piping, and the rest.

The shop's line has expanded through the years to tote bags, suitcases, and jackets, all made from 100 percent cotton. If you buy one of the signature products, you'll be in good company. It's said that Paul Newman, Perry Como, and George C. Scott are among those who have owned an Albury jacket.

ANNIE ALBURY GREW UP SEWING SAIL BAGS AT HER GRANDMOTHER'S SHOP.

Man-O-War just for these sturdy duck bags in all shapes and sizes, hand-sewn by three generations of Alburys.

Bahamas Outfitters (242-367-3312), Bay St., Marsh Harbour. A higher standard of men's, women's, and chil-dren's clothing than most of the local shops. Tommy Bahama and Columbia brands.

✪ **Conch Pearl Galleries** (242-367-0137), Bay St., Marsh Harbour. A nice selection of locally made wares including sea glass jewelry, turned tamarind wood bowls, and boat models.

Ebbtide (242-366-0088), Hope Town, Elbow Cay. One of the town's most well-rounded selections of art, batik clothes, and local books.

✪ **Iggy Biggy** (242-367-5121), Bay St., Marsh Harbour; and (242-366-0354), Hope Town. Fun jewelry and T-shirts, handmade gifts, pottery, and island music.

Island Girl (242-367-0283), Bay St., Marsh Harbour. Everybody's got T-shirts in this town, but these are the best; also soaps, candles, Cuban cigars, and other gifts and clothing.

John Bull (242-367-2473), Bay St., Marsh Harbour. Duty-free name-brand jewelry, watches, perfume, cameras, etc.

✪ **Monkey's Uncle** (242-367-3223), Bay St., Marsh Harbour. Fine tableware and accessories, cigars, and beach and jungle-themed décor items.

Native Creations (242-365-4206), Bay St., New Plymouth, Green Turtle Cay. A collection of everything Bahamian one would want to purchase for souvenirs: happy/sad dolls, mini steel drums, metal sculpture, pottery, Christmas shell ornaments, turned wood, and fine décor items.

The Painted Fish (242-365-6008), Man-O-War Marina, Man-O-War Cay. The closest thing to a conventional store, it still has a varied inventory of clothes, bags, gifts, sunscreen, and marina supplies.

Sammie Boy's Gift Shop (no phone), Man-O-War Cay. This little island is in no way a shopping mecca, but the shops and galleries you find definitely have character. Sammie Boy sells wood cutouts, driftwood lamps,

secondhand items, and an oddball selection of other gifts.

Sunset Souvenirs (242-367-2431), Bay St., Marsh Harbour. Andros Island baskets, Abaco happy/sad dolls, Kalik beer logo wares, cigars, music, and a full array of tacky souvenirs.

✳ Special Events

In the event scheme of things, summer and the winter holidays are busiest. Regatta and fishing tournaments fill the warm months, while Junkanoo is traditionally a Christmas-time celebration. In the past couple of decades, however, islanders get a summer fix of their favorite fun time during a series of weekends. Glimpses of Junkanoo, in fact, appear whenever islanders really get to partying.

January: **Abaco Art Festival** (242-367-2158), Abaco Beach Resort, Marsh Harbour. One weekend at the end of month. Artists and artisans from Abaco display and sell their wares. **New Year's Day Junkanoo** (242-367-3067), Green Turtle Cay. Traditional music, dance, rush-out, and food festival.

February: **Wine Tasting Event** (242-367-3067), Green Turtle Club, Green Turtle Cay. One day in early February. An evening under the stars features fine wine, appetizers, and local entertainment. **Junior & Senior Junkanoo** (242-367-3067), Marsh Harbour. One weekend late in the month. Local students compete for best music, dance, and costumes the first day, then it's time for the grown-ups to take the stage the following day.

March: **Hope Town's Annual Heritage Day** (242-367-3067), Hope Town. Hundreds gather in the center of town to celebrate heritage with historical speakers, school musical groups, a mini boat parade, museum tours, and traditional Bahamian cuisine.

May: **Homer Lowe Memorial Regatta** (242-367-3086), Marsh Harbour. Two days in mid-May. Running 20 years, it departs from the harbor at Snappa's. Sunfish and Optimist classes. **Island Roots Heritage Festival** (242-367-3067), Green Turtle Cay. Three days in early May. A celebration of Bahamian culture, the festival honors its history and connection to sister city, Key West, Florida, with local cuisine, Bahamian crafts, and talks on flora and fauna, bush medicine, archaeological sites, etc.

June: **Treasure Cay Billfish Tournament** (242-365-8801; www.treasure cay.com), Treasure Cay. Six days in early June. More than 25 years old, it is a sanctioned World Billfish Series event. **Junkanoo Summer Festival** (242-367-3067), Marsh Harbour. Four Fridays in June and July. Bahamians can't wait an entire year to celebrate Junkanoo at holiday time, so they throw another celebration each summer with calypso and police bands, food and drink, and arts and crafts. **Green Turtle Club Fishing Tournament** (242-365-4271 or 866-528-0539), Green Turtle Club & Marina; Green Turtle Cay. Four days in mid-June. Twenty-something years old, it focuses on billfish. Awards include the Tipsy Turtle Award for the team with

the largest bar tab, so catching a buzz is a secondary goal.

July: **Regatta** (242-367-2677), throughout the chain. Nearly 35 years old, this regatta runs for nine days among American and Bahamian Independence (July 10) days. Besides boat racing, there's partying going on.

November: **Arts & Crafts Festival** (242-366-0095), Hope Town Harbour Lodge, Hope Town. One day at the end of the month. Local and international artists and vendors sell paintings, jewelry, crafts, wine, and gourmet food. **Guy Fawkes & Bonfire Celebrations** (242-367-3067), Green Turtle Cay. One day in early November. Famous for its British-heritage competitions, including the Best Guy and Dancing of the Guy. Native food, music, and a Junkanoo parade. **Hope Town Big Hill Box Cart Derby** (242-367-3067), Hope Town. One day in late November. Purely West Indian, this competition has junior and senior divisions.

December: **Abaco Christmas Festival** (242-367-3067), Marsh Harbour. One day in early December. Santa delivers free toys and games while choirs, marching and calypso bands, Junkanoo parades, a lighted boat parade, and fireworks entertain. **North Abaco Christmas Celebration** (242-367-3067), Great Abaco Island. One day in mid-December. Christmas Bahamian-style, including a Junkanoo rush-out, arts and crafts, and free toys for the kids.

Andros   4

ANDROS TOWN/FRESH CREEK

NICHOLL'S TOWN

BEHRING POINT

CARGILL CREEK

SOUTH ANDROS

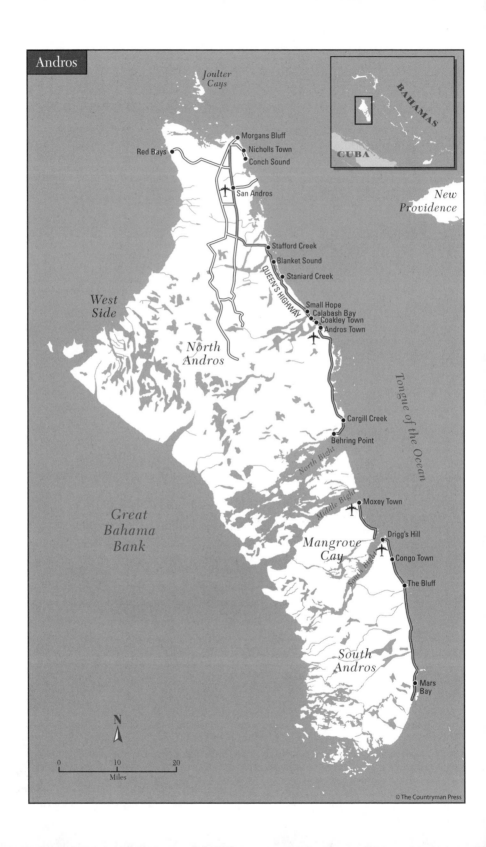

Andros

Joulter Cays

Morgans Bluff
Nicholls Town
Red Bays
Conch Sound

San Andros

New
Providence

Stafford Creek
Blanket Sound
Staniard Creek

West
Side

Small Hope
Calabash Bay
Coakley Town
Andros Town

North
Andros

QUEEN'S HIGHWAY

Tongue of the Ocean

Cargill Creek
Behring Point

North Bight

Great
Bahama
Bank

Middle Bight
Moxey Town

Mangrove
Cay

Drigg's Hill
Congo Town

South Bight

The Bluff

South
Andros

Mars
Bay

N

0   10   20
Miles

© The Countryman Press

BAHAMAS
CUBA

ANDROS

BLUE HOLES & BONEFISH

"The first sight of beach always made us catch our breath, no matter how many times we had walked along the rough path before."
—*Samuel Charters in* The Day Is So Long and the Wages So Small

I will always remember and cherish Andros for ridding my son of his fear of water. He was age 4 and afraid to dunk his head. He clung to me furiously whenever we got into a swimming pool or the sea. That day on Andros, I took a snorkel mask and held it to his face so he could watch a little silvery jackknife fish as it flitted around rocks off the beach. He was mesmerized—completely forgot his head was in the water, and that was the end of his hydrophobia.

Surrounded by sea and so riddled with bights, blue holes, creeks, and lakes, Andros does not allow you to fear water, only to embrace it. It's more part of life here than the craggy land, expansive though that may be. The Bahamas' hugest island, Andros stretches 104 miles and encompasses 2,300 square miles—roughly 50 percent of the nation's land mass, though most of it is uninhabited. With a population of about 8,000, it is one of the northern Out Islands' most lightly settled.

The mazelike swamps and estuaries of its **West Side** have contributed to Andros's reputation as a land of mystery. Spanish explorers first called it "La Isla del Espirito Santo," or "Island of the Holy Spirit" because of its abundance of water, both sea and fresh. The mythical chickcharnie creature and other rich storytelling traditions keep the mystery alive.

Andros Island's history, like that of many of the Bahamian islands, is marked by booms and busts. Its first boom sounded in the 1800s after British Loyalists had fled the States' post-Revolutionary War along with their slaves. Another war caused a small influx of settlers in the north. Fleeing Florida's Seminole Wars, Seminole Indians along with runaway African slaves migrated to the settlement of **Red Bays,** where they hid in secrecy for many decades.

Plantations growing the sisal used in rope-making brought the first true prosperity to the island in the late 1880s, but died within a couple of decades due to

SUNSET ON RED BAYS.

Mexican competition. Next came sponging in the mid-1940s along with the boat-building industry it sparked. A fungus squeezed dry the sponge industry, but boatbuilding continued as islanders turned to commercial fishing. At the same time, logging created jobs and a temporary settlement that thrived through the 1970s.

Tourism had already slowly begun in the 1920s, but didn't really gain steam until the 1960s and the discovery of the island's incredible scuba and bonefishing treasures. Also in the mid-'60s, the U.S. opened its Undersea Test and Evalua-tion Center in the deep waters close to shore for researching anti-submarine warfare for the Western Alliance, using live targets and synthetic torpedoes. Their test sites, which you can see from the eastern shoreline, continue to boost the economy. In the north, agriculture proved a steady new source of income as fruit, vegetable, and livestock farms produced enough to export to Nassau and the U.S.

Today ground crops continue to win bread for Androsians. Besides fruits and vegetables, the island exports 4 to 5 million gallons of fresh water daily to Nassau from its limestone-filtered wells. The karst limestone landscape of Andros is responsible for one of its most striking features: its wealth of blue holes and their underwater cave systems. Whether inland or offshore, they tantalize with their ethereal blue water, plunging depths, and stalagmites and stalactites.

Andros's geology makes it stand out from other Bahama islands in many ways. One islander referred to it as prehistoric in makeup, with its vast pine forests, wild wetlands, Tongue of the Ocean (a trench that plunges 6,000 feet deep) proximity, third largest barrier reef in the world (after Australia's and Belize's), steep ocean wall, and unusual oolitic sand-dune sea bottom north of the island.

Geographywise, the island of Andros is actually three major islands divided by bights, plus hundreds of small mangrove islands. The main, northernmost, 80-mile-long island is politically broken up into two parts: **North Andros** from **Morgan's Bluff** to **Stafford Creek,** and **Central Andros** south to **Behring Point,** which, along with neighboring **Cargill Creek** forms the heart of the island's bonefishing charter industry. North and Middle Bights separate Central from **South Andros.** It consists of the small island of **Mangrove Cay** and, across South Bight, a litany of small settlements ranging about 20 miles long from **Drigg's Hill** down to **Mars Bay.**

The island's two main towns are **Nicholl's Town** in North Andros and **Andros Town** in Central. In between, settlements have names like **Love Hill, Small Hope,** and **Calabash Bay.** Nicholl's Town, once the island's resort hot spot, is now more residential, home to a winter population that has taken up residence in the cute little cottages that were once a part of the erstwhile resort. The beach scene is fun, with colorful conch shacks serving food, and folks playing pool inside Sly Fox and dominoes outside under the trees. This is the agricultural part of the island, so you'll find lots of fresh produce in addition to fish.

Morgan's Bluff, north of Nicholl's Town, is home to Regatta Village, which becomes livelier in summer during the races, but is otherwise quiet despite its close proximity to the government dock and boat harbor. Tourism officials hope to make the Junkanoo-hued Regatta Village a year-round thing where local farmers and artisans could sell their wares.

Conch Sound, just south of Nicholl's Town, still makes its living off fishing, and commercial fishermen sell their catches at a little waterside park under the trees. Mutton fish (snapper) is their most common catch. A blue hole lies near shore on the small beach.

Across the one-lane bridge from Andros Town, **Fresh Creek** is mostly made for the locals with a nod toward tourism. A couple of restaurants and a few shops line the creek.

Drigg's Hill and **Congo Town** lie near the airport in South Andros, where beaches are relatively untouched by human footprints. **The Bluff** offers a commanding view of the Tongue of the Ocean and the beaches below. And water, water as far as the eye can see.

DON'T MISS

- Diving or snorkeling at Small Hope Bay Lodge.
- Hiking to an inland blue hole.
- Casting for the elusive bonefish.
- A visit to Androsia Batik for a demonstration and shopping spree.
- Fresh conch salad in Nicholl's Town.

BAHAMA TALK

Andros: Androsians pronounce it AN-druss or AN-dross. Theories explaining the island's naming have to do with a Sir Edmund Andros, 18th-century governor of several American colonies; a group of 1,200 British colonists who settled here in 1787 with their African slaves from San Andreas; and the Greek sponge traders who settled here in the early 20th century.

SUGGESTED READING *The Day is So Long and the Wages So Small: Music on a Summer Island,* by Samuel Charters, 1999. An excellent retrospect on Andros's rich folk music traditions by an eminent music historian. Available through Amazon.

Folk-Tales of Andros Island, Bahamas, by Elsie Clews Parsons. First published in 1918, but available through Amazon.

The Tales of Andros, an Island in the Sun: The Past Can Come To Life, by Diann M. Hanna-Wilson. A novelette by a native schoolteacher, available through Amazon.

✳ To See

GALLERIES & STUDIOS ✪ **Androsia Batik Works Factory** (242-368-2080; www.androsia.com), Andros Town. What began as a cottage industry to keep the local women employed has turned into the official national fabric of the Bahamas. The enterprise began at Small Hope Bay Lodge in 1973, when then-matriarch Rosi one night melted some candles onto some cloth and dyed it bright colors. The industry moved in 1979 to some derelict resort outbuildings, and today the factory produces hundreds of different tropical patterns in rich shades for local and business use. Visitors can tour the four operation rooms—waxing, dying, cutting, and sewing—and can even arrange ahead of time for a hands-on demonstration of the process. It costs $25 and includes the piece of fabric you batik. The outlet store across the street sells placemats, fabric, shirts, skirts, dresses, swimsuits, you name it—all made from Androsia batik. Both the factory and store close on Sunday.

MUSEUMS & HISTORIC SITES **Andros Lighthouse,** mouth of Fresh Creek in Andros Town, approachable from Lighthouse Marina. Built in 1892 to mark the Fresh Creek Channel, it still stands for those who want to climb to the top of its tower, which was added in 1952 along with three historic cannons. It overlooks a natural beach that is shaded with Australian pines and lightly visited.

MUSIC & NIGHTLIFE **Big Shop** (242-329-2047), Nicholl's Town. Across from the beach, it's where young locals and visitors hang out on weekends.

Cabana (no phone), Drigg's Hill. Reggae music and cheap drinks draw locals to this beach dive.

Colors Beach Club (242-368-6303), Staniard Creek, Central Andros. This "dive bar" attracts a young crowd to groove to the recorded music and play darts.

Conch Stand (no phone), Mangrove Cay. A local hangout for dominoes, backgammon, conch salad, and island music on the box.

Hank's Place (242-368–2447), Fresh Creek, Central Andros. Young and old come hang out creekside for Hank's Saturday night disco. Hanky Panky rum drinks and cold Kalik flow freely.

Pineville Motel (242-329-2788), Nicholl's Town, North Andros. Experience indigenous Out Island entertainment when the local rake 'n' scrape band takes the stage with its entourage of drum, accordion, and toothed saw.

BEST BEACHES Beaching is not usually the first reason visitors come to Andros Island. Not because there's a shortage of such, but because diving and bonefishing trump that pursuit. Most of the best beaches have resorts on them, such as Small Hope Bay Lodge and Andros Lighthouse Yacht Club in Central Andros, and Emerald Bay and Tiamo in South Andros. Most others require some local knowledge to find, so ask around if you want seclusion. North Andros has some nice, easy-to-find and easy-to-reach beaches with facilities nearby.

Nicholl's Town Beach, Nicholl's Town, North Andros. This is a good place to hang out for local color and interaction. A strip of jaunty conch shacks keeps visitors in drinks and food, even a little pool-shooting and dominoes-slapping. More conducive to partying than lounging, it's most lively in the afternoons.

Morgan's Bluff Beach, Morgan's Bluff. Home to the summer regatta and its Regatta Village, this wide, Australian-pine-lined, white-sand beach gets a little action from the boaters who dock in its harbor year-round. But it's typically quiet and within walking distance to restaurants.

BIKING Small Hope Bay Lodge (242-368-2014 or 800-223-6961; www.small hope.com), off Queen's Hwy. has maps for several different bike trips in the Andros Town vicinity, including to Capt. Bill's Blue Hole, Somerset Beach, Love Hill Beach, and the town of Fresh Creek. If you're staying there, you have free use of its bikes.

BLUE HOLES Andros has an estimated 160 inland and offshore blue holes. Here are some of the easiest to reach by land.

✪ **Captain Bill's,** Small Hope. Hike or bike to this popular blue hole with decking and steps down to the water. Watch for birds on your way there.

✪ **Rainbow Blue Hole,** look for the sign near the telephone marked 210 north

RAINBOW BLUE HOLE LIES OFF THE BEATEN PATH NEAR SMALL HOPE.

of Small Hope. A short, half-hour trail marked with bush medicine identification signs takes you through karst, potholed limestone surface to this hidden, undeveloped site. You can easily wade into the pool. Small Hope Bay Lodge has a self-guided tour booklet to the hole.

Uncle Charlie's, North Andros. One of the easiest to get to, a mere 300 yards off the main highway, it measures 40 feet in diameter and 120 feet in depth.

FISHING If you hear it once, you'll hear it a hundred times: Andros is THE best place in the world for bonefishing. There are also deep-sea and reef charters, but bonefishing is defining here. The sport of stalking the elusive "gray ghost" led to the development of fly-fishing right here in Andros.

Prime fishing territory includes the **West Side**—the mangrove-mottled waters of Central and South Andros that take some effort getting to—the **bights** that separate Central and South Andros, **Joulters Cays** (a geological dunes-bottomed phenomenon north of North Andros), and the island's many **creeks.** Guides will pole you through the waterways to sight-cast, and in many places you can find flats where you can walk from shore. West Side is also known for its lobster and tarpon. Deep waters yield grouper, wahoo, and tuna in season.

Charters: The rate for charter fishing varies from $250 to $550 for a half day to $375 to $850 for a full day. Any number of native islanders are ready to take you to their sweet spots.

⚙ **Charlie Neymour** (242-368-4297; www.bigcharlieandros.net), Cargill Creek. Charlie has been guiding since age 13 and specializes in bonefish and tarpon. He offers lodging-fishing-meal packages through his lodge (see *Accommodations*).

Reel Tight Charters (242-554-0031), Drigg's Hill Marina. Deep-sea and reel fishing, diving and spearfishing, and more.

Small Hope Bay Lodge (242-368-2014 or 800-223-6961; www.smallhope.com), Small Hope Bay, Central Andros. Half- and full-day fishing for bone, deep-sea, and reef fish. Its West Side overnight excursion travels to the legendary fishing grounds for a camping-casting adventure.

Andy Smith (242-368-4261 or 242-368-4044) Takes you into the Bights and West, and also has his own small lodge called Broadshad Cay.

HIKING Small Hope Bay Lodge (242-368-2014 or 800-223-6961; www.small hope.com), off Queen's Hwy. Offers a number of self-guided and guided walking tours into the woods. The Bush Medicine Tour interprets a nearby trail's medicinal plants (from gumbo limbo leaves to the so-called "stiff cock" plant—I'm not making that up) and leads across karst, pocked limestone terrain to Rainbow Blue Hole. Other nature programs explore beach, mangrove, and coppice habitat.

HUNTING Wild boar hunting and land crab harvesting offer visitors a true island adventure. Ask your resort staff or talk to the people at the Tourist Office for information.

SO WHAT'S THE BIG DEAL ABOUT BONEFISH?

You don't really want to ask that question out loud on Andros, so "bone up." One of the world's trickiest catches, the thrill is in sight-fishing—spotting the fish and then trying not to spook it while you finesse your lure within its radar. It's not entirely a fly-fisher's sport, but mostly, and Andros made its fame not only with its amazing populations of bonefish, but with its expert fly-fishers and fish-all-day lodges.

Andros's geography is perfectly suited habitat for the bonefish and remains so unspoiled that its West Side nurseries promise to maintain that level of population for the foreseeable future. The fish prefer water temperatures between 70 and 80 degrees, so sand flats, sea grass beds, and mangrove lagoons are their favorite hangouts. Andros has endless habitat that fits that description.

Bonefish school as they are growing up, but later often split into pairs or loners. They are said to be highly intelligent, maddeningly quick, stealthy, and powerful.

The Bahamian government has designed a certification program for fly-fishing guides to ensure a quality experience for visiting anglers. Nearly 20 fishing lodges throughout the island and more than 40 guides can proudly boast their fly-fishing licenses and certifications.

WATER SPORTS *Anchorages:* **Kamalame Cay** (242-368-6281), Kamalame Cay resort, Central Andros. Eight slips and fuel.

Lighthouse Yacht Club & Marina (242-368-2305), Andros Town, Central Andros. This is Andros's main marina, with 18 slips (up to 150-foot boats) and fuel.

Paddling & Ecotours: **Small Hope Bay Lodge** (242-368-2014 or 800-223-6961; www.smallhope.com), Small Hope Bay, Central Andros.

Snorkeling & Diving: Andros's claim to fame in diving circles is its position at the Tongue of the Ocean, its concentration of blue holes, and its famed Andros Barrier Reef **"Over the Wall" dive** invented at Small Hope Bay Lodge. The last is designed to please moderate and deep divers. Multitiered, it goes from 65 to 80 feet deep at the top of the wall and 120 to 185 over the edge. **Blue holes**— entryways into underwater caves named for their deep blue hue—range from depths of 40 feet to more than 200.

Nondivers can become certified within a week or so, or can try out the sport with a resort course. Or they can easily find a snorkel excursion and spots from shore they can swim to. One of the best snorkeling trips takes you to **Trumpet Reef** near Fresh Creek, where you can see elkhorn coral in 15 feet of water.

Recommended Charter: ✪ **Small Hope Bay Lodge** (242-368-2014 or 800-223-6961; www.smallhope.com), Small Hope Bay, Central Andros. Andros's most

THE LEGEND OF THE CHICKCHARNIE

Half-human, half-bird, the legendary Andros chickcharnie has a wee bit of leprechaun in it too. Although it won't lead you to a pot of gold, the elf-sized creature will grace you with years of good luck should you cross one and treat it kindly. Be mean-spirited, and you'll earn yourself a lifetime regretting it.

Many older Androsians swear they've seen the three-fingered, three-toed creature with feathers, wings, and a long tail from which it hangs in the island's tall pine forest. They keep it alive with their strong tradition of story-telling.

"There's some truth to it," islander Ben Pratt says of the legend, which many attribute to the Seminole Indians who settled in North Andros in the 1820s. It may also have arisen from the remains of a very large species of owl that once inhabited the island but is now extinct.

complete and top-rated diving center, it operates with a competent, engaging staff who take out small groups and work with divers of all levels, including beginners, who can take the resort course (also known as "discovery course" in Professional Association of Diving Instructors parlance) and be out in the water the same day. Full certification courses are available through all the different organizations. Its signature "Over the Wall" dive is but one of many on the menu. Devoted divers will do the three-tank dives and try some of the specialty trips such as shark-feeding and night dives. Cavern diving is for the experienced, and **Diana's Dungeons, Alec's Caverns, Cara's Caverns,** and **Coral Caverns** are all beautiful at 90 feet. The **Barge Wreck** and wreck of the *Marian,* both at about 70 feet, are popular with all. Rental equipment is available for snorkel and dive trip participants only. Snorkel safaris go to reefs or Fresh Creek. There's also a shark observation snorkel, and you can snorkel right from shore at the lodge.

WILDLIFE SPOTTING Aside from the mythical chickcharnie, the best spottings above the water on Andros are birds. On the beaches, you'll see black-bellied and Wilson's plovers, ruddy turnstones, gulls, terns, herons, and other shorebirds. In the wooded areas, Cuban peewees, red-legged thrushes, Greater Antillean bullfinches, Cuban emerald and Bahama woodstar hummingbirds, and blue grosbeaks dwell.

✳ Lodging

In the accommodations department, Andros's long suit is its diving and fishing lodges, with more of the latter than the former. The fishing lodges range from four-room guest houses where you eat and live with your fishing guide to 30-room beachfront properties where you can wade out to bonefish once the day's chartering is done. Sixty percent of all Andros lodging is contained in Central Andros, particularly around Andros Town and the Cargill Creek areas.

Price Codes

Inexpensive	Up to $100
Moderate	$100 to $200
Expensive	$200 to $300
Very Expensive	$300 and up

(An asterisk after the pricing designation indicates that the rate includes at least a continental breakfast in the cost of lodging and possibly more extensive meal service as noted in the listing.)

ACCOMMODATIONS

Andros Town

⁰Ⅰ⁰ **Lighthouse Yacht Club and Marina** (242-368-2305 or 800-836-1019; www.androslighthouse.com), off Queen's Highway past Androsia Batik. Boaters and beachers are most likely to take advantage of this property's position on Fresh Creek and the ocean. Despite the "yacht" in its name, its unpretentious rooms make for an affordable stay. The spacious lobby with its vaulted ceiling and restaurant-bar overlook the marina. The 20 rooms are large enough, but the older ones look a bit down at the heels. Ask for a "villa" for nicer accommodations—they're basically rooms with an adjoining room, one on ground level, the other upstairs with no elevator. They come outfitted with ceiling fans, phones, Wi-Fi, and TVs—something of a rarity on this island. All overlook the marina or small pool. Abandoned tennis courts further a feel that this property may be teetering on the edge of closing; the property is currently for sale. The beach, a five-minute walk away, is typically quiet with an old lighthouse you can climb. Moderate.

Behring Point

✪ **Big Charlie's & Fathia's Fishing Lodge** (242-368-4297; www.big charlieandros.net), South Way. This four-room guest house setup again caters to bonefishing, with a fishing dock on Cargill Creek and daily fishing packages. Rates include not only the fishing, but laundry service and all meals and appetizers out on the patio for the fishermen when they return from casting. Meals combine Charlie Neymour's Bahamian background and wife Fathia's Moroccan for an unusual and exotic fusion cuisine, sometimes prepared on the outdoor grill. Breakfast and cocktails are self-serve (alcoholic beverages are not included in the rate). Guests share communal restrooms, tiled and tidy with showers but no bathtubs. Each of the small rooms has its own refrigerator stocked with water and soda upon arrival, in addition to a fruit basket. The only TV and Wi-Fi hot spot are at the bar in the small dining-living area; rooms have no TVs or Internet service. Guests feel part of the family, which includes energetic young Adam, when they stay in this intimate little modern lodge. Very Expensive.⁰ No credit cards.

Cargill Creek

⁰Ⅰ⁰ **Andros Island Bonefish Club** (242-368-5167; www.androsbone fishing.com), Queen's Hwy. It's all about the fishing here, so forget about it if you're not rabid about the sport. One of Andros's largest properties, it has 29 rooms on the old, seen-better-days side, fine for crashing after a day of fishing. Once you've come in from the boat, you may be able to wade offshore and continue if the tide is low enough. The buildings are spread out on the grounds of a 19th-century

ISLAND CHARACTER: CAPT. RUPERT LEADON

"There are nearly as many bonefish guides on Andros Island as there are bonefish, but only one is considered the godfather of them all," *Garden & Gun* magazine reported in its December 2008 issue about Rupert Leadon, owner of Andros Island Bonefish Club.

It's the second fishing lodge that opened on Andros Island back in 1988. Bonefish Charlie's Haven in Behring Point, now closed, was the first.

"I am one of the legends known all over the world," admits Capt. Rupert. He has fished with fly-fishing pioneers and baseball greats George Hummel and Ted Williams. Pictures of other legends and their catches plaster the walls of his lodge's restaurant-bar.

"They're the big boys, the guys who started fly-fishing and pioneered it all over the world," said the charter captain, who has been bonefishing for more than 40 years. His biggest catch weighed in at 15 pounds 4 ounces, caught in the Bights of Andros.

He also fishes for tarpon, permit, mahimahi, and tuna on the legendary West Side of Andros. "West Side has the best fishing in the world," he says. "We call it the land of the giants."

Today his three sons—Brian, Shawn, and Rupert Jr.—and team of fishing guides do most of the charters out of Andros Island Bonefish Club while Capt. Rupert is left with much of the property's administrative duties.

"I'd rather be fishing any day than be in the office," he says.

LEGENDARY BONEFISHING CAPTAIN RUPERT LEADON OWNS AND OPERATES ANDROS ISLAND BONEFISHING CLUB.

sisal plantation; some of the ruins are visible. There's a swimming pool for cooling down after a day in the sun, and two restaurants and bars where meals are part of the rate package. They serve fresh grilled seafood and other Bahamian fare family-style. The main restaurant has a TV (there are none in the rooms, nor phones), Wi-Fi Internet access, and fly-tying tables. The best part is telling fish tales with owner Capt. Rupert Leadon, a fly-fishing pioneer. He does charters occasionally upon special request, but mostly his three sons and other charter guides take over. Very Expensive.°

✪ Mount Pleasant Fishing Lodge (242-368-5171; www.mtpleasantfish .com),off Queen's Hwy. An example of the small lodges many of the local bonefishing guides have opened in recent years, this one may have a low room census—two two-bedroom apartments and two conventional rooms—but the property spreads out along the ocean and a cove perfect for wade fishing. Opened in 2002, it still looks brand spanking new with modern kitchens in the apartments, black-and-white checkered tile bathrooms, small but tidy bedrooms, and a dining room-bar area that serves breakfast and dinner (usually seafood). If you're not an angler or an unabashed beach bum, you may be bored here, down a long road off the beaten path. (There are no phones or TVs in the accommodations, but one satellite TV in the bar.) Beach connoisseurs will wildly appreciate the breezy beach edged with sea grape and Australian pine trees and slung with hammocks. Kayaks, too, are available for guest use. For the fishermen, the main clientele, boating and guided wade-in

fishing packages include lunch and fly-fishing lessons. Expensive.°

Drigg's Hill

❝₁❞ Emerald Palms Resort (242-369-2713; www.emerald-palms.com), The Bluff. It sells the fact that it's the closest Andros resort to the barrier reef, within swimming distance. But unlike some Andros resorts, you don't have to be a snorkeler, diver, or bonefisher to love the away-from-it-all beach and intimacy. Its 18 rooms and 22 one- and two-bedroom villas come with elegant and convenient touches such as four-poster beds in some rooms, Jacuzzi tubs and kitchenettes in the villas, and Wi-Fi and fridges in all (but no TVs or outgoing telephones). Those who do come for the sporting action have access to complimentary bikes and kayaks, a blue-tiled swimming pool, and diving and boating tours. The cabana bar is a good place to start the evening with a view of the jewel-toned sea before moving into the restaurant for dinner with a Bahamian-international flair. Moderate to Very Expensive.

❝₁❞ Tiamo (242-359-2330 or 242-376-4408; www.tiamoresorts.com) Originally built as a high-end ecoresort with no air-conditioning and low-impact design, it recently renovated to add air-conditioning to some units—known as the "cool cottages," as opposed to the "island breeze cottages." Use of reclaimed materials, solar panels, fair trade coffee, and other practices keep it ecoconscious. A private boat delivers guests from South Bight to this dreamy vision of soft and secluded beach, luxurious accommodations, top-notch service, and extravagant dining in the breezy, open-air Great Room. All food and nonalcoholic drinks are included in the rates. The downside is the biting bugs, but mostly in the morning and at sunset. Other times, breezes and sunshine keep them at bay, but bring bug juice in any case. The resort can arrange all manner of Andros recreation, from nature hikes and kayaking to fishing and diving. The new spa features a gym with such an amazing view, you'll forget you're working out. Relax to a massage oceanside or inside. Very Expensive.°

Fresh Creek

Hank's Place Restaurant and Bar (242-368-2447; hanks-place.com) If you want to stay where you can keep your finger on the pulse of busy little Fresh Creek and Andros Town across the bridge, this is a good bet, and affordable to boot. Four rooms have all the small luxuries some of the local lodges don't, including air-conditioning, TV, coffeemaker, and a small fridge. No phones, though. They are simple and clean with tile floors and adjoining rooms. Things get a little noisy on Saturday nights when disco convenes, but if you join in on the party you won't even notice. Inexpensive.

Kamalame Cove

⁰**ᴛ**⁰ **Kamalame Cay** (242-368-6281 or 800-790-7971; www.kamalame.com) Its dozen or so rooms, villas, and cottages are scattered across 96 acres of beach and woodlands on a private island a short ferry or plane ride from Central Andros. Away from everything, the resort provides all the meals, necessities, and luxuries you may require, including a spa, dive trips, and other water sports. Food, drink, and nonmotorized sports (tennis, bicycles, kayaks, snorkeling gear) are included in the all-inclusive rate.

The spacious, open-plan accommodations range from a single room to a three-bedroom villa, and may contain amenities such as private terraces, soaking tubs, kitchens, and such practicalities as wireless Internet, but no TV or phone in the room. Staff can arrange any manner of tour, fishing excursion, or other activity. Sumptuous meals are served in the plantation-style Great House, and cocktails are best enjoyed around the pool. Very Expensive.°

Nicholl's Town

⁰**ᴛ**⁰ **Pineville Motel** (242-329-2788 or 242-557-4354; www.pinevillemotel .com) How to describe this place? Part cultural experience, part quirky, part dorm, part motel. Most of its personality comes from its owner, Eugene Campbell, who has so much energy, he changes the themes and looks of his 16 rooms from time to time to keep things interesting. The Beachside room, for instance, is decorated with fronds, conch shells, and other organic material, while the Rock Creek room has a mattress set atop a rock-cement foundation and driftwood all about. Just wait, it gets quirkier. Tucked into the center of

---

BAHAMA TALK

Kamalame: Pronounced ka-MA-la-mee, it may look Hawaiian, but it's Bahamian for what the tropical U.S. refers to as the gumbo limbo tree. Some islands in the Bahamas spell it quamalame. Because of its red, peely bark, both places often dub it the "tourist tree." Bahamians use it for carving model boats and in bush medicine for insect bites, fever, and diarrhea.

Nicholl's Town, the compound is covered in gardens. Enter and discover an old-island snack stand and bar, disco stage, outdoor theater for movies and sports, bandstand where a local rake 'n' scrape band performs Saturday nights, petting zoo, and buffet serving healthy native food. All of the rooms and two two-bedroom suites (with kitchens) are air-conditioned with TVs and Wi-Fi. For church groups and the like, dorms with bunk beds and communal bathrooms accommodate. Eugene can arrange educational island tours and crabbing and wild boar-hunting excursions. Come here for a unique immersion into Bahamian Out Island life. Inexpensive.

Small Hope
♂ "1" ✪ **Small Hope Bay Lodge** (242-368-2013 or 800-223-6961; www .smallhope.com), off Queen's Hwy. What started out as an environmen-

tally friendly (ecofriendly hadn't even been invented yet) diving resort in the 1960s by Canadian expat Dick Birch has expanded through the years to embrace fishermen, couples, singles, and families. Today it's run by Dick's son, Jeff, and guests still need a little adventure in their blood to want to stay here. First of all, the beachside cottages are on the rustic side, with no phones or TVs and all the ambiance of summer camp except for the bright happiness brought by Androsia batik accents. The family ran the batik enterprise right here on property until it outgrew the resort and moved to Andros Town (see *Galleries & Studios*). The inimitable Small Hope Bay Lodge experience begins when you check in. If it's breakfast time, you repair to the dining room while your taxi driver delivers your bags to your room. Choose the Bahamian breakfast du jour if

HAMMOCKS INVITE LAZING AWAY THE DAYS AT SMALL HOPE BAY LODGE.

you're daring; otherwise, there are plenty of options. If it's evening when you arrive, you'll no doubt check in at the outdoor, beachside bar with a Goombay Smash, No-See-Um, or other signature drink. Folks gather here by day to catch the Wi-Fi signal, nightly for happy hour (when Wi-Fi is shut down) and fresh conch fritters. During the day, you can help yourself to drinks. Meals and beverages are included in the room rate (as are Wi-Fi and calls to the U.S. and Canada), so make yourself at home. Lunch and dinner are buffet-style, either with a Bahamian or international theme. Guests sit together at big tables with one another and staff, so you get to

know everybody quite quickly and warmly. Kids younger than 8 eat separately with a complimentary baby sitter. During the day, most are diving. If you don't dive, you can snorkel, go on a fishing excursion, or take the one-day resort course to learn the basics and get out in the water. Expensive.°

✴ Where to Eat

Andros cuisine is similar to other Out Islands, where conch, fish, lobster (in season), chicken, peas 'n' rice, baked macaroni and cheese, and guava duff are mainstays. In the homes, you'll find oddities such as cassava potatoes, land crab and rice, and sweet potato

Compliments of Small Hope Bay Lodge.
JEFF BIRCH HAS KEPT HIS FATHER'S DREAM ALIVE AT SMALL HOPE BAY LODGE.

ISLAND CHARACTER: JEFF BIRCH
The story of Jeff Birch started long before him, with his father Dick Birch, whom his son and others have described as socialist, atheist, pioneering environmentalist, der-ring-do scuba diver, and brave-new-world resort developer.

Dick Birch, an avid diver who once held the world record for deep diving on compressed air (462 feet), opened Small Hope Bay Lodge as a diving resort in 1960 before there were roads in Central Andros. "Dad's philosophy was 'diving is a sport, not a profes-sion,'" Jeff said. He took scuba out of the hands of professionals and placed it into those of recreational divers. According to Jeff, he invented the resort course (and was banned from certain National Association of Underwater Instructors events because of it), and discovered the Andros Barrier Reef wall with fellow Canadian Dr. Joe McGinnis.

Jeff took over operation of the lodge in 1992 and has expanded its reputa-tion as a more well-rounded destination where guests can experience the cul-ture and natural and social environment of Andros.

"Our atmosphere is our five-star event. We'd maybe get two, three stars bread. North Andros farms grow much of the island's food; the rest is exported to Nassau and the U.S.

Androsians have a long history of harvesting its land crab population as it migrates from low-lying areas flooded by summer rains east. In decades past, some Bahamians looked down upon the crab hunters, but more recently Andros has embraced that heritage with a summertime crab festival and organized crabbing excursions offered to visitors.

It's always best to call ahead before you plan to dine at one of Andros's restaurants. Even the resort restaurants sometimes close, depending upon occupancy.

Price Codes

Inexpensive	Up to $15
Moderate	$15 to $25
Expensive	$25 to $35
Very Expensive	$35 or more

Cost categories are based on the range of dinner entrée prices or, if dinner is not served, on lunch entrées.

Resort restaurants take reservations. For small restaurants, it's a good idea to call ahead to make sure they're open. Often they require that you order your dinner ahead of time from the two or three selections they may offer that evening.

Andros Town
 ♿ **Kristina's Café** (242-368-2182), Queen's Hwy. One of the island's most

for our amenities—we don't have hair dryers or a spa," said Jeff. "So many people live in a small network of friends and don't get other perspectives. We have interesting guests."

Past visitors to Small Hope Bay Lodge have included former Canadian Prime Minister Pierre Trudeau, celebrity diver Jacques Cousteau, astronaut Buzz Aldrin, and *National Geographic* photographer David Doubilet. Thrown together at meal times, guests and staff exchange ideas and perspectives in lively discussions that can range from the day's dive to the decline in family values.

Family is of utmost importance to Small Hope Bay Lodge, and after one day guests feel a part of it. "Ever since Dad started this, it was run as a way of life, not a business," said Jeff, who himself arrived at Andros at age 4 with his two siblings. He grew up on the beach, walking it to get to school in Calabash Bay, about 1½ miles away. For high school, he moved to Nassau to live with his mother, and later attended college in Canada. In 1980, he came home to Small Hope Bay. Along the way he had become a pilot and scuba instructor.

Jeff lost the father he deeply respected in 1996 and continues to operate the lodge in the environmentally sensitive and people-first manner of Dick Birch

"The highest knowledgeable being I know in life is people. What greater calling could I have than serving and sharing with people?"

modern, dependable, and convenient eateries lies along Queen's Highway in a new office square. Choose to sit inside, where the ceiling is vaulted and the handful of long tables have a view of the TV, or outside on the veranda. Despite its modern veneer, it is run like a traditional small Out Island restaurant where the menu is verbal and usually limited to a few items the cook has prepared that day. On my one visit, I tried the baked chicken from a selection that also included cracked conch, cracked lobster, and fish. All came with peas 'n' rice and a selection of coleslaw or potato salad. The chicken was tender, fall-off-the-bone, but the service lagged a bit. Kristina's also does takeout, and you can call ahead. Inexpensive to Moderate.

Conch Sound
&. **Conch Sound Resort Inn Restaurant and Bar** (242-329-2060), Queen's Hwy. For a good, home-cooked Bahamian feed, call and reserve your dinner here. Choose from fresh fish, broiled lobster, pork chops, chicken, and steak with sides of peas 'n' rice, salad, and macaroni and cheese. Conch Sound also serves breakfast and lunch. Like most native restaurants, it occupies a spacious room with tables spaced wide apart. A painted mural decorates the otherwise plain room. The bar is a party hot spot on weekends, as is the outdoor bar next to the resort's pool. Inexpensive to Moderate. No credit cards.

Fresh Creek
&. **Hank's Place Restaurant and Bar** (242-368-2447), on Fresh Creek. On a nice day, you can sit outside on the deck and watch the boat traffic and swaying palms while you dig into

chicken, conch, fish, shrimp, lobster, or a pork chop prepared to your liking, whether that's steamed, fried, or baked. Can't decide? Order one of the seafood combos, but make sure you brought a hearty appetite because the plate comes filled with side dishes to go along with it. Conch fritters, ribs, and steak are other specialties. You'll need a frozen Hanky Panky rum drink to go with that, too. There's also indoor seating around the wood-paneled bar on plastic chairs at tables draped in flowered cloths. Inexpensive to Moderate. Sometimes serves lunch in season.

Small Hope Bay
&. ✪ **Small Hope Bay Lodge Dining Room** (242-368-2013 or 800-223-6961; www.smallhope.com), off Queen's Hwy. Nonguests can drop in (but it's best to call ahead for dinner) and join resort staff and guests for buffet Bahamian lunches and international dinners outside around the beach bar, weather permitting. The experience begins with happy hour cocktails and yummy conch fritters at 6:30. When the bell tolls, the day's cook explains the dishes she has set out for enjoying. At lunch, you'll find such flavors as cracked conch, roasted chicken, baked macaroni and cheese, and guava duff plus a salad and sandwich bar. Dinner offerings can range from pasta to seafood prepared in a variety of styles. Wine flows freely and a party atmosphere prevails. If you decide to eat breakfast here before your diving or fishing excursion, you can help yourself to fruit, toast, and cereal, or order from the day's hot dishes, which always include a few American choices and one Bahamian traditional breakfast such as stew fish or fire engine (corned beef hash with a tomato sauce and

grits)—each with a little eye-opening fire. Very Expensive.

BAKERIES Call the following sources for fresh-baked bread: **Angie's Bread Baking** (242-329-7234), Lowe Sound; **Geneva Braynen** (242-368-5019), Cargill Creek; and **Chickcharnie** (242-368-2025), Fresh Creek.

GROCERS/PRODUCE Mable's Meat Mart (242-368-2926), Calabash Bay. Full line of fresh and canned grocery items and household goods.

Mennonite Tents (no phone), near San Andros. In North Andros, you will often see makeshift tents set up by the local Mennonite missionary community, who sell the produce they grow and the pies, cakes, cookies, and woodwork they make.

SEAFOOD If your timing is right, you can buy directly from the fishermen bringing in their catches in Conch Sound and Red Bays. In South Andros, get in touch with **Mangrove Cay Seafood** (242-369-0881).

TAKE-OUT ✪ **North Andros Conch Stands** (no phone), Nicholl's Town. A handful of colorful shacks line the beach in Nicholl's Town and specialize in conch salad. Locals claim Sly Fox makes the best.

S&M Jerk Stop (no phone), Calabash Bay. Specializing in Jamaican-style jerk chicken and pork.

✸ Selective Shopping

✪ **Androsia Outlet Store** (242-368-2080; www.androsia.com), across Queen's Hwy. from Androsia Batik Factory in Andros Town. Androsia batik is now sold across the Bahamas, but this shop carries the widest selection of bolt fabrics, clothing, bags, placemats, oven mitts, and more.

NORTH ANDROS IS KNOWN FOR ITS CONCH SALAD, MADE FRESH IN THE SHACKS ALONG THE NICHOLL'S TOWN BEACH.

ACROSS THE STREET FROM THE ANDROSIA FACTORY, THE OUTLET STORE SELLS FRESHLY BATIKED FABRIC AND PRODUCTS MADE FROM IT.

✪ **Red Bays.** This intriguing community off the main road in North Andros has a fascinating history of settlement by Seminole Indians and runaway slaves who fled Florida in the 1820s. For many years they were undiscovered, but kept alive traditions of unique basketweaving using the top of the silver thatch palm. Today Red Bays' artisans and children continue weaving (or plaiting, as they call it) and woodcarving, and have opened its tight-knit community to sell its wares to visitors. Many of the baskets are now woven with scraps of Androsia batik for a colorful, sturdy piece of utilitarian art. The road to Red Bays takes you past the homes of the artisans, who often have their work displayed on their front porches.

CRABBY ANDROS

There once was a time when Nassau residents derided the "lowly" land crab catchers of Andros Island. It didn't matter that they were providing them with a well-loved ingredient for a traditional Bahamian dish found exclusively in the home: crab 'n' rice.

Well, the tables have turned, so to speak, and today Androsians embrace and celebrate their crabbing heritage, which was becoming endangered with the loss of habitat on many islands. Andros, with its vast swamplands, still boasts great populations of the crusty critters. To celebrate that heritage and raise awareness of the land crab's plight, they invented Crab Fest several years ago.

The festival takes place in summer to coincide with the migration and harvesting of the skittering crabs. For nine months out of the year, the crabs hibernate in holes on the island's West Side. Then, beginning in May, as the spring rains begin and flood them out of their holes, they emerge to feed and reproduce, moving eastward, heading toward the ocean, where they lay their eggs. (The land crab is one of only a few creatures that begins its life as a marine animal then adapts to the land.)

Crab catchers nab their prey by gently placing their foot on its back, then grabbing it from behind to avoid the working end of the pinching crustacean. They check to make sure it's not a female carrying eggs before considering it for dinner.

Gertrude Gibson (242-329-7736) is one of the best-known names in Andros plaiting. **Henry Wallace** (242-329-7762) is a master carver.

✳ Special Events

January: **Junkanoo** (242-368-2286), Nicholl's Town, North Andros. New Year's Day. Traditional Junkanoo parade and cultural celebration.

✪ *June:* **All Andros Crab Fest** (242-368-2286), Andros Town. Five days mid-June. One of the biggest festivals in the Out Islands, it attracts thousands to celebrate the land crab, of which Androsians are famed hunters. Stands compete and sell crab and rice, crab soup, crab and grits, boiled crab, and more. National musicians entertain.

June through August: **Goombay Festival** (242-368-2286 or 242-368-2514) Every Friday throughout the summer, Androsians celebrate their culture and heritage with local music and dancing, rake 'n' scrape bands, and native dishes.

July: **North Andros-Berry Islands Regatta** (242-368-2286), Regatta Village in Morgan's Bluff, North Andros. Second weekend in July. Bahamian sailing sloop competitions, local cuisine, and entertainment on the beach.

Bimini

ALICE TOWN/NORTH BIMINI

SOUTH BIMINI

BIMINI

FISHING. LEGENDS.

"The water of the (Gulf) Stream was usually a dark blue when you looked out at it when there was no wind. But when you walked out into it there was just the green light of the water over that floury white sand and you could see the shadow of any big fish a long time before he could ever come in close to the beach."

—*Ernest Hemingway in* Islands in the Stream

I started to notice that my cheeks were hurting. I'd been on Bimini for just about an hour, and my face muscles were feeling it.

We were traveling golf cart speed, so I couldn't attribute it to high velocity. More like "the Bimini effect"—you can't help smiling on a little island where everyone waves, and the relative absence of cars means a personal relationship even with strangers. Then too, of course, there's the water. That legendary, can-it-be-real? happy water.

Bimini's past and present loom larger-than-life with other legends—such as its underwater road to the Lost World of Atlantis and visits from Ponce de Leon, Adam Clayton Powell, Martin Luther King, and Ernest Hemingway. Hemingway and Bimini, in fact, are inextricably intertwined in local history. He made the island's fishing and its erstwhile Compleat Angler Hotel famous. While he penned parts of *Islands in the Stream,* he did battle with the big ones and the occasional quarrelsome foe who crossed his path. He immortalized the islands in his book and ensured a rich era of sterling crowds who came to test the water and throw around their wealth at the old Bimini Bay Rod & Gun Club, today resurrected into a modern, polished version of its former self.

The only island in the chain that kept its original, Lucayan-given name—And why not? It's so much fun to say—Bimini has been a way station for sailors since the Spanish first arrived seeking sources of fresh water. According to legend, natives on nearby islands told the great conquistador Ponce de Leon about magical springs that restored youth in a place called Bimini. Whether or not today's

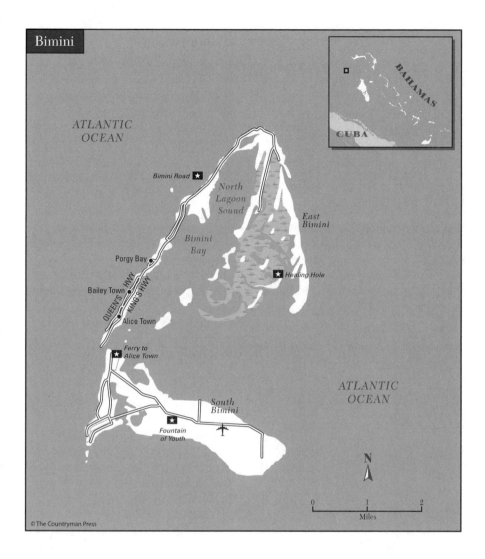

Bimini and Ponce's were the same, South Bimini pays tribute to the legend with a Fountain of Youth park complete with well and nature trails.

Three separate parts actually make up Bimini: **North Bimini,** the long, stretchy main island; **South Bimini,** larger and slightly higher in elevation, but quieter with only one main resort; and **East Bimini,** a cluster of unsettled mangrove islands and cays. Tourism officials are planning a Martin Luther King Jr., memorial in East Bimini at Bonefish Creek, where the civil rights leader came so many years ago to rest and write the acceptance speech for his Nobel Peace Prize in 1964.

Three settlements further divide North Bimini, each running into the other with only a sign to let you know you've crossed a line. **Alice Town,** southernmost and home to the government dock where ferries from the South Bimini airport arrive, is the island's thriving resort and business center. Folks get around its two main streets—Queen's Highway or Top Street (at the top of a sand dune ridge), and King's Highway or Bottom Street—by golf cart, bike, or foot. **Bailey Town** is bright, colorful, and mostly residential. **Porgy Bay** is a smaller continuation of it that reaches to the gates of the Bimini Bay Resort, a new and growing community of marinas, homes, resorts and restaurants, shops, and vacation rentals.

Whereas mariners and fishermen of yore frequented some of the smaller lodges in town, most now enjoy all the modern conveniences of Bimini Bay, meaning some of the classic places, such as Bimini Big Game Hotel, are closing. With Big Game's vacancy and the ruins of Hemingway's haunt, the Compleat Angler, dominating Alice Town, it's beginning to look a little ghostly. Add to that the empty erstwhile Chalk's Airline terminal, once an island landmark but abandoned a few years back after a tragic accident.

> **SIGN ALERT**
> Spotted in Bailey Town: God's Blessing Salon—definitely the place I need for my bad hair days.

On **South Bimini,** a five-minute ferry ride away, staff at Bimini Sands Resort are trying to create a new model for local tourism. Currently, Bimini welcomes most of its visitors in spring and summer, when mild weather and flat seas bring boaters in droves from South Florida, only 50 miles away. Opposite of the other Bahama islands, it has little to no winter trade. Bimini Sands is trying to change that by emphasizing the island's natural qualities and promoting ecotourism.

In the meantime, Bimini's compact, 9-square-mile size and population of 2,000 make it an easy place to meet the people, learn their ways, and smile.

DON'T MISS
- Diving (not driving) the Road to Atlantis.
- A visit to the Sharklab.
- Fishing, whether it's flats fishing for bonefish or deep-sea for blue marlin.
- A conch pizza at Edith's.
- The weekend party at Big John's.

HEMINGWAY ONCE HUNG OUT AT THE COMPLEAT ANGLER HOTEL, NOW REDUCED TO RUINS BY FIRE.

SUGGESTED READING *History of Bimini, Volumes 1 and 2,* by Ashley B. Saunders. The first two in a trilogy the island's historian is writing.

✳ To See

MUSEUMS & HISTORIC SITES **Bimini Museum** (242-347-3038), King's Hwy., Alice Town. Open 9–9 daily. $2. Historic exhibits and artifacts remember Bimini's early heyday with film footage of Ernest Hemingway, Martin Luther King Jr.'s immigration card, and remnants from the historic Bimini Bay Rod & Gun Club in a pretty, circa-1921, two-story jail building in the midst of downtown.

⊘ **Dolphin House** (242-347-3201), off King's Hwy. near Blue Water Marina, Alice Town. Open upon prior appointment. Tours $20 per hour. Part museum, part guest house, this labor of love was started 17 years ago, and construction continues to this day. The island's historian and poet, Ashley Saunders, turned artist in his later years and was inspired to build this indestructible tribute to dolphins out of beach flotsam and salvaged material from local churches and hotels. Stone quarried from South Bimini and local conch shells shore up the house, which has survived five hurricanes. Saunders, who has done 95 percent of the work on the house, will tour you through the upstairs guest accommodations, his own living quarters and library, a small museum, and the town of Alice Town or Bahamian bush medicine, if you so desire.

Wesley Methodist Church (242-347-3329), Queen's Hwy., Alice Town. This picturesque little church with a bell tower and sidekick cemetery dates back to the mid-1800s. It overlooks the ocean at the top of the hill. The nine other churches on North Bimini serve Anglican, Church of God, and Catholic congregations.

SWIMMING WITH DOLPHINS INSPIRED ASHLEY SAUNDERS TO ERECT DOLPHIN HOUSE IN THEIR HONOR.

ISLAND CHARACTER: ASHLEY SAUNDERS

Dolphins changed the direction of Ashley Saunders's life a couple of decades ago after an expert and author on dolphins encouraged him to swim with wild dolphins.

"Upon swimming with them, I became very stimulated," he recalls. "It inspired my outlook, and my values changed. My creativity went up a notch higher. It increased tenfold. My dreams and all changed. I began to see more colors. My imagination flowed so that I had trouble distinguishing between fantasy and reality. I saw such fantastic things in my dreams. I wanted to give back to these dolphins what they gave to me."

Ashley, already known as a great teacher and the island historian and poet, undertook the creation of Dolphin House in 1992. "Seemed like I just wanted to keep making dolphins," he says. Dolphin bas-reliefs decorate the front of the guest house-museum. In all, Ashley has created 27 throughout the house with everything from stained glass to paint.

Quite the Renaissance man, Ashley received his bachelor's degree in philosophy from the University of Wisconsin in Madison and went on to do postgraduate work at Harvard. He has studied and written about Caribbean literature, Bahamian medicinal plants, and Bimini history. He and his vast library have occupied a few small rooms on the ground-level floor of Dolphin House since 2000.

Dolphin House continues to consume his imagination and time. "I'm trying to build something that doesn't look like anybody else's house—not just in Bimini, but in the world," he says.

"I don't know what the building is going to look like," Ashley told me. "It depends upon what I find or what people bring me. It goes by my imagination. I can't give you any idea what the finished product is going to be.

"Some say it'll never be finished," he said in December 2009. "I have a time line of another five years."

MUSIC & NIGHTLIFE Big John's Conch Shell Bar (242-347-3115; www .bigjohnshotel.com), Alice Town. Dance on the boat docks and huge outdoor deck (there's even a small man-made beach) to the music of the Hypnotics Thursday through Saturday. Other times, come in for the game and a cold one.

✪ **End of the World Saloon** (no phone), King's Hwy. near the Compleat Angler ruins, Alice Town. Locals refer to this sand-carpeted, ultracasual party spot as the "Sand Bar." Congressman Adam Clayton Powell made it famous with his visits in the '60s, and a marble plaque honors him. Besides cold drinks, the bar serves lobster and conch pizza.

Mackey's Sand Bar (242-347-4500; www.biminisands.com), Bimini Sands
Resort Beach Club, South Bimini. Come barefoot, if you wish, and dig your toes
into the sand floor. Watch the game, play the ring toss, try your karaoke voice on
Wednesday nights, and mix it up with the locals and visitors, who come all the
way from North Bimini to party here.

✳ To Do

BEST BEACHES Bimini Sands Beach Club, South Bimini. Open to the public, and in fact furnished with public boating docks, Bimini Sands welcomes people arriving by boat, cart, or Bimini Sands Resort shuttle bus to play volleyball,
snorkel right from shore, take a dip in the L-shaped pool, hoist a Kalik at Mackey's Sand Bar, or just wallow in the soft, white sand.

North Bimini Beaches, Alice Town. Three beaches stretch along Bimini's
oceanfront to form a natural chain shaded by Australian pines. They are Radio
Beach, Blister Beach, and Spook Hill, the last named for the cemetery nearby.
The rusting remains of a steel wrecker remembers Bimini's early source of
income on Radio Beach, where colorful little beach bars contribute to a party
atmosphere.

❂ **Shell Beach,** West End, South Bimini. Natural, remote, and lightly used, this
is one of the Bahamas' best. Snorkelers especially appreciate the great snorkeling
venue on its south end, just around the point from Bimini Sands Beach Club.
The only things you'll find at this beach are typically calm waters, railroad vine,
and a small blue-and-white picnic shelter.

FISHING *Charters:* ❂ **Bonefish Ansil Saunders** (242-347-2178), Bailey Town.
Besides being the island's foremost boatbuilder, Ansil holds a record for catching
the world's biggest bonefish right in North Bimini waters in 1971—16 pounds, 3

ISLANDERS STILL BONEFISH THE OLD-FASHIONED WAY BY POLING ACROSS THE FLATS.

ounces. Stop by his Bimini Boat Building to see him at work or arrange a charter.

Bonefish Tommy Sewell (242-347-3234) No guessing what his specialty is. Native-born with 20 years of experience, he's expert at fly-fishing for the elusive "ghost fish."

Capt. Bali (242-473-0898) Half- and full-day deep-sea and reef fishing excursions for wahoo, grouper, and more.

WATER SPORTS *Anchorages:* **Bimini Bay Resort & Marina** (242-347-2900), North Bimini. Its two marinas hold 231 slips, restaurants, showers, a casino, and a Customs and Immigration office. No laundry facilities.

Bimini Blue Water Resort (242-347-3166), Alice Town, North Bimini. Fuel up, dock overnight, or get a room at this complete 32-slip marina in the middle of town. No laundry facilities.

Bimini Sands Resort & Marina (242-347-3500), South Bimini. Fifty slips protect boats in a sheltered harbor with a Customs and Immigration office and full services including laundry and restaurant. This marina is posted as shark-free, meaning the environmentally sensitive resort does not allow bringing in any caught sharks.

Day Cruising: **Bimini Sands Resort** (242-347-3500), South Bimini. It offers a number of sight-seeing/wildlife tours around the island. Most exciting is the educational "Saturday Shark Encounters" tour, where you can ride along as biologists feed lemon and other local sharks.

Paddling & Ecotours: **Bimini Sands Resort** (242-347-3500), South Bimini. Half- and full-day kayak rentals and guided tours into mangroves and creeks with a biologist.

Surf Watersport (242-554-4450 or 242-347-6042), Bimini Bay Resort & Marina, North Bimini. Rent single or double kayaks, or sign up for the three-hour paddle to Healing Hole on East Bimini. Also rents Hobie Cats, paddleboats, snorkel gear, and aqua cycles.

Powerboat Rentals: **Bimini Sands Resort** (242-347-3500), South Bimini. Rents 20- to 22-foot Twin Vee boats for half or full day. Also rents fishing gear.

Snorkeling & Diving: After its fishing, Bimini is highly regarded for its diving. Its most famous dive, **Bimini Road to Atlantis** (also known as just Bimini Road or just Atlantis) consists of a puzzling arrangement of rocks that legend says once led to the Lost World of Atlantis. Just south of South Bimini, the concrete wreck of *Sapona* is a popular spot for snorkelers and day cruisers to gather. Other good spots include **Victory Reef** and **Moray Alley.** Gutsy shark divers head to **Bull Run.** For wall-diving, there's **Nodules.**

Bill & Nowdla Keefe's Bimini Underseas (242-347-3089), Bimini Bay Resort & Marina, North Bimini. In addition to its full-service snorkeling and dive tours and instruction, a wild dolphin snorkeling adventure is offered. Nondivers can get a taste of scuba with its introductory scuba lesson and dive.

Bimini Sands Resort (242-347-3500), South Bimini. Whether you want to join a regularly scheduled trip, hire a private charter, or rent gear to explore on your own, the activities department here can take care of you. Scheduled trips visit the *Sapona* wreck.

WILDLIFE SPOTTING ✪ **Bimini Biological Field Station Sharklab** (242-347-4538 or 305-274-0628 (U.S.); www6.miami.edu/sharklab/news_archive.html), South Bimini. Tours available at low tide. Often featured on Discovery Channel and other TV programs, the lab's 20-year mission has been to study the behavior of local lemon sharks and sharks in general. Its resident and visiting biologists tag and track the sharks in nursery habitats off South Bimini's south shore and in North Bimini's North Sound Lagoon. They will tour you through the facility and take you out into the bay in knee-deep water

STAFF AT THE SHARKLAB HANDLE TEMPORARILY CAPTURED LEMON SHARKS TO DEMYSTIFY AND DEMYTHIFY THE CREATURES FOR GUESTS.

to a fenced pen where they rotate a small stock of sharks for observation. The staff familiarizes guests with the sharks and debunks negative misunderstandings by holding one of the sharks and pointing out its anatomy and incredible coping mechanisms. For more information, e-mail sgruber @rsmas.miami.edu.

✪ **Bimini Sands Resort Nature Trail & Conch House** (242-347-3500; www.biminisands.com), Bimini Sands Resort, South Bimini. Open daily sunrise to sunset. Free admission; tours $12 adults, $6 children. This excellent trail loops a mile into relatively high hardwood forest habitat shaded with gumbo limbo trees, poisonwood, and buttonwood. It's an easy hike with self-guided signage that explains all the local landside fauna and flora, and side paths into mangroves and to benches for sitting and contemplating nature. Along the way, you'll see a non-native green iguana in a cage and an indigenous Bimini boa, which staff rotates on a regular basis so no animal is kept captive for very long. (And they're returned to the exact GPS point where found.) Ruins of the circa-1920 Conch House mark the trail's westernmost point, a good place to catch sunset. Famed Australian swimmer Percy Cavill, also the developer of Bimini Bay Rod & Gun Club on North Bimini, built the house for himself. The best way to experience the trail is by guided tour with the resort biologist, Grant Johnson, who will fondly cradle the nonthreatening boa for you to pet and experience up close.

The Healing Hole, East Bimini. Accessible only by boat, and only with someone who knows the way, this remote freshwater spring is attributed with minerals and healing powers. Local kayak outfits lead kayaking tours to the site if you're interested in taking the plunge. If that doesn't heal you, the glide through placid mangrove-lined backwaters will.

✳ Lodging

Price Codes

Inexpensive	Up to $100	(An asterisk after the pricing designation indicates that the rate includes at least a continental breakfast in the cost of lodging and possibly more extensive meal service as noted in the listing.)
Moderate	$100 to $200	
Expensive	$200 to $300	
Very Expensive	$300 and up	

ISLAND CHARACTER: GRANT JOHNSON

Wherever you see a fledgling coconut tree growing on South Bimini—and you will see them all over the place once you start paying attention—you can thank Grant Johnson. Thank him again if you're lucky enough to see a beautiful, iridescent Bimini boa out in the wilds. Lemon sharks, ditto.

Bimini's foremost ecologist—not surprising—comes originally from Minnesota. Not surprising, because it often takes an outsider to help islanders understand their treasures.

"I've been working at convincing people that you can base tourism on seeing snakes and sharks to a much broader audience," says Grant, who would like to massage ecotourism into an off-season, winter trade.

He arrived in South Bimini in 2001 to work at the Sharklab. He's still passionate about lemon sharks as a biologist, but in 2007 decided to move to a more widespread mission with friend, co-worker, and fellow Minnesotan Katie Grudecki.

They came to an agreement with the owners of Bimini Sands—the island's main resort and marina—to initiate programs to further the island's reputation as an ecodestination. Beyond resort shark-feeding excursions and tours of the nature trail he helped develop, Grant began bringing in the local children for programs and to educate other islanders.

"It's a way to get them involved and happy and proud to live here," he says.

He's still working at getting them to love the snakes, a strong symbol of evil and fear for islanders.

ACCOMMODATIONS

North Bimini

Big John's Hotel (242-347-3117; www.bigjohnshotel.com), King's Hwy., Alice Town. The seven recently renovated rooms here on the harbor are some of the nicest accommodations downtown. They line up over top of Big John's Conch Shell Bar, so be prepared to hear (or take part in) the partying on the deck below Thursday through Saturday. Friendly employees, many of whom worked at the old Compleat Angler for many years, make you feel welcome and at home. Convenient to fishing, boating, and all of downtown's shopping and restaurants, Big John's allows guests to truly become part of the local life. Expensive to Very Expensive.

ⓣ **Bimini Bay Resort & Marina** (242-347-2900 or 305-513-0506 (U.S.); www.biminibayresort.com), north end of the island. On the site of

"I've never been a snake person, but when I first saw the Bimini boa, I fell in love," he told me while cradling a 6-foot specimen.

Grant is convincing locals not to run over the creatures in the road. "Just call us, and we'll come get it," he tells them. Now he gets phone calls in the middle of the night, and happily comes to the boas' rescue.

As for the coconut palms, he started reforesting the population for food and landscaping purposes a couple of years ago, germinating nuts in a garden on the resort's nature trail. In the first year, he planted nearly 500 and has actively campaigned for islanders to start their own coconut palms.

GRANT JOHNSON IS OUT TO SAVE THE BIMINI BOA.

BIMINI BAY RESORT HUGS THE OCEAN ON ONE SIDE, THE BAY ON THE OTHER.

the historic Bimini Bay Rod & Gun Club of the 1920s, which burned down many years ago, a shiny new resort is growing—grand and 800 acres huge. Rentals are available, from suites with kitchenettes to fantastic beach houses and bayside properties with private docks. The décor is as lovely as the setting, reflecting the island's sea legs with seashell and tasteful nautical accents and pastel paint jobs. To date there are close to 200 suites and villas in one- or two-story, Bahamian-style, tin-roofed buildings, but more are being built along with a golf course and a casino, which was expected to open in summer 2010. The casino will sit among the complex at the resort's megayacht marina, along with a free-form, beach-entry, saltwater pool, its flagship Sabor restaurant, poolside cabanas, and a massage tent. Another restaurant, Aqua Grill, and pool—this one with an infinity edge that seems to drop into the ocean—occupy a complex on the other side of the island, a short golf cart drive away. Tennis courts are nearby. The final congregation of facilities clusters at

the resort's entrance, including a sports bar, pizza shop-deli, boutiques, a game and activities room for families, and another marina. This is the kind of place where you could easily spend a week and not run out of things to do. It's steps away from the island's downtown area, but if you're at the north end of the property, you'll want to take the free shuttle to the gate. Service is very friendly here and it is well run while still properly laid-back Bahamas-style. The beach isn't the greatest—pretty to look at, but not particularly conducive to swims or long walks. Expensive to Very Expensive.

Bimini Blue Water Resort (242-347-3166), King's Hwy., Alice Town. One of Bimini's oldest surviving resorts, this property is typical old-island in that it is marina-oriented, simple, and affordable. That is unless you stay in the three-bedroom Marlin Cottage, where Hemingway hid out and described in his *Islands in the Stream*, which he worked on during frequent visits to the island. It'll set you back $300 a night. The rest of the dozen rooms and suites mostly overlook the beach and ocean and are furnished unspectacularly, but do offer air-conditioning and a TV. The Anchorage Restaurant & Bar is a popular spot, especially come sunset. The 32-slip marina hosts a fishing club and tournaments throughout the year. The resort's final claim to fame is that it owns the only gas pumps in town. Inexpensive to Moderate.

Ebbie's Bimini Bonefish Club (242-347-2053 or 242-359-8273 (cell); www.biminibonefishclub.com), King's Hwy., Bailey Town. Native-run and obviously fishing-focused, Ebbie's is also convenient to downtown's restaurants and attractions, plus it has its own food and ship's store on-site. Owner "Bonefish Ebbie" Davis is one of the island's legendary anglers. A typical day here starts with early continental breakfast, then proceeds to a ride out with a fishing guide into Bimini's famed bonefish grounds in the North Sound Lagoon, close to the club. Box lunch is included, and dinner can be right at the docks where the club serves nightly at 7 PM—a popular gathering place for locals and guests. Or you can wander down to Edith's or a number of other options. The five rooms overlook the harbor and have wood-paneled walls, a TV, mini-fridge, microwave, and coffeemaker. Three- to seven-day fishing packages are available, which include all meals. Continental breakfast is included on nonpackage stays. Moderate.°

South Bimini

⁽ı⁾ ✪ Bimini Sands Resort & Marina (242-347-3500; www.biminisands.com), South Bimini. Condos and town houses are still under construction at South Bimini's main resort. To date, it holds 206 one- or two-bed-

room units (80 of which are in the rental pool) that are privately owned and decorated. They ring the safe-harbor marina with its inlet from the sea. The two-story pink stucco buildings make a low impact, and Bimini Sands is all about the island's natural and cultural heritage. Rather than building out to full capacity, it has devoted some of its acreage to a nicely developed nature trail, and its activities department strives to educate locals as well as visitors about local ecology. The units have full kitchens, a patio or balcony, and views of the ocean or marina. From many, you can walk right out to the beach steps away. A funky, brightly painted bus shuttles guests from the resort to the Beach Club, minutes away. Here they can sun on the beach, play volleyball, cool off in the pool, snorkel, watch the game at Mackey's Sand Bar, gaze at the sunset, and have a fine dinner at the Beach Club Restaurant and sushi bar. There's another restaurant, the Petite Conch, on the resort's main campus; it serves breakfast, lunch, and dinner overlooking the pool and 60-slip marina. Moderate to Very Expensive.

✳ Where to Eat

Some of North Bimini's best home-cooking is found in its take-out joints and its conch shacks along the waterfront in Bailey Town. Most of the sit-down restaurants are part of a resort. Every island is known for its specific type of bread, but slightly sweet Bimini bread may be the most famous.

Price Codes

Inexpensive	Up to $15
Moderate	$15 to $25
Expensive	$25 to $35
Very Expensive	$35 or more

AQUA GRILLE LIES POOLSIDE WITH SCENIC VIEWS AT BIMINI BAY RESORT.

Cost categories are based on the range of dinner entrée prices or, if dinner is not served, on lunch entrées.

Resort restaurants take reservations. For small restaurants, it's a good idea to call ahead to make sure they're open. Often they require that you order your dinner ahead of time from the two or three selections they may offer that evening.

North Bimini

⚥ **Aqua Grille** (242-347-2900; www .biminibayresort.com), Bimini Bay Resort & Marina. Paddle fans whir overhead and waves gush below. An infinity pool, surrounded by big round padded chairs for two, seems to empty into the sea from the alfresco tables' view. Practically every Bimini restaurant affords a view of the water, but this feels entirely islandy and relaxing. The simple menu, which is served until 7 PM, offers typical fare on this island that balances Bahamian with American. Appetizers, for instance, include both conch fritters and chicken wings. The mahi sandwich, available grilled or fried, tastes that-day fresh, dressed with a sauce that bites back a bit. Caesar salad, grouper fingers, cracked conch sandwich, burger, and Spook Hill ribs (named for the local cemetery) fill out the offerings. Inexpensive to Moderate.

⚥ **Capt. Bob's** (242-347-3260; www .captainbobsbimini.com), King's Hwy., Alice Town. "Yes We're Open," the sign out front proclaims, propped against painted glass display windows and limestone rock walls. Right in the thick of things, Capt. Bob's is a good place to fuel up before a day on the water or beach. It serves traditional Bahamian breakfasts such as stew fish, tuna and grits, conch omelet, lobster omelet, and pork chops and eggs starting at 6:30 AM. Lunch can be as inexpensive as a $3.50 burger or as elaborate as a $30 seafood platter. The menu, which is also available for dinner in season and on some weekends in the off-season, also lists eclectic dishes such as a pork chop and cheese sandwich, club sandwich, fried lobster, and grouper. Mismatched tables and chairs and fishing pictures plastered on the wall constitute atmosphere. The restaurant serves no alcohol. Inexpensive to Moderate.

✪ **Edith's Pizza** (242-347-2800), King's Hwy., Bailey Town. Edith cooks up more than pizza, but the pizza she does make beats all the rest of her offerings hands down. There's a bit of Bimini bread sweetness and fullness to the crust. Order the conch pizza for a true Bahamian hybrid. Other toppings are more convention-al: barbecue chicken, shrimp, pepper-oni, pineapple and ham, and olive. In addition, Edith cooks up all the Bahamian favorites for lunch and din-ner, including chicken wings, pork chops, ribs, stuffed shrimp, filet mignon, and grouper—either broiled or fried. Order through a slit in the open window out back bayside, have a seat on a wooden bench and table on the deck, and gaze out on the rusting hull of a steel ship while the clear water laps at the small beach. Bring some insect spray, because the no-see-ums can bug you. Inexpensive to Moderate. No credit cards.

& **Sabor** (242-347-2900; www.bimini bayresort.com), Bimini Bay Resort & Marina, North Bimini. Walls of win-dows bank this circular building on the harbor, exposing guests to light and shimmer. The two-tiered restau-rant holds a marble-topped bar with a display kitchen behind it on the top level. Tables spread below the vaulted ceiling and out on the pool deck beneath umbrellas. The menus com-bine Continental and Latin styles with Bahamian comfort food in dishes such as curried lobster spring rolls, snap-per-conch ceviche, blackened or grilled mahi, paella, hibachi steak, and seafood pasta. At night, the lit pool

fountain adds to the festivity of the place. Moderate to Expensive. Reser-vations accepted.

& **Sara's** (242-347-2642), King's Hwy., Bailey Town. Mostly known for its take-out, Sara's does provide a few tables inside and on the deck outside of the new building it occupies on the bay. Breakfast offers a mix of Bahami-an and American favorites—omelets, corned beef and grits, and johnny-cake. For lunch and dinner, there's everything from chicken wings, bologna sandwiches, and burgers to lobster and shrimp. When the cook puts his or her name on a restaurant in the Bahamas, you can be certain you're getting "true true" home cook-ing. Inexpensive. No credit cards.

South Bimini

& ✪ **Beach Club Restaurant** (242-347-4500; www.biminisands.com), Bimini Sands Resort Beach. He must have heard me tell the hostess I want-ed something light, because when I sat down at the sushi bar to peruse the menu, Chef Steven Borela told me he was going to make me some-thing special, and rattled off a few ingredients. I caught tuna and avoca-do, so it sounded great. What it was,

---

BAHAMA TALK

True True: Instead of using adverbs such as very or really, Bahamians have a habit of repeating an adjec-tive for emphasis. One visitor of the 1930s, Gilbert Klingel, described the speech oddity in his book, *Inagua: An Island Sojourn,* thusly: "The Lagoon Christophe was only far, the farm far, far, and Mathew-town was far, far, far."

more accurately, was a complex molded salad of deep red tuna meat, avocado, Asian pear, peppers, and various other fruits and vegetables, all marinated separately then placed on a mango sauce and topped with something creamy, wonderful, and slightly spicy. The sushi bar is a small part of the spacious, elegant-for-Bimini dining room. In addition to the rolls and sushi served there, you can choose from a variety of starters such as conch or shrimp ceviche, lobster bisque, and cream of mushroom soup. Offerings on the entrées menu range from pasta pomodoro and conch linguine to pan-fried or grilled mahimahi and rack of lamb. Inexpensive to Moderate. Reservations accepted.

Petite Conch Restaurant (242-347-4500; www.biminisands.com), Bimini Sands Resort. Situated on the second floor overlooking the resort marina, Petite Conch has an air of coziness and modern with a handful of booths, a vaulted ceiling, and a friendly bar named "Healing Hole" after the mineral springs on East Bimini. The all-day menu is small but varied. The lobster wrap, though a little on the salty side, is excellent with chunks of meat and a spicy sauce. In the sandwich department, there's also a steak wrap, corned beef salad on Bimini bread, chicken or conch burgers, and hamburgers. For something lighter, salads come in lobster, seafood, and tuna varieties. Something more substantial? Try the Kalik-battered fish and chips, minced lobster, spaghetti and meatballs, T-bone steak, or surf and turf. Save room for key lime, coconut cream, or apple pie. At breakfast, the French toast or breakfast sandwich, both made with Bimini bread, are winners. Inexpensive to Moderate.

Thirsty Turtle Yacht Club (242-347-4444; thirstyturtlebimini.com) With its big-screen TVs, huge bar, and pool table, this place seems to be more about the drinking than the eating, yet the all-day menu offers a complete selection of local pleasers and beyond, including pasta, sandwiches, fried chicken, cracked conch, lobster, grouper, steak, spaghetti and meatballs, and shrimp and lobster fettuccine. There's also pizza, which they deliver. Create your own or go for the signature Bimini Bomb—conch, fish, pepperoni, and onion. Inexpensive to Moderate. No credit cards.

BAKERIES Charlie's Bakery (242-347-2416), King's Hwy., Alice Town. Buy your Bimini bread to take home along with other local sweet treats.

GROCERS Most of North Bimini's grocery stores sell a little bit of everything, including (and especially) fishing supplies and bait.

Small's Variety Store (242-347-4032), South Bimini near ferry landing. Pick up canned food items and rent a golf cart at the same spot.

Sue & Joy Variety Store (242-347-3115), King's Hwy., Alice Town. Besides your basic food supplies, it carries liquor, clothing, and souvenirs.

TAKE-OUT Along the lagoon at Porgy Bay and Bailey Town, you'll find little conch shacks such as Stuart Conch Salad and Joe's Conch Shack selling fresh conch salad—so cavalier about their water views that tumble-down structures occupy what would be prime real estate in most places.

J&T's Daily Manna (242-347-2555), King's Hwy., Bailey Town. Sandwiches, tuna or crab platters, vegetable or chicken pasta, and ice cream.

✳ Selective Shopping

Bimini Craft Centre (no phone), near Government Dock in Alice Town. Seventeen stalls sell Bahamian straw goods in this new facility, which sometimes features live entertainment.

Booze & Screws (242-347-4044), South Bimini near the ferry landing. You've gotta love the name of this combo liquor-hardware store.

Dolphin House Gift Shop (242-347-3201), Alice Town. Ashley Saunders sells jewelry and other gifts made from beach glass, coconut shells, seashells, and "stuff the beach coughed up" at his unusual attraction. You can also purchase his two Bimini history books and DVDs about the construction of Dolphin House.

John Bull (242-347-6086), Bimini Bay Resort & Marina, North Bimini. Duty-free jewelry, perfume, and other luxury items.

Splash (242-347-2900), Bimini Bay Resort & Marina, North Bimini. For men's and women's clothing and accessories, this is the best in Bimini.

✳ Special Events

February: **Bahamas Wahoo Challenge** (242-347-2900; www.wahoochallenge.com), Bimini Bay Resort, North Bimini. Four days late in the month. The third and final legs of this tournament take place in Bimini. (The first leg is in November in Bimini; the second leg goes to West End on Grand Bahama Island.)

March/April: **Homecoming,** North Bimini. Easter weekend. Formerly the Bimini Regatta, it welcomes home sons and daughters for a fun celebration of food and music.

CONCH SHACKS LINE THE BAY ON NORTH BIMINI.

July: **Bahamas Boating Flings** (800-32-SPORT) Late July, early August. The Bahamian equivalent of a road trip, its boating flings involve a caravan of boats that crosses the Gulf Stream and island-hops through Bimini and surrounding islands for a week or so.

August: **Bimini Native Tournament** (242-347-3359), Bimini Blue Water Marina, North Bimini. Five days early in the month. This fishing competition started more than 60 years ago.

November: **Bahamas Wahoo Challenge** (242-347-2900; www.wahoo challenge.com), Bimini Bay Resort, North Bimini. Three days early in the month. This three-part tournament kicks off in Bimini waters.

Cat Island 6

THE BIGHT

PORT HOWE

CAT ISLAND

OLD BAHAMIA

"It is not untypical to see trees with bottles filled with dirt, hair, and fingernails to protect the owner's property from thieves."

—Gail Saunders *in* The Bahamas: A Family of Islands

A mere 1,800 people live on this island, counting one doctor. It has just one paved road (Queen's Highway), and Baptist Rev. Cyril Ingraham, who doubles as a tour guide, will tell you: "If you get lost on this island, and I hear about it, I recommend the judge give you six months."

Cat Island feels like a small island because of its delicious isolation and sparse population. It measures, however, 48 miles long and 12 miles at its widest point. The hilliest of the Bahama islands, it "towers" up to 206 feet at Como Hill, aka Mount Alvernia, aka "the Bahamas Alps." Here perches The Hermitage, built by reclusive priest-architect Father Jerome, who began his mission as an Anglican, but later converted to Catholicism. Along with Baptist, they are the island's main faiths, although obeah reportedly survives more strongly here than on other Bahamian islands.

Lying 130 miles southeast of Nassau, it has been called Guanima by the Lucayans, and San Salvador, because it was believed by some to have been Columbus's New World touchdown. After other historians made a case for then-called Waitling Island being the correct spot, names changed.

Two theories explain how the island got its current name. Both involves pirates. One was named Arthur Catt, whose ship wrecked off island shores. This would also explain how Arthur's Town came to be labeled. The second unnamed theoretical pirate is said to have brought cats to the island. I vote for the first theory. In any case,

BAHAMA TALK
Obeah: Often defined as akin to voodoo, it keeps islanders in line with the threat of someone getting "mout' put on dem." That translates as a curse.

pirates obviously played a major role in Cat Island history, especially around **Bennett's Harbour,** where they hid out from the 1600s to the 1800s.

At one point in history, Cat Island, like so many other Bahamian islands, farmed pineapples. More recently, farmers grew tomatoes. At Bennett's Harbour, salt ponds brought cash in the early 1800s.

In 2008, Cat Island got its first bank, and boy are islanders proud. It's the only place on the island, they say, where you have to wear shoes. It's located in **The Bight,** the town's main settlement, divided into **New Bight** and **Old Bight.** Other of the town's businesses multitask, such as the Pass Me Not Bar & Hardware Store and the grocery-laundromat and the inn-rental car agency.

The northernmost and biggest settlement, **Orange Creek** boasts its eponymous natural phenomenon, a creek that turns golden certain times of year. It encompasses the smaller settlements of **Bain Town** and **The Lot,** and lies close to the abandoned **Port Royal** settlement.

The claim to fame of **Arthur's Town,** other than its possible pirate nomenclature, is native son Sidney Poitier, the actor of *Guess Who's Coming To Dinner?* fame. The Poitier surname is still common in these parts.

In between the settlements, scrubby vegetation, swamps, lakes, caves, and blue holes fill in the landscape, providing the adventuresome plenty to explore—with no fear of getting lost or getting thrown in the slammer. A curse? Not as long as you don't wrong anyone.

CAT ISLAND'S MAIN ATTRACTION, THE HERMITAGE, SERVED AS A RELIGIOUS CLOISTER FOR FATHER JEROME.

DON'T MISS

- A hike up to The Hermitage.
- Bonfire at Fernandez Bay Village.
- Surfing, kite surfing, or diving at Port Howe.
- Cold Kalik and dominoes at Hazel's.
- Green turtle roundup (for tagging) with Mark at Fernandez Bay Village.

SUGGESTED READING *An Evening in Guanima,* by Patricia Glinton. The author recalls folktales from her native Cat Island, originally known as Guanima.

Mystical Cat Island, by Eris Moncur and Nick Cripps, $10. Covers the island's history, vegetation, and settlements.

ISLAND CHARACTER: MARK KEASLER, SEA TURTLE SAVIOR

He told us we were going on a sea turtle roundup. It would involve wet suits, two boats, and some tags he would apply to the green turtles who feed in the thick mangrove flats of Cat Island. This a project that Mark Keasler, a nature-lover, adventurer, and 20-year employee of Fernandez Bay Village, pitched in on. It is part of a Bahamawide project to monitor the local sea turtle population, which was once decimated by locals who caught them for their meat. Tameron Armbrister, daughter of FBV's owners, helps out with the efforts.

Mark is happy to take interested guests out on his roundups. "Actually touching and seeing these animals in person goes a long way in helping them survive," he says. "Once you have seen, touched, and swam with them in the wild, it helps when it's time to go in your pocket to save an endangered creature."

A group of about 10 of us split into the two boats and skimmed the shallow back flats, eyes peeled. We saw several of the dark spots we learned to identify as green turtles flitting by. The trick was to get one on its own, then keep it sighted and contained between the two boats until it tired, at which point Mark jumped in to chase it down with snorkel and fins.

MARK KEASLER SCOUTS FOR GREEN TURTLES WITH A HOTEL GUEST.

It took an hour to round up our one tag for the day. Mark hoisted it up to the side of the boat and told us to lift it out. Well, that didn't work; it was way too heavy. Finally he managed to get it in with the help of some guys in the other boat. Tagged, pictured, and admired, it went back to the sea to continue for Mark the story of its travels and life.

CHURCHES & RELIGIOUS SITES Church of the Holy Redeemer (242-342-3029), New Bight. Open 24 hours. One of Father Jerome's masterpieces (also see The Hermitage, below), the limestone church features a bell tower, gargoyles, a painting of Christ, beautiful windows, and stations of the cross.

❍ **The Hermitage,** Pigeon Bay, New Bight. Open daily. The climb up Mount Alvernia, at 206 feet the highest point in the Bahamas, takes visitors past a Bahamian garden and through 14 stations of the cross to a chapel and dwelling that looks like Lilliputians constructed it. John "Father Jerome" Hawes, however, was a tall man, according to locals' descriptions. He built his retreat from the world in small scale to further punish himself in atonement for what sins one can only guess, seeing how he's considered close to sainthood on the island. While cloistered at The Hermitage, he built several Catholic churches on the island, Long Island, and in Nassau, and walked or traveled by boat to minister to local islanders. The assemblage of stone Cat Island buildings the priest-architect built on Mount Alvernia in the early 1940s include the chapel, his small and sparse living space, a bell tower, a guest room, and a kitchen. After dying in 1956, he was buried atop the hill where he lived. Every Good Friday, islanders and visitors gather to follow his stations of the cross. Everyday visitors are rewarded with 360-degree, godly views.

St. Mary's the Virgin Anglican Church, Old Bight. The governor built this church in 1889 as a monument to the emancipation of Bahamian slaves. Many of the plantations they worked are found in this area.

THE HERMITAGE REQUIRES A CLIMB TO THE BAHAMAS' HIGHEST POINT.

MUSEUMS & HISTORIC SITES **Deveaux Plantation Ruins,** Port Howe. Awarded to Capt. Andrew Deveaux from Carolina for ridding Nassau of Spanish invaders in 1783 (unaware that the Brits had already achieved the task), this plantation once grew cotton throughout its thousands of acres. The plantation manor has deteriorated, but stands in mute testament to its previous grandeur and the brief prosperity of the slave-worked plantation era.

MUSIC & NIGHTLIFE Cat Island claims to have invented rake 'n' scrape music, so when you hear it here, it's roots music.

Hazel's Seaside Bar (no phone) Hazel Brown boasts the coldest Kalik and best domino-playing skills on the island.

✳ To Do

ANCHORAGES **Hawk's Nest Resort & Marina** (242-342-7050 or 800-688-4752; www.hawks-nest.com) Cat Island's only marina makes up for the island's lack with full service, including a dive shop. It holds up to 28 boats with modern facilities.

BEST BEACHES **Old Bight Beach,** Old Bight. This 3-mile-long, public beach borders the island's west side, where calm waters prevail.

Orange Beach, Cat Island. At the island's north end, it is said to be one of the island's most beautiful and dramatic. On the leeward side, it gets gentle waves and few people.

FISHING Cat Island has a reputation among deep-sea fishermen, who headquarter at Hawk's Nest Resort for tournaments and hard-core angling.

THE LOCAL RAKE 'N' SCRAPE BAND PERFORMS AT FERNANDEZ BAY VILLAGE.

Hawk's Nest Resort & Marina (242-342-7050 or 800-688-4752; www.hawks -nest.com) If you don't have your own boat, the marina can arrange a charter with guide.

SNORKELING & DIVING You can find a lot of places in Cat Island where you can snorkel from shore, many of them around Fernandez Bay. Ask to see a map at the Fernandez Bay Village office. Dive sites lie 13 to 30 minutes offshore. Some popular dives include **Tartar Bank, The Cave,** and **Vlady's Reef.** Expect to see lots of fish and often huge stingrays.

Dive Cat Island (242-342-7050 or 800-688-4752; www.hawks-nest.com), Hawk's Nest Resort & Marina. A full-service PADI dive center offering rentals, snorkel and scuba trips, and "Discover Scuba" and certification courses.

✳ Lodging
Price Codes
Inexpensive	Up to $100
Moderate	$100 to $200
Expensive	$200 to $300
Very Expensive	$300 and up

(An asterisk after the pricing designation indicates that the rate includes at least a continental breakfast in the cost of lodging and possibly more extensive meal service as noted in the listing.)

ACCOMMODATIONS
Fernandez Bay
❂ **Fernandez Bay Village** (242-342-3043 (office), 954-474-4821 (U.S.), or 800-940-1905; www.fernandezbay village.com), Fernandez Bay, Cat Island. The largest of Cat Island's resort with only 22 rooms, Fernandez Bay is also one of the most easily accessible and full-service of accommodations. Situated on the island's leeward side, its white-sand, natural beach cusps around sparkling, placid waters in shades more precious than gemstones. Tall Australian pines shade hammocks. Activity buzzes around the stone, thatched-roof lobby and restaurant with its adjacent cathedral-ceiling tiki bar and deck. Guests can help themselves to soft and hard drinks at the bar; the resort's store is also on such an honor system. Happy hour starts at 6:30 PM (7:30 in summer), with live music, munchies, and much conviviality led by the owners' extended family. Beachside accommodations range from one-bedroom cottages to two-bedroom houses, none with locks on the doors or any fancy accoutrements such as plush towels and expensive shampoos. The houses have cool outdoor showers and complete kitchen facilities—a little seaworn, but complete. The resort often arranges special island-culture events—cooking classes, for instance—in addition to local bands. Kayak use is complimentary, and boat rentals are available, plus staff can line up any activity you wish. Meal plans are available. The lobby gets Wi-Fi reception, but there are no public computers. Expensive to Very Expensive.

Hawk's Nest
Hawk's Nest Resort & Marina (242-342-7050 or 800-688-4752; www.hawks-nest.com), Hawk's Nest. Boat-in and fly-in visitors and those looking for the most modern accommodations the island has to offer head for this 450-acre destination beach-

LOCALLY QUARRIED ROCK WENT INTO THE BUILDING OF THE COTTAGES AT FERNANDEZ BAY VILLAGE.

front resort that offers newly spruced rooms and rental homes (Very Expensive) to vacationers. Simply furnished with Bahamas standard issue white wicker, the 10 rooms are quite comfortable, with air-conditioning, a TV and VCR, coffeemaker, and terry bathrobes. With three bedrooms and full kitchens, rental homes are suitable for families or sharing couples. The 28-slip marina—the only one on Cat Island—comes complete with air-conditioned fish-cleaning houses. Home to annual wahoo and billfish tournaments, it's conveniently poised for deep-sea and reef fishing. The property's dive shop has it all: rentals, snorkeling and diving excursions, and certification courses. A poolside restaurant and bar serve all your favorite tropical drinks and meals. A second bar is conveniently located at the marina. Expensive.

Port Howe

Flamingo Bay Club (242-342-5069 or 352-383-2477 (U.S.); www.flamingo bayclub.com), off Queen's Hwy. Everything on Cat Island is off-the-

beaten path, but this one is most unusual. It rents two air-conditioned, octagon-shaped villas with kitchenettes that sit atop a hill with a lord's view of the beach and sea below. Each comes with a queen-sized bed, wood deck, TV, DVD player, and selection of DVDs. Guests have access to a pool and Jacuzzi, with surround sound and colorful lighting set in a lovely garden, plus kayaks, bicycles, snorkeling gear, and gas grills. The secluded beach, its trees decorated with buoys and other flotsam that have washed up, is a short walk down the hill. In the evening, owners Jerry and Donna Ornberg serve hors d'oeuvres for guests out on the deck. Moderate (three-night minimum).

Hotel Greenwood Beach Resort & Dive Center (242-342-3054; www.greenwoodbeachresort .com), off Queen's Hwy. Situated on arguably Cat Island's most dramatic, beautiful beach—especially if you're a surfer—this quiet, German-owned inn appeals to sports enthusiasts who spend most of their time in the water.

Divers love the convenience of a dive shop on property and coral reef just offshore. Its 16 simple but cheerful rooms huddle around a garden just steps from the beach, its tiki huts and hammocks. Half of the rooms have air-conditioning, the rest depend upon the typically steady breezes and ceiling fans. They all have small porches, but no telephone or TV. Internet access is available from the guest computer or wireless service in the clubhouse. An open-air restaurant and bar, the latter operated on an honor system, provide daylong service, and meal plans are available. Guests play pool, read, or gather around a bonfire in the evenings. Moderate.

✴ Where to Eat

Cost categories are based on the range of dinner entrée prices or, if dinner is not served, on lunch entrées.

Price Codes

Inexpensive	Up to $15
Moderate	$15 to $25
Expensive	$25 to $35
Very Expensive	$35 or more

Resort restaurants take reservations. For small restaurants, it's a good idea to call ahead to make sure they're open. Often they require that you order your dinner ahead of time from the two or three selections they may offer that evening.

New Bight

Blue Bird Club (242-342-3095), off Queen's Hwy. Typical Cat Island, it requires you call ahead to order your dinner, which you choose from about three nightly selections such as cracked conch, fish, chicken, and lobster, The entrée comes bolstered with Bahamian staples like peas 'n' rice,

potato salad, and coleslaw—all homemade, of course. Murals, drums, and other Bahamian artifacts decorate the simple setting. The restaurant serves no alcohol, but you can bring your own. The night I dined, the cracked conch—tenderized, breaded, and fried—tasted as fresh as that day. Moderate to Expensive. No credit cards.

Bridge Inn Restaurant (242-342-3013 or 800-688-4752; www.bridgeinn catisland.com), Queen's Hwy. For breakfast, Bridge Inn serves a homestyle weekend dish such as the incredible stew fish and grits I relished one Friday morning. Other dishes might include boil' fish or chicken souse—hardy, souplike concoctions known variously as hangover cures and "Bahamian penicillin." Lunch and dinner bring fare more in the American vein—burgers, fried chicken, and seafood. Moderate.

Fernandez Bay

&. ♺ **Fernandez Bay Village** (242-342-3043 (office), 954-474-4821 (U.S.), or 800-940-1905; www.fer nandezbayvillage.com), Fernandez Bay, Cat Island. We feasted on lobster tail the size of my foot. Nearly all the food prepared in this kitchen comes from local fishermen and farmers. The menu varies nightly according to what's fresh, offering guests a choice of two entrées. The restaurant serves buffet-style breakfast (choice of continental or full), lunch, and dinner. The lunch menu caters mostly to American tastes with deli sandwiches, burgers, and salads. Its conch chowder and conch fritters are among the best I've tasted anywhere, accompanied by local bread, sweet and freshly made daily. The dining room, with its imposing rock fireplace, makes a cozy

CONCH SALAD IN A FLASH

One afternoon during my stay at Fernandez Bay Village, a team of conch fishermen, shuckers, and cooks gave a conch salad demonstration on the beach. Before our eyes, the guys shucked the conchs with a machete, cleaned them, and handed them over to the women to chop up with fresh local tomatoes, onions, green peppers, and hot finger peppers for the cevichelike conch salad, a true island delicacy. To "cook" the conch, they squeezed in lime juice, then orange juice—"to cut the sharpness of the lime." This of-the-moment dish is ready in no time and is best eaten on the spot, on the beach, with a local Kalik beer in hand.

CONCH SALAD: AN OF-THE-MOMENT DISH PREPARED WITH THE FRESHEST INGREDIENTS AND "COOKED" BY A CHEMICAL REACTION FROM LIME JUICE.

evening scene. Lunch is best enjoyed alfresco overlooking the beach. Very Expensive. Call ahead to order your dinner.

Hawk's Nest
& **Hawk's Nest Restaurant** (242-342-7050 or 800-688-4752; www .hawks-nest.com), Hawk's Nest Resort, Devil's Point. Part of a spiffy resort and marina complex, its restaurant and porch look out over the swimming pool. Its menu mixes regulation Bahamian fare such as burgers, Greek salad, chicken wings, Caribbean chicken (marinated in herbs and served with sweet and sour sauce), grilled pork tenderloin, and rib-eye steak. For dinner (served promptly at 7 PM), call in your selection by 3 PM. Service is island-paced, but with sea breezes blowing and the swimming pool for refreshing dips,

you may as well stay awhile. Try the Bahamian cinnamon toast for breakfast, touched too with nutmeg and vanilla. The bar also serves munchies such as conch fritters and fish fingers. Moderate to Expensive. Call ahead to order your dinner.

✳ Special Events

January: **Wahoo Tournament** (242-342-7050 or 800-688-4752), Hawk's Nest Resort & Marina. Four days midmonth. Big purses and lots of action.

May: **Billfish Blast Release Tournament** (242-342-7050 or 800-688-4752), Hawk's Nest Resort & Marina. Five days midmonth. The resort offers free docking for the tourney.

June: **Rake 'n' Scrape Festival,** Cat Island. First weekend in June. Musical competitions and a celebration of folk culture.

START OUT YOUR MEAL AT HAWK'S NEST WITH A TRUE BAHAMIAN TRADITION.

Eleuthera 7

HARBOUR ISLAND

GOVERNOR'S HARBOUR

GREGORY TOWN

SOUTH ELEUTHERA

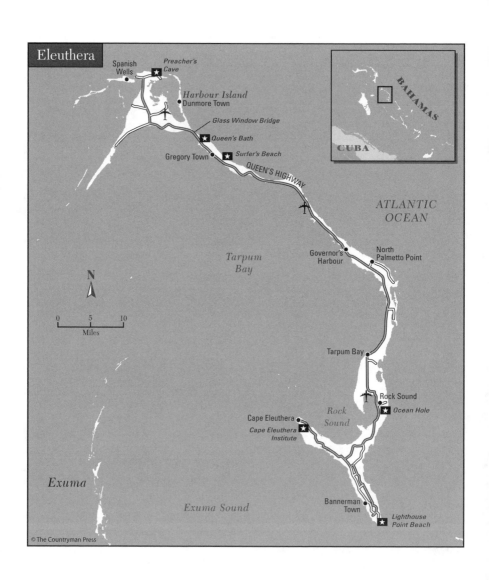

Eleuthera

Spanish Wells
Preacher's Cave
Harbour Island
Dunmore Town
Glass Window Bridge
Queen's Bath
Gregory Town
Surfer's Beach
QUEEN'S HIGHWAY

ATLANTIC OCEAN

Tarpum Bay

Governor's Harbour
North Palmetto Point

N

0   5   10
Miles

Tarpum Bay

Rock Sound
Ocean Hole
Rock Sound

Cape Eleuthera
Cape Eleuthera Institute

Exuma

Exuma Sound

Bannerman Town
Lighthouse Point Beach

BAHAMAS

CUBA

© The Countryman Press

ELEUTHERA

BEACHES IS WE

"The famous pink sand of Harbour Island, which is actually more of a salmon color, was taking on the hue of a slightly bruised peach as the sun went down. It is truly remarkable, the sand here, finer than sugar and of a color I've never seen anywhere else."

—Bob Morris *in* Bahamarama

"Head up dat road a piece past dat brown pickup, see? To a white house and follow de pat' to de kitchen door."

Such were the directions the Bahamian grocery store guy gave me to find johnnycake in Gregory Town, one of North Eleuthera's main villages. And that's how I found myself in Nappy's kitchen on a bright Sunday morning, slurping chicken souse and talking (well, mostly listening to) local politics. The men (whose wives had sent them out to pick up breakfast) jabbered rapid-fire about what the prime minister was up to and how it would affect their sleepy island.

As Nappy wrapped my johnnycake in foil to go, I sniffed around the bubbling pots on her stove to discover she had made one of my other favorite Bahamian breakfast foods: souse. I asked if she minded me eating some at her kitchen table because I was on foot. As I relished the limey, peppery soup, the men streamed in with their orders and opinions. Meaning I scored local entertainment as well as food.

The local scene and the resort scene intertwine on this unusually hilly (for the Bahamas), quiet island that stretches 110 miles long and skinny like a tawny cat in the sunshine. Islanders are friendly, if a bit reserved, and are crucial amenities at the resorts, which are typically small, intimate, casual, and intrinsically relaxing.

Visitors come in search of what most Out Island Bahamian tourists want: fishing, beaches, diving, boating, and ultimately escape. Eleuthera remains rooted in a fishing-farming village attitude that runs on a schedule dictated by seasons, tides, and cocktail hour. And not all that strictly by season: Holiday decorations still hung over the one-person customs desk at North Eleuthera International Airport when I arrived in April.

Early risers typically hit **Gregory Town** at 7 AM to catch the fresh fish arrival and yeasty-sweet perfume of fresh bread and pineapple tarts pulled from bakery ovens. In June, it's the scene of Pineapple Festival, which celebrates the town's long-standing reputation for farming the sweet fruit and nurturing the hospitality it represents.

After breakfast, pick a beach, any beach; the selection beats Baskin-Robbins. If there's wave action, and there almost always is, those in the know hike to hidden Surfer's Beach, the best surfing in the Bahamas with a funky hangout shack totally surfer-style. Lunch is a drive down the squiggly road over the gorgeous Glass Window Bridge with its double-sided sea view to the Eleutheran capital (and once Bahamian capital) of **Governor's Harbour.** One of the prettiest towns in the Bahamas, it huddles around an ample bay with Victorian buildings and the only movie theater in all of the Out Islands.

A trip down-island to south Eleuthera opens up a whole new side of the island, with its deserted roads but lively main settlement of **Rock Sound.** Beaches here, as in most of Eleuthera, lie hidden down potholed roads. Most dramatic, **Lighthouse Point** punctuates the end of the island. At nearby **Bannerman Town,** Princess Cruise Lines maintains its "private island destination" known as Princess Cay.

Throw in a water sports excursion and a day exploring the Loyalist-founded settlement of **Harbour Island,** and there you have the sum demands on your time in Eleuthera. Many people rent a golf cart to explore Harbour Island's art galleries, shops, restaurants, and bustling waterfront. You can do it by foot if you're energetic and sunscreened. Stroll along the straw market on the harbor and stop for a Kalik beer and conch fritters. Harbour Island, shortcutted to Bri-

THE FAMED PEACHY-PINK SANDS OF HARBOUR ISLAND.

land in local parlance, encompasses the charming cottages and historic buildings of British Loyalists' **Dunmore Town** and one of the world's most famous pink beaches.

The more intrepid make the ferry ride to **Spanish Wells** to explore the beaches, parks, and insular society that remains a bit aloof from the rest of the islands. It's almost entirely populated with Loyalist descendants, and a bit inbred some say.

Originally called Cigatoo by the Lucayans, Eleuthera occupies 200 square miles 60 miles east of Nassau, 240 miles southeast of Miami, and a world away from . . . well, the world.

DON'T MISS
- The pink-sand beach and historic architecture of Harbour Island.
- Driving the torturous road for the reward of Lighthouse Beach.
- Governor Harbour's Victorian lovelies.
- Visiting the Hot Tubs (a.k.a. Queen's Bath) among the limestone bluffs north of Gregory Town.
- A day trip to quirky Spanish Wells.

SUGGESTED READING *Bahamarama,* by Bob Morris. A good beach-read murder-mystery set in Harbour Island.

The Elusive Beaches of Eleuthera, by Geoffrey and Vicky Wells. Detailed directions (including GPS points) to more than 60 beaches along with recipes, hidden attractions, and other tidbits. $24.95 from Amazon.

The Harbour Island Story, by Anne and Jim Lawlor, Macmillan Caribbean, $36.95.

✳ To See

GALLERIES & STUDIOS Glass Window Art Gallery (242-359-7467), next to Laughing Lizard Café, Gregory Town. It features an assortment of work by local artists, including oil and acrylic paintings, photographs, and driftwood furniture.

MUSEUMS & HISTORIC SITES Haynes Library (242-332-2877; www .hayneslibrary.org), 1 Haynes Ave. at Queen's Hwy., Governor's Harbour. Open 9–6 Mon.–Thurs., 9–5 Fri., 9–4 Sat. Built in 1896 in pretty Victorian style, this historic library closed in later years, and the building was destined for demolition. In 1994, the community formed Friends of the Library to reclaim, restore, and reopen the landmark. Today it houses more than 11,000 books, plus computers and children's programs for islanders and visitors.

Preacher's Cave, North Eleuthera. It gets its name from its reputation as the site of the island's first Christian service. A huge boulder shaped like a pulpit furthers the illusion.

> **BAHAMA TALK**
> Up south, down north: "We can't get it right," one Bahamian woman told me regarding this conflicted colloquialism.

South Eleuthera Mission (242-334-2948; www.southeleutheramission.com), Rock Sound. Open 10–6 Mon.–Thurs., 11:30–4:30 Fri., 10–1 Sat. Once a Methodist missionary manse in the early 1800s, it later served as a medical center. When it closed in 2003, the government granted the locals' petition to use the building, and it has since reopened as a place of resource for island children. A small museum is in the works. The beautiful, two-story home has a bit of New Orleans style, and its rich interior woodwork was donated by local craftsmen. It's worth a stop to admire the architecture and artifacts collection, and to see what kind of programs the mission is offering.

> **BAHAMA TALK**
> Kupunkled up: If someone says this about you, perhaps it's time to put your nightlife to bed. Translation: drunk.

HAYNES LIBRARY WAS RECENTLY RESTORED TO ITS CIRCA-1896 PURPOSE.

MUSIC & NIGHTLIFE Dr. Seabreeze gets around on the island with his acoustic guitar and sometimes a steel-drum banger. Look for him at local resort restaurants, where he plays his own special brand of island music. As for rake 'n' scrape, Spider & the Boys do it right.

⊙ **Elvina's Bar and Restaurant** (242-335-5032), off Queen's Hwy., Gregory Town. Tuesday and Thursday nights, locals and visitors hit this favorite hangout for open mic jam sessions—everyone's invited to sing or play. Music ranges from rake 'n' scrape to folk to classic rock to roots reggae. Sometimes rocker Lenny Kravitz, a local homeowner, joins in.

Fish Fry, Anchors Bay, Governor's Harbour; and Rock Sound. Every Friday night, locals and visitors join together for this end-of-the-week blow-off with live entertainment and native dishes.

Tippy's (242-332-3331; www.pineapplefields.com/restaurant.html), Banks Rd. at Pineapple Fields resort, Governor's Harbour. Live music on the beach Friday and Saturday in season.

BEST BEACHES Harbour Island Beach, Harbour Island. By far Eleuthera's most famous beach, its reputation comes from its pink sand and 3 miles of reef-protected shoreline—meaning calm, shallow, friendly waters. It is one of the few Eleuthera beaches that is groomed and is lined with resorts and restaurants. Sip Sip restaurant is a good place to anchor your beach day. Harbour Island is accessible by ferryboat from North Eleuthera.

○ **Lighthouse Point Beach,** Bannerman Town, South Eleuthera. Sculpted limestone cliffs, caves, and what's left of the tower that gave the point its name reward the explorer to this exquisite windward beach. With its pink sand and sheer drama, it is much prettier than Harbour Island's famed beach, but less discovered because the drive to it is notably torturous and hard to find. The pot-holed dirt and limestone road goes for more than 3 miles. Keep driving after you first spot a beach; Lighthouse Point is off to the right on the other side of some sand dunes.

Rock Sound Beach, Rock Sound, South Eleuthera. Look for the sign just south of the Rock Sound Airport and follow the pocked road to a wave-crashing beach at the end. Picturesque with limestone outcroppings and a fringe of sea oats and sea grapes, it offers seclusion and a coarse sand beach for dreaming.

Spanish Wells Beach, Spanish Wells. Less-visited than Harbour Island, the small island of Spanish Wells (accessible by ferry) is rimmed with beach, but most prefer the leeward shore, where the soft, white sand invites strolling and playing in the gentle waves.

Sunset Beach, Cape Eleuthera, South Eleuthera. Hammocks, tiki roofs, and a spread of inviting white sand edged in shiny green scavola bushes welcome visitors to this pleasant beach—one of the island's easiest to drive to. On property at Cape Eleuthera Resort, it is accessible to the public. On certain nights the resort does bonfire parties.

TYPICALLY OFF THE BEATEN PATH, ROCK SOUND BEACH REQUIRES A BIT OF A BUMPY RIDE, BUT REWARDS WITH ITS VIEWS.

✪ **Surfer's Beach,** Gregory Town, North Eleuthera. Look for the sign to Surfer's Beach Manor hotel and resort to make your turn toward this top-rated wave beach. Then prepare for some four-wheeling road or hiking until you reach the windblown beach with its little shack that looks like it

> **BAHAMA TALK**
> Eleuthera: Islanders pronounce it Eleut'ra. Its name comes from the Greek word for "freedom," coined by British settlers who were fleeing religious persecution in 1647.

could blow away at any minute. There are some rocks to make surfing a bit tricky; for nonsurfers, it has soft, deep sand and lots of room for exploring.

Tarpum Bay Beach, Tarpum Bay, South Eleuthera. This charming little town is edged by a leeward narrow white sand beach shaded by Australian pines. If you're there about 2 PM, the local fishermen will be bringing in their day's catch to sell at the fish stand. That's the extent of facilities along the pretty stretch.

WATER SPORTS *Anchorages:* There are six government dock ports of entry in Eleuthera: Governor's Harbour, North Eleuthera/Harbour Island, Rock Sound, Spanish Wells, Hatchet Bay, and Current.

Cape Eleuthera Yacht Club (242-334-8500; www.capeeleuthera.com), Rock Sound, South Eleuthera. Eleuthera's grandest marina with 55 slips to accommodate boats and yachts up 200 feet and longer. It's full service with electricity, fuel, Internet, laundry facilities, picnic and gas grill pavilion, and showers.

Harbour Island Club & Marina (242-333-2427), Harbour Island. No laundry facilities or groceries, but otherwise this 23-slip marina takes care of all boaters' needs. It closes mid-September through mid-November.

Spanish Wells Yacht Haven (242-333-4255), Spanish Wells. Forty slips, a restaurant, laundry facilities, showers, and hook-ups.

Snorkeling & Diving: Diving in Eleuthera is every bit as varied and spectacular as on other Bahama Islands. Some of the best sites include **Hole in the Wall,** a crevice in the reef at 75 feet that opens into Exuma Sound; the 20- to 50-foot cavern **Tunnel Rock; Ike's Reef,** 10 to 40 feet; **Rock Sound Blue Holes,** which reach a depth of 130 feet; **The Fish Cage,** an aquaculture research cage at 50 to 130 feet; the **Glass Window Bridge** reef; and **Smuggler's Plane Wreck,** at 50 to 130 feet and popular with loggerhead turtles.

Cape Eleuthera Divers (242-470-8242 or 888-270-9642 (U.S.); www.cape eleuthera.com), Cape Eleuthera Resort & Yacht Club, South Eleuthera. It offers daily two-tank dives and afternoon one-tankers, plus weekly night dives, day excursions to offshore islands, NAUI and PADI instructions, and Oceanic equipment rentals.

WILDLIFE SPOTTING Seven or so wild horses inhabit the island's bush in addition to indigenous and migrating birds.

Nature Preserves & Eco-Attractions: ✪ **Awesome Blossoms** (242-332-6351), Savannah Sound, South Eleuthera. Open 8–4 Mon.–Sat. From the street, this may look like an ordinary nursery, but stop in to visit Dorothy and Robert Rah-

ISLAND CHARACTER: DOROTHY RAHMING

"I always had a special love for plants," retired economics and music teacher Dorothy Rahming says as she first introduced me to her sprawling garden. She grew up among farmers and women who tended beautiful gardens.

"Back then, you had to know how to cook, do music, sew, and learn to garden," she says. She added to those talents those of an artist, accomplished musician, and straw plaiter—Eleuthera's Renaissance woman. Dorothy trained at the Royal School of Music and took her exam in London.

Upon retiring from Central Eleuthera High School in 2005, she and her husband set about transforming bush into an oasis of poincianas, pigeon plum, calabash, neem, sugar apple, and banana trees; native orchids; and rose bushes, fevergrass, and other decorative, food, and medicinal plants. As we walked among her plants, we tasted sugar apple and sapodilla (dilly) fruit, and learned what plant cured what ailment.

After the tour, we sat a spell on the benches under the generous shade of Miss Dorothy's garden, sipping sodas, tasting tarts from a nearby bakery, and admiring her straw work and paintings of local scenes and fish.

DOROTHY RAHMING: GARDENER, MUSICIAN, TEACHER, ARTIST.

ming and discover a 3-acre horticultural enclave that combines art and flora.

✪ **Cape Eleuthera Institute/The Island School** (242-334-8552; www
.ceibahamas.org), Cape Eleuthera, South Eleuthera. Tours by advance reservation at 11 and 1 Mon.–Fri., 11 only on Sat. $25 fee suggested; program fees vary.
Children ages 10 and younger pay half price. Home to a live-in, semester-long,
ecological-intensive high school program, CEI makes groundbreaking progress
in environmental research and implementation of sustainable practices. During a
tour of the campus, guests learn earth-friendly alternatives such as solar-heating,
rainwater collection, biodiesel fuel production from used cruise ship vegetable
oil, wind turbines, and wastewater recycling. Special programs take you on a
shark-tagging mission, a snorkeling or diving expedition to its fish cage 90 feet
down, archaeological explorations on nearby islands, an exploration of aquaponic
farming and aquaculture, and more. Students here learn math and other disci-
plines by practical application, such as scuba diving, for which they all earn certification.

Ocean Hole Park, Tarpum Bay, South Eleuthera. Locals say there's no bottom
to this great inland saltwater blue hole. At least it hasn't been measured. It's
where many of them learned how to swim and all of them, at one time or another, come to feed bread to the fish.

Queen's Baths (Hot Tubs), north of Gregory Town (look for sign on east side
of road). Natural tidal pools have formed in the limestone cliffs here. Warmed
by the sun, they reputedly provide a warm place for soaking and sunning, but it's
a treacherous climb down to reach them. The dramatic scenery is best and most
safely appreciated from above.

THE QUEEN'S BATHS PROVIDE A UNIQUE SCAPE OF KARST AND OCEAN.

✳ Lodging

Price Codes

Inexpensive	Up to $100
Moderate	$100 to $200
Expensive	$200 to $300
Very Expensive	$300 and up

ACCOMMODATIONS

Governor's Harbour

⁙ ✪ **Pineapple Fields** (242-332-2221 or 877-677-9539; www.pine applefields.com), Banks Road. Named for its adjacent five-acre pineapple farm, Pineapple Fields is a delightful, 32-unit complex of bright yellow, Bahamian-style condo buildings outside of Governor's Harbour. The Bahamas National Trust's Botanical Gardens are at its back door and the Atlantic Ocean at its front, creating a pretty enclave with modern accoutrements. The units come with pull-out sofas, flat-screen TVs, DVD players, and full kitchens with marble bar and stainless steel appliances. Bright pastel and white cottage-style furnishings and decorations create a cheerful feel in the individually owned one- and two-bedroom units spread through eight two-story buildings, each with its own outdoor shower. Vegetation-crowded pathways lead from one to the other and to the resort's deli, gift shop, and free-form pool. Across the street, Tippy's serves lunch and dinner in Bahamian beach-shack style. Expensive.

Gregory Town

⁙ ✪ **The Cove** (242-335-5142, 214-764-4400 (U.S.), or 800-552-5960; www.thecoveeleuthera.com), Queen's Hwy., North Eleuthera. The perfect intersection of Bahamian style and American comfort, The Cove's 26 units are built island-style with rock

coral accent walls, vaulted wood ceilings, luxurious bed linens, white tile floors, and ocean views, but no phones or TVs. Glass cube shower stalls add a quirky touch. The accommodations scatter down a hillside that slides into the ocean at a toasty sand beach suitable for swimming, kayaking, and sipping rum at the new tiki bar. The main house, restaurant, and pool overlook that beach and the one on the other side of the rocky hill, more secluded and better for snorkeling. For guests' recreation, there's also complimentary tennis, a fitness center, kayaks, and bicycles (Gregory Town is a short, but hilly, ride away). Staff can also arrange all manner of boating or touring expeditions, including scuba and horseback riding. Plus, iPod checkouts and wireless Internet are free. The bar and pool deck get lively around 6 PM as happy hour kicks in with Wallace behind the bar. Dinner is a sumptuous affair at the casual yet elegant restaurant, which also serves breakfast and dinner. Note: To experience the north and south ends of Eleuthera in one vacation, ask about its Island Package with Cape Eleuthera. Expensive to Very Expensive. Closed six to eight weeks in September and October.

⁙ **Sky Beach Club** (242-332-3422 or 800-605-9869; www.skybeachclub .com), off Queen's Hwy. in Governor's Harbour. If you're looking for affordable, you're looking at the wrong place, but the shiny-new gated prop-

---

SIGN ALERT
Seen inside one of Pineapple Fields' condos: "Island living keeps you conchious."

ELEUTHERA

erty's three bungalows are your best bet. They're close to the beach, pool, restaurant, and bar—where all the action is. Plenty roomy for two at 549 square feet, the bungalows feature spacious patios with love seats, iPod docking stations, a beverage center, whirlpool tubs, rain showers, and state-of-the-art bathroom fixtures. The four four-bedroom homes loom on the hillside above and afford more privacy, but require a bit of a walk or a short drive (golf cart is included with rental) down to beach level. They come in one-story or split-level floor plans and are the utmost in cutting-edge design and décor—sort of Miami Beach meets Asia meets Scandinavia. Ultraspacious with a private pool and hot tub, the most modern kitchen appliances, and other conveniences, they truly exude an air of privilege and creativity. The property's Bistro restaurant is the hottest new eatery on the island, specializing in globally prepared seafood and precious views. Moderate to Very Expensive.

⁰**ᵀ⁰ Surfers Beach Manor** (242-335-5300; www.surfersmanor.com), Eleuthera Island Shores, North Eleuthera. Near to its eponymous beach, Surfers Beach decorates its lobby with surfboards and rents them to guests, but Flloyddeia Walkes, the affable manager, says that most of her guests are nonsurfers looking for simple and affordable accommodations near the beach. The 14 rooms have TVs and DVDs (with free library available), small refrigerators, coffeemakers, paddle fans, and a barefoot feel. Most rooms have a sofa and dining table. Guests can hook up to wireless connection in the comfortable, sprawling rattan-furnished bar. Moderate.

Harbour Island

⁰**ᵀ⁰ Dunmore Beach Club** (242-333-2200 or 877-891-3100; www.dunmorebeach.com), Gaol Lane. Created more than 35 years ago for the Duke and Duchess of Windsor, this beyond-charming 8-acre resort still exudes that air of privileged, exclusive holidays in the sun. Its 16 thoroughly Bahamian cottages are scattered among gardens bursting with color. Some are more plush and newly furnished than others, but all provide a good measure of luxury, down to monogrammed bathrobes (but no TVs or phones). They range in size from one to four bedrooms. The restaurant is one of Eleuthera's most formal, requiring jackets and collared shirts for dinner, which kicks off with a traditional cocktail hour at 6:30. Meal plans are available. The resort overlooks the 3-mile stretch of beach, a short walk down the dunes. Very Expensive. Closed September and October.

⁰**ᵀ⁰ Pink Sands** (242-333-2030; www.pinksandsresort.com), Chapel St. The open lobby welcomes you with an oddly Indonesian feel to a lush 20-acre garden of riotous color and ultrasecluded cottages—25 in all ranging from one- to two-bedroom. Louvered wood doors open to views of the ocean and the resort's namesake beach or the gardens. They feature chunky teak furnishings, high-luxury bedding, plasma TVs with DVDs, iPod docking stations (including complimentary use of "loaded" iPods), mini-bars, and big space. The Blue Bar restaurant has gone the Japanese route for dinner, and is also open for breakfast and lunch. The resort caters to honeymooners, celebs, and others with unlimited budgets; a night's lodging bill can reach into four

figures for the two-bedroom cottages. Plus there's a three- to seven-night minimum stay. Sure, there are nice touches such as turndown service, sunbeds around the pool, and complimentary use of snorkeling equipment and kayaks—but it's still out of the reasonable range of even the occasional splurge. Very Expensive. Closed September and early October.

Tingum Village (242-333-2161), Colebrook St. Lodging can be spendy on trendy Harbour Island, but here's a down-to-earth spot close enough to the beach but far enough away not to burn up your cash. And it stays open year-round, one of the few on the island. Its 16 rooms and one three-bedroom cottage are comfortable and tropically inclined, if a little dated and worn at the edges. The cottages have kitchens and whirlpool tubs, and some of the rooms have refrigerators, too. Overgrown by lush vegetation, the property also holds a small spa. Owned by a Bahamian family, it feels close-knit and a little disheveled, as most families do. Ma Ruby runs her eponymous restaurant, colorful, hung with baseball caps, and known for its Jimmy Buffett–class cheeseburgers. Moderate to Expensive.

North Palmetto Point
❀ ⁺ɪ⁺ **Unique Village** (242-332-1830 or 877-610-3874; www.uniquevillage .com) An incredible value considering the view and room amenities, this 18-

year-old property perches on a cliff above the windward sea, tucked off the main burst of activity along the road to Governor's Harbour. Its 10 rooms, stacked two high in white stucco structures, are all done up in sturdy white tile and white rattan with an ocean view, patio or balcony, TV, phone, little fridge, coffeemaker, hair dryer, and complimentary wireless Internet. The four villas have fully equipped kitchens, but no phones for some reason. Two of them are two-bedroom, the other two one-bedroom. Guests have use of the sea-view pool, tennis courts, snorkeling equipment, and hard-to-resist hammocks. Its spacious restaurant serves breakfast, lunch, dinner, and delicious views. Inexpensive to Moderate.

Rock Sound
✪ ⁺ɪ⁺ **Cape Eleuthera Resort & Yacht Club** (242-334-8500; www .capeeleuthera.com), South Eleuthera. This was, once upon some 35 years ago, THE place. Hidden, but posh, it attracted boaters to its safe harbor and vacationers to its ends-of-the-earth sense of escape. Built on the cusp of an earlier U.S. economic collapse, it withered away until a few years back, when new owners bulldozed most of its buildings to start anew, this time as a chic condo resort. Again, enter American economics, so for now the building is stalled at 19 rental town houses, a couple of homes left over from the previous enterprise, a coffee shop-deli, and the massive marina. The resort clasps Powell Pointe, where plans call for 40-some more homes, a golf course where the old one used to be, a pool, and restaurants. Until then, guests can take advantage of kayaking, wind surfing, fishing, and other day excursions out

---

BAHAMA TALK

Tingum: Sort of a combination of "thing" and "um, I can't think of what it's called," it's the Bahamian equivalent of "whatchama-callit."

Cape Eleuthera Resort & Yacht Club.

SOUTH ELEUTHERA'S NEWEST PROPERTY RESTORES CAPE ELEUTHERA TO ITS RIGHTFUL REPUTATION FOR CATERING TO YACHTERS AND VACATIONERS WHO LOVE SECLUSION AT THE BEACH.

to sea, including snorkeling, scuba, and conch diving. The town houses and homes are luxuriously decorated and equipped, but in a style compatible with island living—everything from stainless steel kitchens to flat-screen TVs with DVD players (and free rentals). If you're arriving by air, you should fly into Rock Sound Airport and rent a car—it's a half-hour away. Expensive to Very Expensive.

HOME & CONDO RENTALS
Spanish Wells Harbourside Rentals (242-333-5022; www.spanish wellsharboursiderentals.com) Apartments, cottages, and time-share suites on Spanish Wells.

✳ Where to Eat

Cost categories are based on the range of dinner entrée prices or, if dinner is not served, on lunch entrées. Resort restaurants usually take reservations.

Price Codes

Inexpensive	Up to $15
Moderate	$15 to $25
Expensive	$25 to $35
Very Expensive	$35 or more

For small restaurants, it's a good idea to call ahead to make sure they're open. Often they require that you order your dinner ahead of time from the two or three selections they may offer that evening.

Governor's Harbour
&. **The Bistro** (242-332-3422 or 800-605-9869; www.skybeachclub.com), at Sky Beach Club. Feel like one of the beautiful people no matter what meal you're doing here. Custom designer furnishings scattered along the deck and inside the open-plan restaurant, a view of waters that inspire grace, and a chi-chi infinity pool with seats at the bar: One feels nourished even before ordering. Local catches determine the day's specials: Grab the hog snapper if it's offered. The dinner menu spends

most of its time in the tropics. Smart menu! There's a bit of Asian influence in dishes such as edamame and grilled lamb chops with sweet chili sauce. Entrées, however, tend toward Mediterranean (pan-seared ahi tuna with Mediterranean ragout and seafood linguine) and Caribbean (pan-roasted lobster tail and jerk chicken). Lunch offerings range from cheeseburgers to vegetarian lasagna and steak. Moderate to Expensive. Credit cards have 3 percent fee.

&. ✪ **Tippy's Restaurant, Bar & Beach** (242-332-2221 or 877-677-9539; www.pineapplefields.com/restaurant.html), Banks Rd. at Pineapple Fields resort. You've gotta try a Tippy's Sunrise drink—at least one. Too many, though, and your sun may be setting. Kick off your shoes, dig your toes in the sand, and contemplate the chalkboard menu (or the foolishness of ever leaving this place). Find a spot at a table made from old house shutters beneath one of the clustered gazebos. Selections change daily; try the lobster pizza with caramelized onions in lobster season. Other selections range into creative mode: lobster salad with avocado and roasted peppers, fish cakes, conch bruschetta, pecan-crusted grouper with sweet-sour relish, and coconut crème brûlée. Moderate to Expensive.

Gregory Town

&. **Laughing Lizard Café** (242-470-6992; www.laughinglizardcafe.com), Queen's Hwy. You might find Lenny Kravitz noshing here when he's staying at his place on-island. It has a totally hip, young vibe with its bright colors, comfortable lounging nooks, counter seating, and balcony tables overlooking Gregory Town. Paninis

and wraps are its come-on, and locals rave about the jerk chicken with mango chutney wrap. Specials change daily, with offerings such as Rasta veggie wrap and "smashed Italian panini"—turkey, mozzarella, kalamata olives, tomatoes, and fresh pesto. For dessert, try something insanely rich and wonderful such as warm coconut-chocolate brownie à la mode. On the liquid side, there are smoothies, beer, and wine. Saturday brings dinner-and-a-movie nights (westerns, surf flicks, etc.), with gourmet pizzas such as mozzarella and pesto or The Mexican. Moderate. Serving dinner on Saturday only; closed Sunday.

&. ✪ **Surfers Beach Manor** (242-335-5300; www.surfersmanor.com), off Queen's Hwy. Two cool things in this above-average resort restaurant: the lobster balls and the fighting fish that decorate the glass vases of lucky bamboo at each table. Open to the resort's lobby, it's a casual place that attracts beachgoers as well as hotel guests. Bahamian to the bone, it serves stew fish and conch for breakfast, fried chicken, conch, shrimp, grouper, and lobster (aka lobster balls) for lunch; and a few more far-reaching dinner entrées such as conch or lobster fettuccine, grilled steak, honey barbecued chicken, and a

BAHAMA TALK

Hog snapper: You'll see this deep-water, speared fish on menus as hogfish, hog snapper, or hogfish snapper. Always the hog word, but there's nothing swine-ish about it. Its delicate flavor, in fact, defies such a boorish, or should I say boarish, name.

seafood platter. Signature is the grouper in mushroom sauce. On Sunday, a rake 'n' scrape band plays. Moderate.

Harbour Island
&. ✪ **Sip Sip** (242-333-3316), Court St. Named for the Bahamian word for "gossip," you can also take it to mean drink drink—the Sip Sip Rum Punch, for example, made with pineapple, guava, and passion fruit juices and dark and gold rums. After one of those, the chartreuse walls won't hurt your eyes so much. Focus instead on the local primitive-style art and historic photos. Some of the house specialties, aside from drinking, include hot and spicy conch chili and conch chili cheese dogs. Total American-Bahamian fusion! Other dishes and changing specials introduce different tropical influences: curried chicken salad with mango chutney and green apple, baba ganoush, and lobster quesadilla with chipotle lime crema and tropical salsa, for instance. Do not neglect its famous carrot cake with ginger caramel no matter how full you're feeling. The fave of the young and famous, it crowds early and closes at 4. Moderate. Closed Tuesday year-round and also Wednesday in off-season. Closed late August to just before Thanksgiving.

North Palmetto Point
Sea View Restaurant (242-332-1830 or 877-610-3874; www.uniquevillage .com), at Unique Village. Drink in the view while you quaff a rum punch at the bar, then move into the in-the-round dining area with its vaulted ceiling and generous windows, or opt for the patio, where the ocean below comes into even sharper focus, providing a rhythm section for your dining experience. Breakfast and lunch

offerings are a typical mixture of things conchy and American. Dinner specialties include grilled pork chops, barbecued ribs, baked lamb chops, seafood pasta, vegetable stir-fry, steak Diane, baked salmon, and lobster scampi. During high season (Jan.–May), the restaurant spreads a buffet on Tuesday and Saturday nights, when live musicians come to entertain. Inexpensive to Expensive.

Rock Sound
&. ✪ **Coco Plum Restaurant & Bar** (242-334-2962), Queen's Hwy. Avian, aka "Coco," is one of the main attractions here—he and the on-the-spot conch salad he makes in a little shack across the street. It goes great with a cold Kalik and the conversation of locals who drop by for a to-go cup on their way home in the evenings. With his big laugh and sly humor, Coco keeps the talk lively and sometimes a bit naughty. In the main restaurant, things are slightly more formal. Known for its jerk chicken and pork, it also serves chicken, snapper, cracked conch, shrimp, steak, and lobster in "snack" and dinner portions. Inexpensive to Expensive. No credit cards.### Spanish Wells

The Generation Gap (242-333-4464) Should you decide to check out this unusual little island for the day, stop here for take-out or sit-down lunch. It's plain like most local-yocal Bahamian diners, with counter seating in the front and a small dining area where plastic chairs are as fancy as it gets. Choose from a long list of sandwiches, subs, and burgers, or go for a big meal of chicken, turtle, T-bone steak, lobster tails, or fried pork chops. For the sweet tooth, there's mud pie and chocolate éclairs. Moderate. Closed Sunday. No credit cards.

BAKERIES Arthur's Bakery (242-333-2285), Harbour Island. Fresh bread, pastries, cakes, breakfast croissant sandwiches, banana pancakes, and luncheon salads and sandwiches.

Governor's Harbour Bakery (242-332-2017), Governor's Harbour. Follow your nose to fresh-baked bread and desserts. Don't pass up the homemade conch, beef, and chicken patties.

ISLAND CHARACTER: HENRY SANDS

He began our interview with a strong, strong handshake and ended it with a proposal of marriage.

Cards from Queen Elizabeth and pictures of the royal family and Lord and Lady Brabourne fill the walls and shelves of Henry Sands's cozy little living room in Savannah Sound. His proudest piece frames the wedding invitation to Prince Charles and Lady Diana's wedding in London in 1982.

"I got the invitation and I went with my wife," he remembers. "They had a car for us. I didn't like it very much, because it was like you had a dream, and when you woke up, it was over," he finishes with his sly sense of fun.

How did a bread baker come to be invited to St. Paul's Cathedral for a royal wedding? It all started with the bread.

Lord and Lady Brabourne discovered the warm, sweet bread Henry and his wife baked on one of their first visits to Eleuthera. So naturally, when they made arrangements for Charles and Di's stays in the 1980s, they introduced Henry to the newlyweds, and he became the official royal Eleutheran baker.

HENRY SANDS, BAKER AND BUDDY TO THE ROYAL FAMILY.

"When my wife was here, she'd bake the bread. Prince Charles would come here and eat bread here," he says, gesturing to his humble home.

Henry still hears from Queen Elizabeth and Prince Charles almost every year. "If he writes to me he don't get his secretary to sign it. He sign it."

Kathy's Bakery (242-333-4405), Spanish Wells. Pies, cakes, and other desserts.

Miss Gibson (242-332-2932), Savannah Sound, South Eleuthera. Call ahead to order her coconut or pineapple (or half-and-half) tart—a cakelike pastry smeared with fruit and topped with pretty dough lattice.

✪ **Sands Bakery** (242-332-6143), Savannah Sound, South Eleuthera. Home of the "Prince Loaf"—fresh bread and rolls once favored by Prince Charles and Lady Di on visits to the island.

COFFEE Bahama Coffee Company (242-334-8500), Cape Eleuthera Resort & Yacht Club. Good steaming hot coffee and espresso, pastries, desserts, sandwiches, and pizza.

GROCERS The Marketplace (242-334-2254), Rock Sound, South Eleuthera. Stop at this modern complex between the airport and heading south to Cape Eleuthera. Buy all your groceries and other necessities. There's also a liquor store.

TAKE-OUT South of Rock Sound, take-out joints are all you can find as far as prepared food. North Eleuthera offers more in the way of sit-down dining, but still has its preferred take-out places, some of them in unmarked homes that only the locals know about, so ask around.

✪ **Cush's Place** (242-335-5301), Queen's Hwy., between Gregory Town and Hatchet Bay. Home-cooked Bahamian and American dishes.

✳ Selective Shopping

More known for its outdoors pleasures than its shopping treasures, Eleuthera does have some fun shops, particularly in Harbour Island and Governor's Harbour.

Bay Street Market, Harbour Island. Vendors selling straw items, fruits, vegetables, fish, and more in stalls that line the waterfront.

Blue Rooster (242-333-2240), Dunmore St., Harbour Island. Luxury boutique featuring delicate tunics, island scarves, colorful bathing suits, exotic jewelry, and shoes. Also offers household accessories. Pricey but nice.

Briland Androsia (242-333-2342), Bay St., Harbour Island. Clothing and household accessories made from brightly dyed Androsia batik, the Bahamas' official national fabric.

Dilly Dally (242-333-3109), King and Dunmore Streets, Harbour Island. Colorful outside and in with pottery, photography, T-shirts, and other arts and souvenirs.

Dornell's Treasures (242-332-2932), Governor's Harbour. It carries the paintings and straw work of Dorothy Rahming and other crafts and souvenirs.

✪ **Island Made Shop** (242-335-5369), Queen's Highway, Gregory Town. A fun selection of Bahamian arts and crafts, Androsia batiks, Abaco ceramics, conch shell crafts, and more, including the glasswork and driftwood jewelry of owner Pam Thompson, who likes to claim that she's half-mermaid.

Salt Water Boutique (242-335-0294), Rainbow Bay. Features a colorful assortment of island apparel: tunics, swimwear, beach cover-ups, flip-flops, and homemade jewelry.

✳ Special Events

○ *June:* **Pineapple Festival,** Gregory Town. First week of the month. The island's biggest event, it celebrates Eleuthera's pineapple growing with yummy pineapple dishes, music, and more.

October: **North Eleuthera Sailing Regatta** (242-333-2275 or 242-333-2621), Harbour Island. Six days early in the month. In the water, Class A, B, and C boats race the wind while live band performances, cultural shows, and Bahamian cooking happens onshore.

December: **Junkanoo** (242-332-2141), Harbour Island, Rock Sound, and Tarpum Bay. Dec. 26. Bahamians continue to party the day after Christmas with a don't-sleep, party-'til-you-drop form of energy called Junkanoo. A throwback to slavery days, it's a noisy parade of bands and brightly costumed revelers.

Exuma 8

GEORGE TOWN

WILLIAMS TOWN

EMERALD BAY

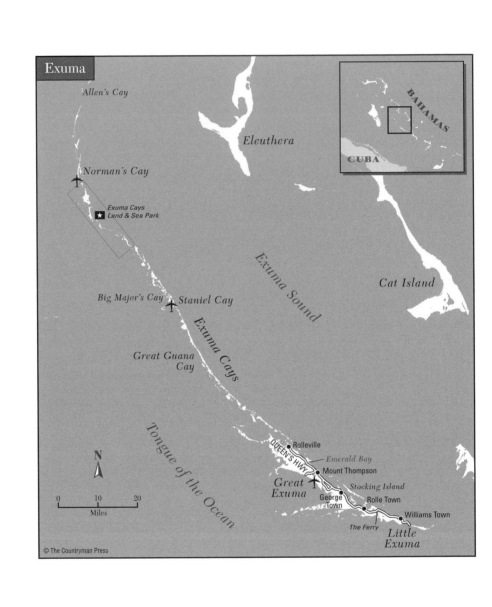

Exuma

Allen's Cay

Eleuthera

BAHAMAS

CUBA

Norman's Cay

*Exuma Cays
Land & Sea Park*

Exuma Sound

Cat Island

Big Major's Cay Staniel Cay

Exuma Cays

Great Guana
Cay

Tongue of the Ocean

N

0   10   20
Miles

Rolleville
QUEEN'S HWY
Emerald Bay
Mount Thompson
Great
Exuma
George
Town
Stocking Island
Rolle Town
Williams Town
The Ferry *Little
Exuma*

© The Countryman Press

EXUMA

SO MANY ISLES, SO LITTLE TIME

"There were more clumps, the ink splashes of sea eggs, crowds of small glittering reef fish, a small forest of sea fans that beckoned and waved with the ebb and the flow like the hair of drowned women."

—*Ian Fleming in* Thunderball

It was Friday night and sleepy George Town finally woke up. Wait, make that Friday afternoon: Exumans don't wait until dark to celebrate the conclusion of their workweek. The party started around 2 PM, I noticed as I walked to the corner liquor store to survey the selection. Maurice, a charming bloke I had met earlier on a vacation home construction site, threw his arm around my shoulder, called me "baby," and insisted on buying me a bottle of his favorite cabernet sauvignon.

I had already caught onto that "baby" thing—a term of affection rather than derision among the Bahamians, but hadn't yet been enlightened as to the tradition of Exuma men and their offers to buy drinks. Where I live, it means they expect something. Where they live, it means a gesture of gleeful largesse, gallantry, and sighing relief that it's Friday. I tactfully turned Maurice down, but it wasn't the final offer of the evening.

I'm all about meeting the weekend with a cheer and a toast, but I had been in Exuma for only a couple of days, and I was already so relaxed I hadn't realized Friday had arrived until I stepped out onto George Town's one street.

There's not a lot of sightseeing on the island to get in the way of serious languish, and the drop-dead gorgeous beaches invite quiet reclining, mental defragmenting, and deep exhaling (often known as snoozing). A 60-mile-long stretch of some 365 islands and cays at Nassau's southeastern doorstep, the Exumas have long been a secret of the yachting and angling crowds, crazy about the chain's profusion of safe harbors and bona fide bonefishing. Annual spring sailing regattas fill the harbor around **George Town** with sailors from all corners of the planet, and services in the capital city focus on their needs. Outside of George

Town on **Great Exuma,** the largest of the isles, bridged to **Little Exuma** in the south, lodges cater to hard-core anglers in search of the enigmatic "gray ghost fish," as the flats-dwelling bonefish is known.

In recent years, Exuma's secret has leaked out. Since the opening of Four Seasons (now a Sandals resort) on the north end of Great Exuma in 2003, the islands register on the radar of travelers looking for some serious escape. Sandals occupies the most gorgeous of the island's many beaches, **Emerald Bay,** which succinctly describes the color of its breeze-whipped waters.

In Little Exuma's hushed, historic **Williams Town,** cotton plantations and salt-raking once earned livelihood. Ruins of The Hermitage plantation manor and an unmarked secluded beach, where you can step into the Tropic of Cancer, bring a dribble of visitors across a one-lane bridge at a settlement known as **The Ferry** (because a ferry made the crossing prebridge), through time-stilled villages to this southernmost point.

The true Bahama experience lies between the two extremes of Emerald Bay and Williams Town around George Town, a capital city with about 350 people and no traffic lights. The island's old-style resorts huddle around, giving visitors an opportunity to mingle and experience Out Island lifestyles.

George Town is an easy-to-walk village convenient to Government Dock. Beaching, kayaking, snorkeling, fishing, and boating fill lazy days on Great Exuma. George Town's local eateries and resort clubs while away the evenings with local bands and Bahamian eats. Different resorts and clubs take turns hosting live entertainment, so there's something going on most nights.

EXUMA CAYS LAND AND SEA PARK OFFERS ADVENTURE BY SEA AND TRAILS TO EXPLORE ON SOME OF THE CAYS.
Bahamas Ministry of Tourism.

Exumans like to say they have an island for every day of the year. Some are privately owned, a few by celebrities such as Faith Hill, Tim McGraw, and Johnny Depp. One, **Musha Cay,** holds a private-island resort. Others are accessible to island-hoppers and hold unusual surprises such as Thunderball Grotto, named for the Bond movie filmed here (**Staniel Cay**), ruins of a reputedly haunted castle (**Darby Island**), a herd of wild pigs that swim out to meet approaching boats (**Big Major Cay**), iguanas galore (**Allen's Cay**), an NOAA research facility (**Lee Stocking Island**), and the beach filming location for *Pirates of the Caribbean* (**Sandy Cay**). Many of the islands are preserved under the national park umbrella as **Exuma Cays Land & Sea Park.**

BAHAMA TALK

Snack: Many Bahamian restaurant menus designate snack- and dinner-sized meals. "Snack" usually means smaller portions and without all the side dishes that come with a dinner—peas 'n' rice, salad or coleslaw, and baked macaroni and cheese.

With its Loyalist plantation roots, Exuma's past mimics that of a lot of other Bahama islands. One British subject in particular impacted local history and nomenclature. The English government awarded Denys Rolle 7,000 acres on the island. He and later his son, Lord John Rolle, built the island's largest cotton plantation with 325 slaves. In the end, the plantation failed, and Rolle left his property and surname to his slaves. Today their descendants occupy the towns of Rolleville, Rolle Town, and Mount Thompson—generational land that anyone with the last name Rolle (which accounts for about half of the island's population) is allowed to build upon.

DON'T MISS

- A trip to Stocking Island for beaching or hangin' at Chat 'N' Chill.
- Island-hopping to Exuma Cays Land and Sea Park and beyond.
- Fish Fry outside of George Town.
- Snorkeling or diving a blue hole or reef.
- A drive to Little Exuma to eat Johnny Depp's favorite conch fritters and explore the island's past.

SUGGESTED READING *The Exuma Guide: A Cruising Guide to the Exuma Cays: Approaches, Routes, Anchorages, Dive Sights, Flora, Fauna, History, and Lore of the Exuma Cays,* by Stephen J. Pavlidis (Paperback; 2007).

Thunderball, by Ian Fleming. The book doesn't refer directly to Exuma, but the James Bond movie it inspired was filmed in these islands.

✻ To See

MUSEUMS & HISTORIC SITES Crab Cay Ruins, Crab Cay, one mile southeast of George Town. The gardens steal the show at this 18th-century plantation. Owner William Walker, who once represented Exuma in the House of Assembly, planted exotic trees and plants such as breadfruit, cinnamon, Chinese tallow, Spanish chestnut, and mango. Stone columns on both sides of the island mark the entrance to the ruins.

Hermitage Estate Ruins, Williams Town, Little Exuma. A reminder of the Exuma's short-lived cotton plantation era, it includes the foundation of the manor and four tombs dating back

BAHAMA TALK

Dilly crabs: In the Exumas, they call their land crabs by this name because of their preferred diet of "dilly," aka sapodilla—a sweet fruit that tastes like brown sugar and whose bark sap, chicle, puts the snap in chewing gum.

to the 18th century, when the Ferguson family relocated here from the Carolinas. One tomb marks the grave of family member Henderson Ferguson (1772-1825), two others bear other names, and one unmarked grave is believed to be that of a slave.

MUSIC & NIGHTLIFE Just north of town, **Fish Fry** is a hot spot. A jumble of Bahamian beachside shacks serve fish, barbecue, beer, and Bahama Mamas to islanders and visitors 'til midnight or so. Money spends as freely as the rum flows while everyone tries to buy the next round for the ladies. It doesn't take long to shed your homeland mores, loosen up, and sigh in total appreciation of people who know how to wind down in a way that's easily contagious. On Monday nights, there's usually a rake 'n' scrape band.

Club Peace & Plenty (242-336-2552; www.peaceandplenty.com), Queen's Hwy., George Town. DJ music and barbecue in the outdoor poolside bar Friday nights, live jam sessions Wednesday and Saturday nights, live Bahamian musicians Sunday nights.

Eddie's Edgewater (242-336-2050), George Town. Rake 'n' scrape band Mondays, jerk and DJ music Fridays.

✳ To Do

BEST BEACHES ✪ **Stocking Island,** Elizabeth Harbour. The Peace & Plenty hotel's ferry shuttle delivers beachgoers ($10 for nonguests) to this offshore beach, minutes away but soundly removed from worldly worries. The hotel maintains a beach club there with an ultracasual restaurant. Grab a conch burger and plant yourself along the 2-mile beach. Ferries and charters from Government Dock take you to amiable Chat 'N' Chill, the ultimate yachties haunt at the island's south end—on the other side of a hill and shallow pool of water from the Peace & Plenty beach. You can rent a sailboat in town to go on your own and explore Hurricane Hole along the way. Be sure to pack snorkel equipment.

Other beautiful beaches include the **Tropic of Cancer Beach** in Little Exuma, **Three Sisters Beach** at Mount Thompson, **Sandy Cay** (site of *Pirates of the Caribbean* filming), and **Exuma Cays Land and Sea Park.** Norman's Cay boasts 10 miles of untrammeled beach where you can grab a cocktail or lunch at **Norman's Cay Beach Club at MacDuff's** (242-357-8846).

FISHING As on most Bahama Out Islands, bonefish is the quarry. The Exumas boast a number of certified bonefish guides such as **Alston "Rambo" Rolle** (242-345-5555), **Barraterre Bonefish Lodge** (242-355-5052), and **Steve Ferguson** (242-345-0153). For deep-sea fishing in Exuma Sound, **Fish Charters** (242-357-0870) can take up to six people to find marlin, sailfish, and wahoo.

GOLFING Sandals Emerald Reef Golf Club (888-SANDALS; www.sandals .com), Emerald Bay. One of the Out Islands' two golf courses, this 18-hole championship course was designed by Greg Norman. It is open to the public, but be prepared to pay the big green. It also has a driving range and rentals.

Bahamas Ministry of Tourism.

THE SPORT OF FLY-FISHING FOR BONEFISH HAS HELPED EXUMA MAKE IT BIG ON SPORTSMEN'S RADAR.

WATER SPORTS *Anchorages:* Government Dock in George Town is an official port of entry.

Exuma Docking Services (242-336-2578), Kidd Cove, Great Exuma. Full service with 52 slips, groceries, laundry facilities, showers, and a restaurant.

Staniel Cay Marina (242-355-2024), Staniel Cay. Small (18 slips), but complete with everything from fuel and water to groceries and a restaurant.

Day Cruising: **Off Island Adventures** (242-524-0524) Capt. Steven Cole will take you on snorkeling, sight-seeing, and other excursions that can last from two hours to an entire day.

Reggae Boat Adventures (242-524-4039; reggaeboatadventures.com), based at Chat 'N' Chill on Stocking Island and Beach Inn Exuma on Great Exuma. Day island-hopping trips to Sandy, Staniel, and Big Major Cays.

Starfish the Exuma Adventure Center (242-336-3033 or 541-359-1496 (U.S.); www.starfishexuma.com), George Town, Great Exuma. Its Sunday Chat 'N' Chill Tour stops at a blue hole and cave for snorkeling en route to the pig roast on Stocking Island.

Paddling & Ecotours: **Starfish the Exuma Adventure Center** (242-336-3033 or 541-359-1496 (U.S.); www.starfishexuma.com), George Town, Great Exuma. Kayaking rentals and tours into Elizabeth Harbour and to a national park on Moriah Cay. Also full-moon excursions.

Powerboat Rentals: **Minns Water Sports** (242-336-3483), George Town. Rents boats 15 to 20 feet and can provide dockage and storage for boat owners. Also has a marine store.

Sailboat Rentals: **Starfish the Exuma Adventure Center** (242-336-3033 or 541-359-1496 (U.S.); www.starfishexuma.com), George Town, Great Exuma.

Sandals Emerald Bay

OCEAN VIEWS ADD THE LUXE OF GOLFING SANDALS' TWO COURSES.

Rent a Hobie Wave for an excursion to Stocking Island and beyond. Rentals available by the half day, full day, and week.

Snorkeling & Diving: On the east side, the barrier reef wall drops thousands of feet. To the west and leeward, the shallower waters of the Great Bahama Bank provide a different sort of reef diving experience. Some of the islands' most popular dive sites include the blue hole **Thunderball Grotto** (which appeared in the eponymous Bond flick), **Stocking Island Mystery Cave,** the wreck of the *Austin Smith,* the **Exuma and Pillar walls, Angel Fish Blue Hole,** and a number of reefs: **Dog Rocks, Wax Cut Drift, Whale Shark Reef,** and **Sharks Amberjack Reef.** Some dive operations specialize in lobster harvesting and stingray dives.

Snorkeling excursions take in the marine life-rich waters of **Exuma Land and Sea Park,** where fishing is prohibited.

Charters: **Dive Exuma** (242-357-0313; www.dive-exuma.com), Peace & Plenty Inn, George Town, Great Exuma Island. Snorkeling and diving excursions in and around Elizabeth Harbour include blue holes, wrecks, walls, and sharks.

Starfish the Exuma Adventure Center (242-336-3033 or 541-359-1496 (U.S.); www.starfishexuma.com), George Town, Great Exuma. Snorkeling excursions to various reefs, blue holes, and other sites include free use of gear and transportation from hotel.

WILDLIFE SPOTTING Rent or charter a boat to visit the colony of native iguanas on Allen's Cay. Birding is high sport on other boat-accessible cays, particularly in the **Exuma Cays Land and Sea Park** (contact Ray Darville at 242-359-1821), a cluster of a dozen or so small, uninhabited islands stretching from Wax Cay Cut in the north to Conch Cay Cut in the south. Established in 1958, it was the first of its kind in the world and became a no-fishing zone in 1986. You'll also see iguanas on some of these cays, which are also habitat for a rare, large rodent known as the Bahama hutia. Unfortunately, some of the unique wildlife spotting experiences here and elsewhere in the Bahamas are due to feeding wild animals. At Compass Cay, for instance, tamed sharks swarm under the dock, waiting to be fed. On Big Major Cay, wild pigs swim out to greet approaching boats for the same reason.

Nature Preserves & Eco-Attractions: **Moriah Harbour Cay National Park,** offshore between Great and Little Exuma. The Bahamas National Trust has preserved 13,440 acres here as vital bird-nesting habitat. Along its beaches, mangrove creeks, and sea grass beds, terns, nighthawks, plovers, ospreys, and oystercatchers nest. Access is by boat only, and local operators lead kayak excursions to the island.

✷ Lodging

Winter to spring is high season for Exuma, and resort rates reflect supply and demand. They are highest around holidays and during Regatta Week in April, especially in and around George Town.

(An asterisk after the pricing designation indicates that the rate includes at least a continental breakfast in the cost of lodging and possibly more extensive meal service as noted in the listing.)

Price Codes

Inexpensive	Up to $100
Moderate	$100 to $200
Expensive	$200 to $300
Very Expensive	$300 and up

ACCOMMODATIONS

Emerald Bay

Grand Island Resort and Spa
(242-358-5000 or 888-472-6310; www
.grandisleresort.com) One of the
island's newest and most luxurious

ISLAND-HOPPING THROUGH THE CAYS OF EXUMA LAND AND SEA PARK IS A FAVORITE PASTIME. VISITORS CHARTER A BOAT OR RENT THEIR OWN FOR THE ADVENTURE.

Bahamas Ministry of Tourism.

resorts is situated on arguably Great Exuma's most beautiful beach. Its 78 two-story villas range from one to four bedrooms and are nothing short of elegant. You'll need for nothing here, where DVD players, wireless Internet, full kitchens, and washers and dryers take care of creature comforts. A restaurant and full-service spa raise the comfort level another notch. Guests can play the nearby 18-hole golf course at Sandals. Beach bums will find their happy place. Water sports enthusiasts can snorkel the resort's underwater trail, kayak, sign on for a fishing trip, or hop aboard the tour boat to explore the nearby cays. Very Expensive.

⚟ **Sandals Emerald Bay** (888-SANDALS; www.sandals.com) Formerly a Four Seasons Hotel, this Sandals climbs a clear rung above some of the brand's other Caribbean resorts as part of the company's new Sandals Luxury Included brand. Two of the 500-acre all-inclusive's best features are its butlers, trained to the

standards of the Guild of Professional English Butlers, and its complimentary scuba diving. Sequestered on a fantasy half-moon beach miles from George Town, it nonetheless provides all of its guests' needs with five restaurants, an 18-hole Greg Norman golf course, six Har-Tru tennis courts, a 150-slip marina, three pools, a full spa, wind surfing, snorkeling, and other water sports. (Spa treatments, golfing, private pool cabanas, and island tours cost extra.) The restaurants serve Italian, Bahamian, and other global cuisines, all included in the rates along with unlimited Beringer wine and premium brand drinks. Room service is also available 24 hours to its 183 units, which range from rooms and suites to beachfront villas, all luxuriously decorated with all the modern conveniences, including iPod decking systems. Very Expensive.°

The Ferry
⚟ ✪ **Peace & Plenty Bonefish Lodge** (242-345-5555; www.ppbone

BRIGHT, WHITE SAND SETS OFF THE PASTEL, CARIBBEAN-STYLE ACCOMMODATIONS AT SANDALS.

Sandals Emerald Bay

fishlodge.net), Queen's Hwy. Only the fishing-frenzied need apply. Like most Bahama bonefishing lodges, this is parked far from other resorts or restaurants. Guests spend days out on the water casting away to their hearts' content. Ergo, its eight rooms are on the plain side of fancy, but roomy and boasting private balconies with views of the water. Don't expect phones or a TV in the room, but they do provide Wi-Fi access. Head to the lodge if you need a TV fix; that's where most of the off-the-water-action takes place anyway. It has a true lodge feel, complete with wood siding. It holds the dining room, honor bar, library, dart board, pool table, poker table, and a table for tying flies. There's also a saltwater swimming pool, kayaks, and bicycles. Staff can arrange anything from car rentals to scuba diving, just in case you want to bring along a non-fishing type. Most guests opt for fishing packages of three days or more, which include meals. Expensive. Closed late June through October.

George Town

Augusta Bay (242-336-2251 or 800-525-2210; www.augustabaybahamas .com), Queen's Hwy. Recently renovated to top luxury (with a change of name from Exuma Beach Inn), the 16 rooms of this resort look out onto a narrow strip of beach lapped by waters in gemstone shades. Beautifully decorated, the rooms feature stone tiled floors, glass-encased rain showers, pillow-top mattresses, down comforters, and myriad other special touches and comforts. Air-conditioning and paddle fans keep it cool indoors, while kayaking, snorkeling, sailing, and a pool make it cool to be outside. Its restaurant is full-service and laundry service is available. Expensive.

✪ **Club Peace & Plenty** (242-336-2552 or 800-525-2210; www.peace andplenty.com), Queen's Hwy. The island's first and one of its finest hotels, it's right in the thick of activity in George Town, overlooking Elizabeth Harbour. Named for Lord Denys Rolle's British trading ship that made the voyage to Exuma in 1783, it dates back to colonial days. The grand nephew of Florida railroad builder Henry Flagler first built a hotel on the spot. Today, its 29 rooms and three suites offer a bit of charm and all the modern conveniences. Leman "Doc" Rolle tends the outdoor pool bar and has for as long as anyone can remember. Every Monday the resort throws a party here for its guests. People from all over the island come for a lively evening of entertainment at Friday night barbecue and at Wednesday, Saturday, and Sunday nights' jam sessions. The inside air-conditioned bar in the property's historic slave kitchen was the scene of a live broadcast of Johnny Depp accepting the People's Choice Award in 2006. The resort's restaurant serves some of the finest cuisine on the island. Moderate to Very Expensive.

"♫" **Coconut Cove Hotel** (242-336-2659; www.exumabahamas.com/coconutcove.html), Queen's Hwy. One of the most affordable options for beachfront accommodations on Great Exuma, it has a nice, intimate, easygoing vibe enhanced by its casual Sandbar poolside bar. Breakfast and dinner are served in the main dining room Wednesday through Sunday. The 11 guest rooms either face the beach or are steps away. All have refrigerators, air-conditioning, TV, Wi-Fi, and bathrobes, but no phones. The Paradise Suite (Expensive) is roomier, with a private terrace and oversized bathroom with a black marble Jacuzzi. Moderate.

Palm Bay Beach Club (242-336-2787 or 888-396-0606; www.palmbay beachclub.com), Queen's Hwy. Envisioning a perfect Bahamian village with bungalows and villas painted the colors of local flora, Palm Bay Beach Club is as ideal for a romantic couple as a family, with its span of 70 studios to three-bedroom villas, all sunny and modern in décor. They cluster around the pool and popular Splash restaurant and bar, and across the street and up a hillside for more privacy. All have kitchen facilities of some sort, plus telephones and TVs. The resort is a mile from George Town, and a free shuttle takes you there and back.

FOLKS TRAVEL BY GOLF CART AROUND TINY STANIEL CAY.
Bahamas Ministry of Tourism.

A sandy beach, kayaks, and Hobie Cats entice guests out to enjoy the inimitably clear waters of Exuma. Moderate to Very Expensive.

Staniel Cay

☝ Staniel Cay Yacht Club (242-355-2024 or 954-467-8920 (U.S.); www.stanielcay.com), Queen's Hwy. An island getaway in every sense of the word, this property occupies a tiny island less than a mile wide, and is within walking distance to its settlement. Golf carts are available for rent if you'd prefer not to walk. By-boat is the preferred mode of transportation, and if you opt for the all-inclusive rate, you have free use of a Boston Whaler (including fuel) and an ocean kayak. All meals and airport transportation are also included with the package, but not bar drinks or snacks. The island has its own private airstrip, and many guests arrive by private plane or boat. They stay in the nine different colored cottages recently renovated and equipped with wireless Internet access, but no phones or TVs. Kayu Maya is a luxury villa that holds up to eight guests (Very Expensive; includes golf carts and other sporting concessions). A full-service marina accommodates 18 boats, plus there's a pool, sand beach, and plenty of tours and diving excursions to while away the days. Moderate to Expensive.

HOME & CONDO RENTALS February Point Resort Estates (242-336-2693 or 877-839-4253; www.februarypoint.com), Queen's Hwy., George Town. Some 40 villas from two- to six-bedroom are available to rent in this 42-home community. Guests enjoy use of its fitness center, tennis courts, pool, and restaurant.

✳ Where to Eat

Cost categories are based on the range of dinner entrée prices or, if dinner is not served, on lunch entrées.

Price Codes

Inexpensive	Up to $15
Moderate	$15 to $25
Expensive	$25 to $35
Very Expensive	$35 or more

Resort restaurants usually take reservations. For small restaurants, it's a good idea to call ahead to make sure they're open. Often they require that you order your dinner ahead of time from the two or three selections they may offer that evening.

George Town

⅃ **Cheater's Restaurant & Bar** (242-336-2335), Great Exuma. One of the more formal nonresort restaurants on the islands, Cheater's sets a pretty table with floral tablecloths covered with glass and brocade napkins. Steaks, including a juicy porterhouse, are a specialty, but its nightly changing menu also does due justice to the local seafood with grouper, lobster, and garlic shrimp. Call ahead for the night's menu and to order your entrée. Save room (you'll need it) for the luscious rum cake or, when available, tuxedo cheesecake with caramel. The local place got its name from an islander who ran so fast in high school, they nicknamed him "Chee-tah." Evidently he fared better in sports than in academics because he didn't know how to spell that, and the rest is Exuman culinary history. Moderate to Expensive. No credit cards. Reservations required.

⅃ **Club Peace & Plenty** (242-336-2552 or 800-525-2210; www.peaceand plenty.com), Great Exuma. George Town's top option as far as cuisine and ambiance, Club Peace & Plenty breaks out of the Out Island mold with specialties such as sweet-and-sour chicken, Danish babyback ribs, French rack of lamb, and porterhouse steak. For local treats, try the fresh grouper prepared to your liking, conch in spicy tomato sauce, or guava upside-down cake. Rattan chairs and rock walls accent the bright setting with its white wood vaulted ceiling and windowed doors out to the pool deck. Moderate to Expensive. Reservations suggested.

❂ **Sam's Place** (242-336-2579), Great Exuma. Sam Gray is a big name on this island, and this is his place. You'll see him breakfasting at his reserved table every morning, which is a good time to go for some traditional Bahamian eye-openers such as an excellent stew fish and fresh johnnycake, boil' fish, souse, or tuna and grits as well as omelets and other Americanized dishes. The locals are lined up for their take-out orders, so you know you've hit a winner. Lunch is more typical with sandwiches, burgers, and salads. Moderate.

Ramsey

⅃ **Iva Bowe's Central Highway Inn** (242-345-7014), Great Exuma. Legendary for its best-of-the-best native cuisine, this is a good place to stop before or after the airport. Nothing like a good home-cooked meal in a totally Out Island setting to start or end your vacation. Iva marinates her conch in lime juice before deep-frying it to add to its tenderness and appeal. Other favorites include coconut beer shrimp and spicy Cajun shrimp (call in advance to order either), lobster linguine, garlic snapper, and shrimp scampi. Moderate. No credit cards. Closed Sunday.

Stocking Island

Chat 'N' Chill (242-336-2700 or 954-323-8668 (U.S.); www.chatnchill.com), Great Exuma. Native Exuman Kenneth "KB" Bowe is host and cook at this boat-in haven that has been welcoming boaters, diners, chatters, and chillers since 1998. You can catch a five-minute water taxi from Government Dock and spend the day snorkeling and funning, or rent a boat and make it part of a day's island-hopping. With the beach right outside the door and a full all-day menu of happy meals from hot dogs to conch salad, conch burgers, grilled fish, and barbecued ribs, you'll have plenty to balance your intake of Kalik beers, guava daiquiris, and Bahama Mamas. Sunday's pig roasts start at noon with a spread of pulled pork, peas 'n' rice, KB's famous garlic slaw, and more ($20 per plate). Volleyball begins at 2:30 daily, or whenever there's enough for a game. Dolphins and stingrays swim with you in the sandy-bottomed, crystalline waters. Inexpensive. No credit cards.

BAKERIES Mom's Bakery (no phone), George Town. You'll see this van parked in the middle of town loaded with bread, pastries, and meat patties.

GROCERS Smitty's Convenience Store (242-336-2144), Hoopers Bay. Snacks, groceries, and the usual array of necessities.

TAKE-OUT ✪ Stop at seaside cabana **Santana's Grill** (242-345-4102) in Williams Town, which anyone will tell you makes the finest conch fritters in Exuma. It was a favorite hangout for Johnny Depp, they say, while he was in the islands in 2005 filming sequels to *Pirates of the Caribbean.*

✹ Selective Shopping

Exuma Straw Market, George Town. 'Neath the shade of an ample ficus tree, locals sell souvenirs.

Sandpiper Arts & Crafts (242-336-2084), Queen's Hwy., George Town, Great Exuma. A higher quality of souvenirs than you'll find at the straw market: It sells art, batik clothing, books, and cards.

✹ Special Events

◉ *Every Month:* **People-To-People Teas** (242-336-2430) On the last Friday of each month, island guests are invited to this event to learn about local culture through bush medicine, musical, culinary, and other demonstrations. The location changes every month, so check with your hotel.

March: **Bahamian Music and Heritage Festival,** Regatta Park, George Town. Nine days starting midmonth. Get to know Exuma's past through its music and cultural festivities. **George Town Cruising Regatta** (242-336-2430), George Town. Midmonth. Regatta season kicks off with this weeklong racing event, which attracts more than 500 yachts from outside the area.

April: **National Family Island Regatta** (242-345-6163 or 242-336-3766), Elizabeth Harbour, George Town. Five days at the end of month. This 60-year-old regatta pays homage to the Bahamas' rich boatbuilding heritage and includes a race for junior boatbuilders. There's lots of sailing by day and partying by night.

May: **Farmer's Cay Conch Festival** (242-355-4006 or 242-355-4017) Third Saturday. Cooking and conch-blowing competitions, live entertainment.

July: **Independence Day Celebration** (242-336-2430), Roker's Point. July 10. Traditional Bahamian activities such a plaiting the maypole, climbing the grease pole, and relishing native food prevail.

August: **Rolleville Regatta and Homecoming** (242-336-2430), Rolleville. Emancipation Day weekend. Beside boat races, islands compete in talent contests, a fun run, and more.

Long Island

DEADMAN'S CAY

CLARENCE TOWN

STELLA MARIS

ONEIL'S

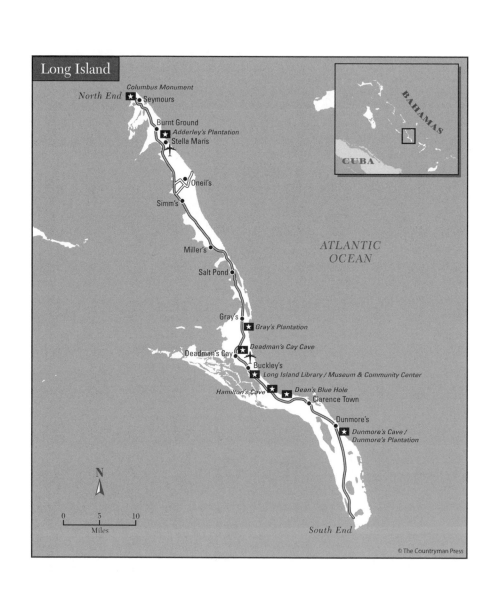

Long Island

North End

Columbus Monument
Seymours

Burnt Ground
Adderley's Plantation
Stella Maris

Oneil's

Simm's

Miller's

Salt Pond

Gray's
Gray's Plantation

Deadman's Cay
Deadman's Cay Cave
Buckley's
Long Island Library / Museum & Community Center

Hamilton's Cave
Dean's Blue Hole
Clarence Town

Dunmore's
Dunmore's Cave /
Dunmore's Plantation

ATLANTIC
OCEAN

BAHAMAS

CUBA

N

0   5   10
Miles

South End

© The Countryman Press

LONG ISLAND

KEEPER OF TRADITION

First impressions: From the sky it looked like an oasis in the middle of the desert. With the water so shallow and clear on its leeward side, it became invisible, leaving only sand bottom to make that initial impact. Its stretch profile confirmed its name, but the sparseness of settlement surprised me. As we floated into the Deadman's Cay airport, I spotted first the white steeples of a church, then a school bus, a few banana groves whose broad, flat leaves stood out against the blur of bush, and houses in different stages of completion. (In the Bahama Out Islands, people don't take mortgages out to build a house, they work on it in dribs and drabs as their paychecks allow.)

The plane was full that day—people from around the world arriving for the free dive competition held semiannually in its 663-foot-deep blue hole, an island icon Long Islanders proudly claim to be the deepest inland blue hole in the world. Who am I to argue? In South Eleuthera, they claim no one knows how deep theirs is. On Long Island, Jacques Cousteau himself once plumbed its depth and after 600 feet

LONG ISLAND REMEMBERS ERAS GONE BY WITH AN EXTENSIVE SELECTION OF PLANTATION RUINS.

proclaimed there was no bottom. Later, researchers dropped a measure to come up with current official reading. I do know one thing: It's about the prettiest blue hole I've seen in all the Bahamas.

Aside from its limestone sinkhole, Long Island culls its identity from a time-mired island way of life that includes raising goats and sheep, weaving basketry the old-fashioned way, storytelling, and other age-old arts.

Originally called Yuma by the Lucayans, it got its name change from Columbus, who dubbed it Fernandina Island when he stopped here on his first visit to the New World in 1492. He also called it "the most beautiful island in the world."

At 80 miles long (4 miles at widest) and 80 churches full, it has an average of one church per mile—mostly Anglican, followed by Baptist and Catholic. Its 3,400 people occupy 35 settlements in North Long Island and South Long Island. Loyalty to being a north islander or a south islander is nearly as fierce as among the U.S.'s northerners and southerners. Churches further the separation: In the north they're trimmed in red; in the south, blue. Islanders even use the term "Deep South" to refer to settlements down around **Gordons** and **Mortimer.**

The main southern towns of **Deadman's Cay** and **Clarence Town** are the island's biggest and prettiest with their groomed gardens, but most of the resort business lies to the north, particularly in **Stella Maris.** The off-road settlement of **Oneil's** is worth a stop to visit the shops of the island's traditional straw plaiters. **Salt Pond,** the north's main town, is home of Government Dock and the annual regatta. In between the settlements, huge mango trees, poincianas, frangipani, tamarind trees, bougainvillea, sea grapes, and jumby trees flourish.

Long Island's economic patterns followed that of most Out Islands: Loyalists, cotton plantations, failed crops, emancipation, farming, and fishing. In the town of **Hard Bargain,** Morton Salt once operated a salt plant. Farmers here, however, began raising sheep and goats early on, and continue to do so today. They also

GOAT FARMING REMAINS AN IMPORTANT ECONOMIC AND HERITAGE INDICATOR FOR LONG ISLANDERS.

grow ground crops, which the mailboat picks up once a week at the government dock to take to Nassau.

The southernmost of the Bahamas' major islands, Long Island lies 160 miles southeast of Nassau, and crosses the Tropic of Cancer. It has some of the Bahamas' most ideal weather, warmed by the Gulf Stream in winter and cooled by trade winds in summer. Visitors come mainly for the diving and reef and bonefishing, but then discover its culture—one of the most intact of the Bahamas.

Although there's talk of a new big development called Port St. George in Stella Maris, Long Island promises to cling tightly to the traditions of its elders as they pass them from generation to generation on an island that tricks the eyes when seen from above, one's sense of time when experienced at ground level.

DON'T MISS 41. A dip into Deal's Blue Hole and beach time.
42. Conch salad at Max's.
43. The churches of Clarence Town.
44. The straw plaiters of Oneil's.
45. Cave spelunking.

✸ To See

CHURCHES & RELIGIOUS SITES St. Mary's Church, The Bight. The Spaniards built the island's oldest church, a Catholic one, in the 18th century. Catholics turned it over to the Anglicans after a tidal wave destroyed it.

❂ St. Paul's Anglican Church (242-337-3002), Clarence Town. Built by Father Jerome Hawes, the priest most famous for his Hermitage religious retreat site on Cat Island, while he was Anglican. The priest-architect later converted to Catholicism. The rustic twin-tower structure was built in 1940 and assumes a heavenly stance atop a hill.

❂ St. Peter's Roman Catholic Church, Clarence Town. Another circa-1940 Father Jerome construction on another hill in Clarence Town, its standout feature is its two rounded towers.

THE FAMOUS HERMIT OF CAT ISLAND BUILT TWO CHURCHES IN CLARENCE TOWN, INCLUDING ST. PAUL'S ANGLICAN.

MUSEUMS & HISTORIC SITES
❂ Adderley's Plantation, North Island, near Stella Maris Resort. Look for the small sign on the west side of the road and follow the potholed road to the beach. If you walk along the beach, following the signs; you'll pick up the steep, rocky trail that leads to the extensive plantation ruins at the top of the hill and down the other side. The kitchen and its chimney are

still intact, but roofless, as are six other buildings. Once a cotton plantation established in 1780 by Abraham Adderley and later expanded by son William, it is the best preserved of the island's three sites. Owners of Stella Maris Resort have contributed greatly to clearing a trail and maintaining the site.

Columbus Monument, Columbus Point, Seymours. The inscription on this stone obelisk monument where Columbus purportedly first made Long Island landfall reads: "This monument is dedicated to the gentle peaceful and happy aboriginal people of Long Island the Lucayans and to the arrival of Christopher Columbus on Oct. 17, 1492." The trek up the hill requires sneakers.

Deadman's Cay Cave, Deadman's Cay. The cave has two tunnels, one that leads to the sea and has not yet been fully explored. Two chiseled designs, believed to be Lucayan, decorate the wall.

Dunmore's Cave, Dunmore's. Native Lucayans and pirates have used this cave in times gone by, according to native lore.

Dunmore's Plantation, Dunmore's. Once a slave plantation, its ruins include six gate posts and a house with two fireplaces and drawings of sailing ships on the wall. Like most plantation manors of the period, it perches upon a hill to catch breezes, with sea views on three sides. Lord Dunmore, for whom Harbour Island's Dunmore Town was named, built the plantation.

Gray's Plantation, Gray's. It includes at least three house ruins; one of them has two chimneys intact. Not much is known about the plantation's history.

Hamilton's Cave, Hamilton's. The largest Bahamian cave, it measures up to 50 feet wide in some parts. Lucayan artifacts and drawings were discovered here in 1935. For tours, contact Leonard Cartwright (242-337-0235).

✪ **The Long Island Library, Museum and Community Centre** (242-337-0500), Buckley's. Open 8–4 Mon.–Fri., 9–1 Sat. $3 adults, 50 cents children age 12 and younger. Not far from the airport, this is a good place to stop to get your historical and cultural bearings on Long Island. Its tagline, "Dis We Tings," begins the story in local dialect, roughly translated: "Here's Our Stuff." The charming Bahamian–New England style cottage devotes several rooms to different aspects of Long Island heritage. A homestead vignette demonstrates some of the survival methods on the island before electricity and other modern conveniences. A dugout canoe and duhos, Lucayan chieftain thrones re-created from three found locally, represent the native American presence. Straw work, seashell crafts, and Junkanoo displays showcase Long Island's richest traditions.

MUSIC & NIGHTLIFE Long Island Breeze Resort (242-338-0170), Queen's Hwy., Salt Pond. Live music by local bands on certain Friday nights; cover charge.

✴ To Do

BEST BEACHES ✪ **Cape Santa Maria Bay and Beach,** Stella Maris, North Long Island. Named by Columbus after one of his ships, it is hands-down the prettiest beach on the island—some say in all of the Bahamas. Its bleached white-powder sands stretch more than 3 miles, past the resort that takes its name. Beachers can stop in at the resort for lunch or a drink.

Deal's Beach, Deal's, South Long Island. A favorite with the locals, its calm, shallow, jewel-toned, leeward waters border a long, coved stretch of casuarinas-shaded sands. Local picnics and charity functions often take place here.

Salt Pond Beach, Salt Pond. An Atlantic-side beach, its crashing waves and craggy formations are typical of Long Island's windward ocean beaches.

FISHING Bonefish, especially in flats on the northern part of the island, are the prized catch, but charters will also take you to reefs and deep seas to pull in the big ones—grouper, yellowtail and red snapper, mahimahi, king mackerel, tuna, marlin, and barracuda.

Charters: The going rate for charter fishing is $325 to $450 per day for bonefishing, and $450 to $650 for reef and deep-sea fishing. Resorts can arrange charters for you, or look for signs advertising services.

Bahamas Discovery Quest (242-472-2605; www.bahamasdiscoveryquest.com) Half- and full-day deep-sea and reef fishing excursions.

Bonafide Bonefishing (242-338-2025; www.bonafidebonefishing.com) Docky can show you where the bonefish are hiding on the flats and how to bait them. Full- and half-day charters; also permit and reef fishing excursions.

TJs Bonefishing & Guide Services (242-338-8978; www.tjsresortactivities .com), Miller's. Capt. Presley Pinder includes lunch on his all-day trips. Also snorkeling and sight-seeing tours; free airport pickup.

HIKING Bahamas Discovery Quest (242-472-2605; www.bahamasdiscovery quest.com) Explore three secluded beaches for shelling, flamingo-watching, and Bahamian history and culture. Its "Night Quest" program offers an authentic Bahamian experience—hunting down land crabs, which the locals love to eat.

WATER SPORTS *Anchorages:* Stella Maris Marina is Long Island's port of entry. For customs, call 242-338-2012.

Flying Fish Marina (242-337-3430; www.flyingfish-marina.com), Lighthouse Point Rd., Clarence Town. Eighteen dock slips accommodate boat-ins who can use the resort's showers and stay for lunch or dinner, drinks, a dip in the pool, and partying on the spacious seaside deck.

⁰1⁰ **Long Island Breeze Resort** (242-338-0170), Queen's Hwy., Salt Pond. Dock for the day to take advantage of its showers, pool deck, laundry facilities, Wi-Fi, and restaurant and bar.

Stella Maris Marina (242-338-2055; www.stellamarisresort.com), Stella Maris. Full service with 12 slips, a port of entry, a restaurant and bars, showers, boat hauling and launching, and repair services.

BAHAMA TALK
Crab picker: Better known by birders as a yellow-crowned night heron, the Bahamians renamed it for its choice of diet.

BOATERS APPRECIATE THE POOL, VIEW, AND OTHER ACCOMMODATIONS AT LONG ISLAND
BREEZE RESORT.

Snorkeling & Diving: **Bahamas Discovery Quest** (242-472-2605; www
.bahamasdiscoveryquest.com) Separate tours take you reef snorkeling or pluck-
ing and cleaning sponges. Snorkel equipment available for rent.

WILDLIFE SPOTTING ❂ Dean's Blue Hole, Dean's, near Clarence Town.
Open daily. One of Long Island's greatest attractions, islanders claim it to be the
world's deepest inland blue hole. Many Bahamian islands, with their limestone
foundations, boast blue holes. Besides being the deepest, this is certainly the
prettiest and most visitor friendly, with a beach that faces craggy cliffs that look
down upon its 663-foot depth. Its oval shape ranges in diameter from 80 to 120
feet. Site of a biannual international free diving competition, it has recorded a
diving world's record of 300 feet. Currents can be strong in the hole, so don't
attempt swimming unless you're a strong swimmer.

✳ Lodging

Long Island's 15 hotels and guest
houses account for 144 rooms. The
northern half of the island holds the
most rooms in its larger, foreign-
owned resorts. Accommodations in
the south are small, locally owned
guest houses for the most part.

Price Codes

Inexpensive	Up to $100
Moderate	$100 to $200
Expensive	$200 to $300
Very Expensive	$300 and up

ACCOMMODATIONS

Clarence Town

Winter Haven (242-337-3062; www .winterhavenbahamas.com) One of south Long Island's newest and most complete resorts, its eight rooms occupy two pastel-hued Bahamian-style buildings framed in pretty vegetation. All have a view of the craggy coastline here. Paddle fans, seashell-motif curtains, and plantation-style furnishings make for a pleasant, clean feel. Social activities center around the oceanside pool, its tiki bar, and the modern, sprawling dining room next to it. The restaurant, Rowdy Boy's, serves local and American favorites for breakfast, lunch, and dinner, and its V-shaped bar is a popular hangout for islanders come happy hour. Moderate.

Salt Pond

☼ Long Island Breeze Resort (242-338-0170; www.longislandbreeze resort.com), Queen's Hwy. Where to watch the sun set? From a chaise on the palm-fringed, white-sand beach? Or the balcony of your blithely decorated cottage room? Perhaps enjoying a cocktail from the second-floor restaurant and bar? Or maybe submerged in the freshwater pool that overlooks the harbor and its fishing boats plying fishbowl-clear waters? It doesn't matter where, just don't miss the grand finale. It's one of the property's best features, along with a handy location right off Queen's Highway (no torturous dirt roads to navigate as at other island resorts) and central to the sights of both northern and southern Long Island. Plus, the surf-swept beach is but a 15-minute walk away. New and operated by a sanitary-conscious pair from the U.S. and England, this resort shines spotless and is well-furnished with amenities. Next to Government Dock and at the threshold of popular commercial fishing grounds, it is perfectly poised for gazing at the harbor from the resort's capacious deck. If you require something more active, the owners can arrange car rentals, kayaking, diving, boating, and island tours. Recreational boaters often stop in when the resort hosts live entertainment, or to catch a shower and hot meal. Currently, the property consists of four

THE POOL DECK AT LONG ISLAND BREEZE RESORT: A PERFECT SPOT FOR SUNSET.

units in one cottage that can be rented separately or in unison. The top floor unit has one bedroom, a great room, a powder room, a kitchen, and laundry facilities. The others are roomy and have separate locked entrances on the first floor. Pastel hues, botanical prints, and board-and-bead motif create an island cottage feel. The owners will be building more cottages, which are available for private ownership, with a planned build-out of eight. For now, TV is available only in the bar, where a lovely wood compass rose is set into the floor, but the rooms contain DVD players and movies are available. Moderate to Expensive. No credit cards.

Stella Maris

⁰**1**⁰ **Cape Santa Maria** (242-338-5273, 800-663-7090 reservations, or 800-926-9704 direct; www.capesanta maria.com) Private jet-setters frequent this Canadian-owned property, but it's equally inviting to families and couples wanting to get away without sacrificing the conveniences of home. Here those conveniences include a fitness center, a library with a big-screen TV and video games, complimentary laundry facilities, tennis, and a bright two-tiered restaurant-bar overlooking the island's most eye-popping lay of beach. Inconveniences? One of Long Island's famous torturous road entrances and far distance to other restaurants. The majority and original accommodations line up along the beach in two-unit bungalows, which feel like slipping into comfy flip-flops. Each of the 20 bungalows contains one bedroom unit. With some you have the option of adding on a bedroom. All have screened porches facing the beach,

where charming roofed cabanas provide shade. For bigger, better, and newer, the villas are individually owned and decorated, with two bedrooms, a spacious kitchen with stainless steel appliances, TV, and jetted tubs. To date five buildings with four villas each have been completed, with five more expected in years to come. (There is a three-night minimum stay in the villas.) The resort provides all the water sports rentals and charter hook-ups you may require. This end of the island is particularly known for its bonefishing, so much of the clientele has that on its agenda. Meal plans are available. Expensive to Very Expensive.

✪ **Stella Maris Resort Club** (242-338-2050 or 954-359-8236 (U.S.); www.stellamarisresort.com) Classic island hospitality spreads over 15 lushly landscaped acres at this hilltop bastion. The one-bedroom cottages and two- to four-bedroom bungalows are not the most modern with their white wicker and faded spreads, but they have plenty of room and amenities, including a water view and minifridge or kitchenette (but no phones or TVs). Some of the three- and four-bedroom bungalows have their own swimming pools. Other guests can take advantage of the two other freshwater pools and one saltwater infinity pool. Or they can wade off the small private beach or into the sea's "natural pools"—some created by the sea, others with a little help from the resort's German owners. A breeze-cooled restaurant, bar, pool, deck area, and library with a big-screen TV sit at the top of the hill, and the 20 accommodation units tumble down it to the pool, bar, rocky cliffs, and beach at sea's edge. A play-

AMONG THE MOST UNUSUAL FEATURES OF STELLA MARIS RESORT, ITS "NATURAL POOLS" AFFORD GUESTS A ONE-OF-A-KIND SEA BATH.

ground, tiki cabanas, and hammocks make the beach a popular spot to while away sunny days. Convenient to the airport and great bottom and deep-sea fishing, Stella Maris has attracted sportsmen and escape artists since 1965. A full-service marina, scuba, snorkeling, and fishing charters fulfill all watery whims. Rental bikes, scooters, and cars are available for island exploration, and there are two AstroTurf tennis courts. Moderate to Very Expensive. Closed September.

✳ Where to Eat

Most restaurants close at least during September, sometimes longer.

Price Codes

Inexpensive	Up to $15
Moderate	$15 to $25
Expensive	$25 to $35
Very Expensive	$35 or more

Cost categories are based on the range of dinner entrée prices or, if dinner is not served, on lunch entrées.

Resort restaurants usually take reservations. For small restaurants, it's a good idea to call ahead to make sure they're open. Often they require that you order your dinner ahead of time from the two or three selections they may offer that evening.

Clarence Town

&. **Rowdy Boy's Bar & Grill** (242-337-3062; www.winterhavenbahamas .com), at Winter Haven. Whether you want to watch the game or the waves, Rowdy Boy's can entertain you in its spacious, modern dining room overlooking the resort's pool and the ocean. Sturdy, cushioned rattan chairs and tables and a V-shaped bar provide plenty of seating space. Chef Gregory Bowe adds a bit more flair to his

Bahamian specialties than most island chefs, so in addition to the usual cracked conch and broiled lobster, you might find pan-broiled grouper with lemon butter, grilled pork chops with barbecue sauce and sautéed onions, New York strip steak, and barbecued ribs. Eileen's bread pudding with bourbon sauce is famous. For kicks, order a Blonde Moment cocktail with lemon rum, blue Curaçao, grenadine, sweet and sour, and a splash of soda. Moderate. Reservations accepted.

Deadman's Cay

✪ **Max's Conch Bar & Grill** (242-337-0056; www.maxconchbar.com), Queen's Hwy., near airport. More than just a place to stop for a hearty meal or a drink before the airport, Max's (his name is actually Gary) place is a way to plug into the island's local life and catch up with the news and gossip. Fluttering flags on the west side of the road mark this little dot on the map. A circular, open-air hut with a thatched roof is the hub of

MAX'S HUMBLE TIKI BAR AND CONCH SHACK ARE AN ISLAND INSTITUTION.

the restaurant, which also has some randomly strewn covered tables. In fact, "random" suitably describes the whole attitude of the place. License plates, pinup pix, dollar bills, and quirky bric-a-brac cram every possible bit of space. Max chops up fresh conch salad as traditional Bahamian stews and grills scent the place in mouthwatering aromas. A couple of unusual specialties include stuffed breadfruit and crawfish-stuffed potatoes. Inexpensive to Moderate. No credit cards.

McKann's

♿ **Club Washington** (242-338-0021), Queen's Hwy. Sky-blue stucco on the outside, sparkling clean and roomy on the inside, this is a typical no-frills Bahamian restaurant that feels and tastes like a home. Five tables are spaced wide apart and dressed with bright tropical tablecloths and the kind of fish-shaped straw placemats made right here on Long Island. The unwritten menu depends upon what the cook decided to whip up that day and if any fresh fish came in. Chicken, ribs, and cracked conch show up regularly. Specials may include okra soup with salt beef, lobster, grouper, pot roast, and steamed mutton—all served with the best coleslaw ever or baked mac and cheese. The bar serves a full array of liquor. Moderate. No credit cards. Closed September. Call ahead to order dinner.

Miller's

✪ **Chez Pierre** (242-338-8809; www.chezpierrebahamas.com) Arguably the best non-native food you'll find on this island, it tends toward Italian rather than the French its name implies. Quebecois by birth but happily naturalized onto Bahamian soil, Pierre runs a rustic, romantic cottage inn on a stretch of off-the-main-Queen's-Highway beach. Guests and locals come for his pasta and seafood specials in a simple setting cooled by breezes and enlivened by sparkling conversation. The penne gorgonzola is frightfully rich and delicious. Other choices: pâté foie gras appetizer, pizza five ways, pasta rustica (with tomato sauce, garlic, black olives, and onions), steak and fries, and shrimp scampi. Chef Pierre, who often turns up at the table taking orders and delivering food, is a charming fellow with a cutting wit that keeps customers entertained. Moderate to Expensive. Closed August through mid-October. Reservations recommended.

Salt Pond

Long Island Breeze Restaurant (242-338-0170; www.longislandbreeze resort.com), Queen's Hwy. Whether you choose to sit poolside or on the second-floor restaurant and deck, the views are delicious and the meals executed with the utmost care for freshness. Choose from an array of burgers and sandwiches at lunchtime. For dinner, the variety runs from pizza and blackened fish to broiled or cracked lobster, fettuccine Alfredo, penne vodka with pancetta, crumb-crusted lamb chops, and rib-eye steak. The feeling of spaciousness starts at the fully stocked bar and spreads to the dining room and vast pool deck below, which is gaining popularity with the boating crowd. Moderate. No credit cards. Closed Monday. Reservations suggested.

Stella Maris

& **Stella Maris Restaurant** (242-338-2050, 800-426-0466, or 954-359-8236 (U.S.); www.stellamarisresort .com), at Stella Maris Resort. Take a step back to an era of congenial island dining and hospitality at this classic

A STROLL ALONG THE BEACH AT SUNSET HIGHLIGHTS DINNER AT CHEZ PIERRE.

resort. Limestone rock walls accent the high rafter, hilltop dining room cooled by breezes and paddle fans. Live plants flourish out of huge pots, and natural rattan chairs invite sinking into. At lunch, there's salads, soup, cracked conch, pizza, and sandwiches with an island strain. I tasted a thick and delicious pumpkin soup of the day and a roast beef sandwich doctored with the Rasta Bahama All-Natural Hot Pepper Tonic from a bottle on the table. Lunches come with a small side salad and four types of dressing. The poppy mango is best. After lunch or before dinner, walk down to the natural pool and beachfront, then perhaps rest at the bar for a rum punch to bolster yourself for the climb back up. The kitchen offers two entrées every evening such as poached Nova Scotia salmon with caper sauce, roast Angus sirloin with béarnaise, roast spring leg of lamb with rosemary gravy, and braised chicken breast with basil stuffing and black truffle sauce. Side dishes include okra soup, French onion soup, peas 'n' rice, broccoli rabe, and *pommes Duchesse.* Expensive. Reservations essential.

ISLAND CHARACTER: ELSIE KNOWLES

Turn off Queen's Highway to discover the settlement of Oneil's. Here a European woman named Ivy Simms began producing handbags, hats, placemats, and other items from the hand-plaited straw work of local women. Simms has since passed on, but a number of women continue to do the hand-plaiting of silver thatch and coconut palms to machine-sew into remarkable works of art.

This is the true straw market of the Bahamas. (The markets in Nassau and other places get their stock from Taiwan and other foreign importers.) The plaiters wait for the full moon to harvest the palms, then dry them in the sun before working them into intricate patterns with names such as pineapple, spider web, fish gill, and fish pot.

Elsie Knowles can do more than 150 different patterns, many of which she invented herself. She started doing the work in 1949 at age 5. "I learned from my great-granmaddy. She had hair white as snow," Elsie recalls. "It comes from an African tradition. Sally Bongo was one of the old greats that taught it to us. So many great t'ings I learned from my ancestors. They were very artistic. They were very smart."

Today Elsie continues the tradition, teaching the craft locally and once demonstrating her skills at the Smithsonian Institution. Instead of drying the silver thatch palm, she singes the fronds over an open fire. "That method was invented right over here at Oneil's," she says. "It turns the palm brown, but the silver remains. Some, they smoke over kerosene lamp. I found out it works better with a flambeau. All over the Bahamas they use the silver thatch, but only on Long Island do they singe."

BAKERIES Ritchies (242-337-0004), Deadman's Cay. Locally recommended for its breads and pastries.

✳ Selective Shopping

Cheryl's Creations (242-338-8322), Queen's Hwy., Millerton. Ask the local women where to find the most creative straw handbags, and they will point you to this cute little roadside shop. Cheryl incorporates the island's goatskins into some designs, but most popular are her coconut-straw bags.

✪ **Elsie's Authentic Crafts** (242-338-8881), off Queen's Hwy., Oneil's. Besides her extensive line of hand-plaited straw work, Elsie carries shell works, beach towels, T-shirts, and other souvenirs.

✪ **Everglades Souvenir Shop** (no phone), Burnt Ground. Look for the giant conch shell along the road, and stop in at this unique shop to see and purchase the intricate shell work of Allan Dixon. He makes wall hangings, lamps, and other decorative items out of local shells.

Elsie remembers a time back in the '80s when the Long Island art of straw plaiting almost dried up because of competition from Nassau markets and their foreign products.

"They tried to push me out of work because I was too native-y," says the feisty, outspoken lady. "It's more durable if plaited by hand." She believes the strong plaiting tradition began on Long Island and here it should continue, even if she has to see to it herself.

"I enjoy passing it on to people. I never hide it. The grave is rich with a lot of people with a lot of knowledge that never passed it on."

STRAW MATRIARCH ELSIE KNOWLES POSES OUTSIDE HER SHOP WITH SOME OF HER HANDIWORK.

DIVERS FROM AROUND THE WORLD PREPARE FOR THE FREEDIVING WORLD CHAMPIONSHIP AT DEAN'S BLUE HOLE.

✴ Special Events

Regatta season and fishing tournaments fill the summer months. September marks the opening of bird hunting season, where sportsmen beat the bush for coot, whistling ducks, and white-crowned pigeons. It runs through December.

February: **Agro/Expo & Muttonfest** (242-338-8668) One weekend mid-month. A celebration of the island's livestock farming traditions.

❂ *April:* **AIDA Freediving World Championship** (www.verticalblue .net), Dean's Blue Hole. Late in the month. For the past few years, 53 of the planet's greatest free divers from 17 nations have competed at the 663-foot-deep blue hole. Diving to depths of more than 300 feet on a single

breath, they vie for titles in the with and without fins categories. Training and competitions take place for 11 days. Live commentary, drinks, and conch salad add to the entertainment on competition days.

May: **All Tackle Fishing Tournament** (242-337-0199), Flying Fish Marina, Clarence Town. One weekend late in the month. Cartie Co and Chamcem Boats hosts this annual event.

June: **Long Island Regatta,** Salt Pond. One weekend early in the month. The 40-year-old annual race takes place midisland.

November: **AIDA Freediving World Championship** (www.verticalblue .net), Dean's Blue Hole. Late November to early December. See April.

Other Out Islands 10

BERRY ISLANDS

SAN SALVADOR

GREAT INAGUA

OTHER OUT ISLANDS

REMOTE & DREAMY

"We looked up and froze in our tracks. From the interior of the island was coming a great flock of scarlet flamingo, wings ablaze in the setting sun. . . . The place was an ornithologist's paradise."

—*Gilbert Klingel in* Inagua: An Island Sojourn, *published 1940*

Our tour guide, an elderly gent in a suit jacket despite the heavy August tropic air, turned passionate at the historic grave site of the Reverend P. Chrysostomus Schreiner, a Catholic priest who studied San Salvador's all-consuming, never-ending Columbus controversy. The debate goes on, disputing whether or not this was Christopher Columbus's first landfall—the only, although small, disturbance on this totally peaceful island.

As the Bahamas' Out Islands head south, they become increasingly sere and sparse humanwise. **San Salvador** is by far the most populated and tourist friendly with its Club Med and a handful of other concessions to vacationers. The northernmost of this last group, it is most vegetated, but not fertile enough to keep its colonial cotton plantations vital. Columbus compared its 12-by-7-mile oval shape to a lima bean.

Wildlifewise, the populations grow heading south, peaking at southernmost **Inagua**—the third largest Bahama island and known for its great populations of iguanas, flamingos, parrots, and other birds and reptiles. Here we've reached the extreme remote Bahamas on a latitude par with the Turks and Caicos, a separate archipelago still under British governance. Not known for its great beaches, Inagua's virgin reefs and excellent bonefishing draw experienced sportsmen prepared to outfit themselves independent of guides, which are virtually nonexistent here. Tourism infrastructure on the 2.5-by-4.5-mile, flat, scrubby **Great Inagua Island** is limited to a few guest houses and restaurants in block-long **Matthew Town.** Its Morton Salt operation employs a majority of its 1,000 inhabitants. The island's desolate isolation meant it experienced brief prosperity in the '80s as a drug-smuggling waypoint.

Crooked and Acklins Islands also claim a healthy flamingo population, much more robust than its human population of only about 400. A narrow passage separates Crooked from Acklins to the south. **Long Cay,** south again of Acklins, is home to 500-some of the honking, graceful, pink birds. North of Crooked, the 3,600-foot-deep Crooked Island Passage insulates the remote islands from its nearest neighbor, Long Island. Infrastructure here too is spotty at best. Some areas have no electric or phone service and islanders must plug into generators. Its 45-mile barrier reef also brings intrepid divers.

Mayaguana Island lies to the east of Crooked and Acklins Islands, on the other side of the Mayaguana Passage. The few tourists who come to this 24-mile-long island are intrepid beach-lovers and fishermen. Many of its 300 inhabitants migrated from nearby Turks and Caicos.

The final island group covered in this chapter of small, lightly visited islands lies far to the north of the rest, near Bimini and Andros Islands. **Berry Islands** consists of 10-mile-long Great Harbour Cay—the most populated with about 700 residents, resort island **Chub Cay,** private resort island **Little Whale Cay,** and another 20 or so small islands and a hundred little cays. Poised at the Tongue of the Ocean, it attracts divers as well as fishermen. Resorts in the main town of **Bullock's Harbour,** aka **The Village,** line the beach north of the boat harbor.

This last chapter of Bahama Islands covers parts of the archipelago that appeal to a very specialized traveler looking for an experience like Gilbert Klingel recorded in his book—a place where time has frozen under tropic sun.

DON'T MISS 46. Bonefishing on any of the islands.
47. Spotting flamingos on Great Inagua or Long Cay.
48. Snorkeling or diving the caverns and reefs around San Salvador.
49. Climbing the lighthouse on San Salvador.
50. Escaping to the secluded beaches of Great Harbour Cay in the Berry Islands.

SUGGESTED READING *Inagua: An Island Sojourn,* by Gilbert Kringel. An account of a scientist's stranding on the island with a friend in the late 1930s.

✳ To See

MUSEUMS & HISTORIC SITES Crooked Island Ruins, north end of Crooked Island. Open 24 hours. The so-called Marine Farm site is believed to have been used as a fort that was ransacked by American-based pirates in the early 19th century. Spanish guns have been found there. The Bahamas National Trust maintains lovely gardens at Hope Great House.

Dixon Hill Lighthouse, south of Graham's Harbour, San Salvador. Open 24 hours. Donations requested.

BAHAMA TALK
Waving: Every motorist in the Out Islands—whether they know each other or not—uses this nonverbal form of friendly salutation to oncoming cars, golf carts, or anyone they see alongside the road.

This lighthouse still runs on kerosene and requires the keeper to crank it by hand. Built in 1956, its height of 160 feet affords a fabulous view of the island's oceanfront and interior lakes. The keeper will let you climb the tower if you knock on his door and ask.

Erickson Museum & Library (242-339-1863), Gregory St., Matthew Town. Open 9–5 daily. Morton Salt established this sweet little facility in the historic home of the Erickson family, who came to Inagua to run the company in 1934. It interlinks island and company history with exhibits such as photographs of the Bahamian salt industry from small to large scale. The museum collaborates with the Bahamas National Trust (BNT) for its permanent exhibit about the flamingo, the national bird of the Bahamas. It includes photos of the three wardens, the Nixon brothers, who worked with BNT and the Audubon Society in the 1960s to enforce laws that would protect the birds.

Great Inagua Lighthouse, Southwest Point, Great Inagua. Open 24 hours. Donations requested. You can see Cuba on a clear day from this circa-1870 white tower, one of four hand-operated kerosene lamps that have survived in the Bahamas. The point's treacherous reefs make it a handy navigational tool still today.

✪ **Landfall Park,** Fernandez Bay, San Salvador. Open 24 hours. A white, 9-foot cross marks the spot where Columbus first walked in the New World, according to most historians, anyway. Despite the disputes, locals and others cling tenaciously to the story, and this park pays homage with flags from the 32 countries of the Organization of American States and other related monuments, including a sculpture recalling the Olympic torch that passed through here with the 1968 Olympics.

New World Museum (no phone), near North Victoria Hill, San Salvador. Open by appointment. Your hotel can make arrangements to view this small collection of Lucayan and other pre-Columbian artifacts assembled by Columbus scholar Ruth C. Durlacher Wolper Malvin.

Watling's Castle Ruins, Sandy Point, San Salvador. Open 24 hours. Local legend attributes the hilltop ruins here to a 17th-century pirate by the name of George Watling. He stayed on the island from time to time and even changed its name to Watling's Island. The government, however, restored its supposedly Columbus-given name in 1926. Some historians say it's more likely that these are the ruins of a plantation manor.

✳ To Do

FISHING Crooked Island has terrific bonefishing, but is known equally for its deep-sea and reef charters. On San Salvador, Pigeon Creek, which dumps into the ocean, is a sweet spot for bonefish.

Charters: **Captain Robbie Gibson** (242-344-2007), Crooked Island. THE guy to see for offshore fishing on Crooked Island. A number of guides specialize in bonefishing, including **Elton "Bonefish Shakey" McKinney** (242-344-2038) and **Jeff Moss** (242-344-2029).

FISHERMEN GO AFTER THEIR CATCHES THE OLD-FASHIONED WAY BY POLING BOATS ACROSS THE FLATS IN THE REMOTE OUT ISLANDS.

NATURE PRESERVES & ECO-ATTRACTIONS ✪ **Inagua National Park** (242-393-1317 (Bahamas National Trust Nassau office) or 242-339-1616 (local warden Henry Nixon); www.bnt.bs), Great Inagua. Open by reservation. $25 adults, $10 for students plus guide tip. Once upon a time, West Indian flamingos inhabited all of the Bahamas. Now they're mostly concentrated in this 183,000-acre preserve on Great Inagua's west coast. The brackish Lake Windsor draws more than 50,000 flamingos as they feed, mate, or fly through in small flocks. Best time to find them is November through June, especially later in the season when you might be lucky enough to see the fuzzy, clumsy hatchlings. An abundance of other birds, including the rare Bahamas parrot, plus sea turtles and wild donkeys also make this a boon to birders and nature-lovers. To tour the park, you must reserve a tour with a BNT official.

PINK FLAMINGO, THE ALWAYS DELIGHTFUL NATIONAL BIRD OF THE BAHAMAS.

WATER SPORTS *Anchorages:*
Chub Cay Club Marina (242-325-1490 or 877-234-CHUB; www.chub cay.com) The marina's 110 slips accommodate yachts up to 200 feet. Customs and immigration, airport, fuel.

Great Harbour Cay Marina (242-367-8005) Eighty slips for boats up to 150 feet; full-service and safe harbor.

Powerboat Rentals: **Happy People's** (242-367-8117), Great Harbour Cay, Berry Islands. Rents boats by the day or longer.

Snorkeling & Diving: **The Wall in Crooked Passage,** between Crooked and Acklins Islands, starts at 45 feet of water and plunges to 3,500, which of course means it's a magnet for divers.

Visitors also flock to San Salvador. Its best dive sites include the **Double Caves** at 115 feet, **North Pole Cave** (a wall drop from 40 to 150-plus feet), and **Doolittle's Grotto** at 140 feet.

✳ Lodging

Besides a few resorts, Crooked Island has a number of small guest houses where you get to know your hosts well. Great Inagua has only small guest houses, the largest with six rooms.

Price Codes

Inexpensive	Up to $100
Moderate	$100 to $200
Expensive	$200 to $300
Very Expensive	$300 and up

(An asterisk after the pricing designation indicates that the rate includes at least a continental breakfast in the cost of lodging and possibly more extensive meal service as noted in the listing.)

ACCOMMODATIONS

Berry Islands

Chub Cay Marina and Resort (242-325-1490; www.chubcay.com), Chub Cay. A resort in progress, Chub Cay builds upon the foundation of a 40-year-old resort that has been a magnet for fishermen, divers, and other water sports fans since the beginning. It recently renovated the original hotel rooms in Harbour House hotel, where the restaurant serves breakfast, lunch, and dinner. There are also villas for rent, with more to come. The marina holds 110 boats up to 200 feet in length, and customs and immigration services are available. It hosts a major wahoo tournament every winter. For now, amenities include a beautiful sweep of beach, an infinity-edged pool, bar, laundry facilities, and guiding services. To come: a three-level clubhouse with another restaurant, more villas, more restaurants and bars, and a marina-side shopping village. Moderate.

Great Harbour Inn (242-367-8117), Bullock Harbour, Great Harbour Cay. No frills and straightforward, here's an affordable place marina-side and convenient to the local shops and restaurants. The five rooms are basic and tidy with small kitchens, but no telephones, Internet, or TVs. Typically Out Island laid-back, service is often slow to nonexistent. But you can't beat it for price and location. Inexpensive. No credit cards.

¶ Little Whale Cay (800-783-6904; www.littlewhalecay.com) If your fantasy envisions hanging out on an island that you and your 11 closest friends have all to yourselves, meet Little Whale Cay, a 93-acre, beachy-keen island containing three individual villas. They are fully stocked with air-conditioning, flat-screen TVs, Wi-Fi, phones, terraces, and spacious living areas. The main house, Little Whale House, has a bar and two bedrooms. Flamingo House has four bedrooms and three baths, and Peacock House one bedroom. At guests' disposal is a marina with a number of boats and kayaks, spa facilities, a gym, an infinity-edged pool, a tennis court, and a staff of 13. The staff prepares healthy, organic meals and can do everything from massages to captaining a fishing excursion or a trip to the main Berry Island, Great Harbour Cay. All this for only around $10,000 a day, minimum of five days—definitely a fantasy. Very Expensive.*

Crooked Island

"1" **Crooked Island Lodge** (242-344-2507; www.pittstownpoint.com), Pittstown Point Landings. This pretty, green, palmy property caters largely to bonefishers, divers, and pilots, but also has a pleasant beach, overlooking the historic Bird Rock Lighthouse, for soaking up the rays. Its 12 rooms are comfortable, island-style with no frills, no phones, no TVs, but with Wi-Fi and some with air-conditioning. A restaurant, bar, library, and plenty of fishing, snorkeling, and diving excursions engage guests in the island lifestyle. Or hop on a bike and explore the quietest part of a quiet island. The restaurant serves American and Bahamian food, and meal packages are available—a good idea because this is the best restaurant around. It is near an airstrip for small planes in case you own one and want to zip off to another island for lunch. Expensive.

"1" **Tranquility on the Bay Resort** (242-344-2563), Major's Cay. Small but complete with a restaurant, gift shop, and beauty salon, this small, family-owned property delivers what its name promises. Situated on a 3-mile swoop of beach, it encourages merely lounging your days away with an occasional dip into its clear, warm waters for a swim or snorkel. It provides free transportation to and from the airport, plus arranges tours such as the three-island boat excursion (Crooked Island, Acklins Island, and Long Cay), nature walks, or bonefishing. All-inclusive meal packages are available. Rooms are simple in a one-story motel setting footsteps from the beach. Moderate.

Great Inagua

Main House (242-339-1266 or 242-339-1267 (reservations); www.inaguamainhouse.com), Kortwright St., Matthew Town. Operated by Morton Salt, this little two-story hotel is convenient to the town's restaurants and activities, but is also close to the company's power plant, which can be a little noisy. Its six second-story, air-conditioned rooms share a central living area with the guest house's only guest telephone. The first-floor restaurant is open for lunch and dinner. Inexpensive. No credit cards.

Mayaguana

"1" **Baycaner Beach Hotel** (242-339-3726; baycanerbeach.com), Pirate's Well. A fusion in name of Mayaguana's pirate past and water-wonderful present, low-key, one-story Baycaner sits on a sand beach steps away from the gem-toned ocean. Its 16 rooms won't win any design awards, but are perfect for beach bums. They do have TVs, a rarity for the outflung islands. For the more active sort, the resort has or can arrange bike, car, canoe, and boat rentals, plus bonefishing and snorkeling or diving excursions. (You must bring your own gear for the latter three.) There's also a restaurant and bar on-site. Moderate.

San Salvador

"1" ✪ **Club Med–Columbus Isle** (242-331-2000 or 888-932-2582; www.clubmed.com), near Riding Rock Point. To avoid confusion with the capital city of El Salvador, Club

Med calls the island Columbus Isle, a marketing ploy that hasn't caught on beyond its 89 acres of beachfront village. It's a shining star in the Club Med chain, especially among divers but not among families—bringing children is discouraged. Activities do not end with diving. Sailing, tennis, wind surfing, biking, and snorkeling are part of the all-inclusive package (diving is not). Spa treatments are also extra, as are island and boating excursions. All meals, nonalcoholic beverages, and beer and wine with meals are also included. Club Med, a French chain, has a nice international flair. Staff, known as GOs (*gentils organisateurs*) are attentive, well-traveled, multilingual, young, and personable. They share meals with guests and even are allowed to hang out with them in the bars. The main dining room overlooks the free-form pool and serves sumptuous buffets for breakfast, lunch, and dinner—loaded with local specialties, imported cheeses, homemade bread, and yummy desserts. Two other restaurants specialize in seafood and Brazilian fare for dinner. Entertainment keeps the property lively night and day. Asian-style, custom furniture lends style to the guest rooms, which all have their own private porch or balcony. Very Expensive.°

HOME & CONDO RENTALS Tat's Rental (242-367-8123 or 242-464-4361; www.tatsrental.com), Great Harbour Cay, Berry Islands. Rental agency for Beach Villas—town homes with private docks for boats up to 30 feet.

✳ Where to Eat

The menu looks much the same on the least-visited islands of the Bahamas, although restaurants may be few and far between. One unusual find in Inagua is a dish known as "kickin' beef," a clever name for donkey meat—similar to beef and quite tender when prepared as the Inaguans do.

Price Codes

Inexpensive	Up to $15
Moderate	$15 to $25
Expensive	$25 to $35
Very Expensive	$35 or more

CLUB MED ACCOMMODATIONS CONFORM TO BAHAMIAN STYLE.

Club Med

Cost categories are based on the range of dinner entrée prices or, if dinner is not served, on lunch entrées.

Regarding reservations, it's a good idea to call ahead to make sure a restaurant is open. Small restaurants may require that you order your dinner ahead of time from the two or three selections they offer that evening.

Berry Islands

& **Coolie Mae's** (242-367-8730), Bullock Harbour, Great Harbour Cay. Probably the best choice for fresh, home-cooked grub on the island, Coolie Mae's changes its menu daily. Everything on the menu is good, but some favorites include conch salad, conch fritters, cracked conch, pan-fried grouper, burgers, peas 'n' rice, and baked macaroni and cheese. Casual, island-style, local art often decorates the walls. Inexpensive to Moderate. No credit cards. Closed Sunday.

Crooked Island

& **Sea Side Café** (242-344-2035), Landrail Point. Andy Gibson catches 'em, his wife Marcia cooks 'em—grilled or fried with all the fixings. Folks rave about her fresh, home-made bread. Other specialties include grilled conch with tamarind sauce and minced lobster Creole. Meat-lovers can feast on barbecued chicken, barbecued ribs, or steak—all at incredibly reasonable prices. Bring your own booze for happy hour from 5-6 PM with free fresh conch salad. Inexpensive. No credit cards.

Great Inagua

& **COZY CORNER** (242-339-1440), Matthew Town. Known simply as Cozy's, it is voted the most likely to be open of all the independent, nonhotel Inagua restaurants. (Other restaurants open upon need and whim.) Its fresh johnnycake is worth a visit on its own merit. At lunchtime, there's the usual hamburger, conch burger, chicken tenders, and local "sip sip" (Bahamian for gossip) going on. Dinner is often by advance request and may include anything from steamed lobster or grilled snapper to baked chicken and cracked conch. The experience requires a rum punch or Kalik at the bar. Inexpensive. No credit cards. Closed Sunday.

San Salvador

& **Riding Rock Inn Restaurant** (242-331-2631; www.ridingrock.com), Riding Rock Resort, Riding Rock Point. Part of a resort but also biking distance from the Club Med, it sets a perky table inside or outside by the pool. Breakfast offers the usual array of pancakes, eggs, fresh fruit, and freshly baked bread buffet-style or served to order. Sandwiches, burgers, and pizza satisfy lunchtime appetites, but at dinner, things get slightly more formal with soup (conch chowder or okra soup) and salad before entrées are served. Grilled fresh catch of the day is the specialty, but there's also stuffed lobster in season, steamed grouper, steaks, and chicken. The price also includes a glass of wine and dessert. Very Expensive.

✸ Special Events

July: **Regatta,** Spring Point, Acklins and Crooked Islands. Last weekend of the month.

October: **Regatta,** Grahams Harbour, San Salvador. One weekend mid-month.

Information 11

INFORMATION

PRACTICAL MATTERS

We hope that you never need a doctor or police officer, but in case you should, we provide that information here, as well as information on other topics.

✳ Emergency/Medical Services Information

Nassau/Paradise Island

Ambulance: **Air Ambulance Service Ltd.** (242-323-2186 or 242-380-6666 pager)

Bahamas Air Sea Rescue Association (242-325-8864)

Crisis Center (242-328-0922)

Doctors Hospital Ambulance Services (242-302-4747)

EMS (919, 242-323-2597, or 242-323-2580)

Med-Evac (242-322-2881)

Police/Fire: 911 or 919

Medical Services: **Doctors Hospital** (242-322-8411 or 242-302-4600)

Princess Margaret Hospital (242-322-2861)

Grand Bahama Island

Ambulance: **Bahamas Air Sea Rescue Association** (242-325–2628 or 242-325-2772)

Police/Fire: 911

Fire Department (242-352-8888)

Medical Services: **Rand Memorial Hospital** (242-352–5101 or 242-352-6735)

Abaco

Police/Fire/Ambulance: 919

Bahamas Air Sea Rescue Association (242-366-0500)

Royal Bahamas Police Force (242-367-2560)

Green Turtle Cay Fire Department (242-365-4133 or 242-365-4019)

Man-O-War Fire Department (242-365-6911)

Marsh Harbour Fire Department (242-367-2000)

Treasure Cay Fire Department (242-365-9112)

South Andros Police (242-369-4733)

Medical Services **Abaco Family Medicine** (242-367-2295)

Auskell Advance Medical (242-367-0020; Marsh Harbour)

Corbett Medical Center (242-365-8288)

Cooper's Town Government Clinic (242-365-0300)

Hope Town Government Clinic (242-366-0108)

Marsh Harbour Medical Centre (242-367-0049)

Sandy Point Government Clinic (242-366-4010)

Andros Island
Police/Fire/Ambulance: **North Andros Police** (242-329-2353 or 242-329-2103)

Central Andros Police (242-368-2626 or 242-368-2625; Fresh Creek)

Mangrove Cay Police (242-369-0083)

South Andros Police (242-369-4733)

Medical Services: **North Andros Government Clinic** (242-329-2055)

Central Andros Government Clinic (242-368-2038)

South Andros Government Clinic (242-369-4849)

Bimini
Police/Fire/Ambulance: 919

Fire Rescue (242-347-3144)

Police (242-347-3144; Alice Town)

Medical Services: **Bailey Town Government Clinic** (242-347-2210)

Eleuthera
Police/Fire/Ambulance: **Governor's Harbour Police** (242-332-2117)

Governor's Harbour Airport Police (242-332-2323)

Harbour Island Police (242-333-2111)

Spanish Wells Police (242-333-4030)

Medical Services: **Governor's Harbour Government Clinic** (242-332-2774)

Harbour Island Government Clinic (242-333-2227)

Spanish Wells Government Clinic (242-333-4064)

Exuma
Police/Fire/Ambulance: 919

Farmer's Cay Police (242-355-4034)

George Town Police (242-336-2666)

Rolleville Police (242-345-6066)

Staniel Cay Police (242-355-2042)

Medical Services **Black Point Government Clinic** (242-355-3007)

George Town Health Clinic (242-336-2088)

Steventon Government Clinic (242-358-0053)

Long Island
Police/Fire/Ambulance: 919

Clarence Town Police (242-337-3919)

Deadman's Cay Police (242-337-0999)

Simm's Police (242-338-8555)

Stella Maris Police (242-338-2222)

Medical Services: **Clarence Town Government Clinic** (242-337-3333)

Deadman's Cay Government Clinic (242-337-1222)

Roses Government Clinic (242-337-1100)

Simm's Government Clinic (242-338-8488)

Other Out Islands
Police/Fire/Ambulance: **Crooked Island Police** (242-333-2599)

Great Harbour Cay (Berry Islands) Police (242-367-8344)

Inagua Police (242-339-1263)

Medical Services: **Great Harbour Cay** (Berry Islands) Medical Clinic (242-367-8400)

Inagua Hospital (242-339-12490

Landrail Point (Crooked Island) Government Clinic (242-344-2166)

San Salvador Medical Clinic (242-336-2105)

Spring Point (Acklins Island) Government Clinic (242-344-3172)

✳ Climate, Seasons, and What to Wear

Because the length of the Bahamas runs about six minutes in latitude—from off-coast West Palm Beach, Florida, to the southernmost tip of Cuba—temperature and climate fluctuate accordingly. Thermometer readings can vary 5 to 10 degrees on any given day.

Bahama weather tends to be warmer than its Florida counterparts in winter, thanks to its insulating surround-waters, and cooler in the summer, thanks again to insulation and also trade winds.

Surprising to many, the Bahamas do experience seasonal changes, especially in the north, where winter temperatures can dip into the 50s, but average around 70 degrees. Those temps, however, mean warmth to visitors from colder climes. On most islands, high tourist season kicks in around Christmas and continues into the warmer spring months through Easter. Hotel rates are highest then, and traffic, especially in Nassau, is at its peak.

Summers can be brutal and stifling to those unaccustomed with temperatures

SUNSHINE IS THE BEST FORM OF ENERGY ON THE ISLANDS, AND SUNSETS THE GRANDEST SHOW.

in the upper 90s and high humidity, but those who plan to spend time in the water or on a boat prefer it. In fact, some islands—especially those closest to Florida, such as Bimini, Berry Islands, and Andros—experience a high season in spring and summer. Many restaurants and even some inns have no air-conditioning, especially in the Out Islands. Warm weather also means more biting mosquitoes and sand flies. June through November marks hurricane season—another thing to consider when scheduling. Summer is also the rainy season, but that rarely ruins a vacation day; most showers fall briefly in the afternoon, when it's time for siesta. Or happy hour.

Fall is a pleasant time to visit because it's quiet, inexpensive, and cooler. Many businesses, however, close during August, September, and even October.

Naturally, your vacation wardrobe will depend upon the time of year you're visiting, but in general it should be loose-fitting, comfortable, and casual. There may be a call for dressing up in Nassau, and some of the old-school Out Island inns have a jacket-required dress code for dinner. But in general, everyone abides by the flip-flop-and-shorts uniform. (Small Bay Hope Lodge on Andros Island actually forbids neckties.)

Most importantly, pack swimsuits: More than one is advisable because the islands' humidity slows down the drying process. Bring your favorite snorkel and fins, or rent at many resorts or other rental outlets. Bring hats to protect your face from the sun.

You'll want some out-on-the-town outfits—sundresses for the ladies, khakis and nice tropical shirts for the men. Bring a light wrap, even in summer when some restaurants jack up the air-conditioning. If you're spending time on the water, park more layers and something waterproof. Include other sportswear according to the activities you plan to participate in. A pair of sneakers and some water shoes usually come in handy. In the summer, an umbrella is a good idea.

Other necessities: lots of sunscreen, bug spray, aloe vera products if you tend to burn, first-aid supplies, and plastic bags for transporting wet clothes home.

TIP: DON'T FORGET YOUR PASSPORT. It's your only way in and out of the Bahamas.

✳ Tourist Information

For information and visitors guides for all of the Bahamas, contact the following agencies. Information sources by island follow.

Bahamas Chamber of Commerce (242-322-2145; www.thebahamaschamber .com) Distributes some tourism information, but mostly business.

Bahamas Ministry of Tourism (800-BAHAMAS; www.bahamas.com) The MOT Web site is not always current or correct, so double-check info gleaned from it.

Bahamas Out Island Promotion Board (954-759-2210 (U.S.) or 800-688-4752; www.myoutislands.com)

Nassau/Paradise Island

Ministry of Tourism (242-322-7500 or 242-302-2000; www.bahamas.com) Tourist information booths at the airport (242-323-3182) and the Welcome Center at Festival Place near Prince George Wharf in Nassau (242-323-3183).

Nassau-Paradise Island Promotion Board (www.nassauparadiseisland.com)

Grand Bahama Island

Ministry of Tourism (242-352-8044 or 800-448-3386; www.grandbahama .bahamas.com) Visitor centers are located at the Fidelity Financial Center in Freeport, Grand Bahama International Airport, Lucayan Harbour, and Port Lucaya Marketplace.

Abaco

Abaco Tourist Office (242-367-3067; www.bahama.com) Office in Marsh Harbour, Great Abaco Island.

Andros

Andros Tourism Office (242-369-1688; www.andros.bahamas.com) Office in Fresh Creek for Central Andros (242-368-2286) and South Andros (242-369-1688); tourism contact on Mangrove Cay (242-369-0331).

Bimini

Bimini Tourism Office (242-347-3529; www.bimini.bahamas.com)

Cat Island

Cat Tourism Office (www.catisland.bahamas.com)

Eleuthera

Eleuthera Tourism Office (242-332-2142, Queen's Hwy., Governor's Harbour; or 242-333-2621, Dunmore St., Harbour Island; www.eleuthera.bahamas.com)

Exuma

Exuma Tourism Office (242-336-2430; www.exuma.bahamas.com) Office in George Town at Turnquest Star Plaza above Royal Bank of Canada.

Long Island

Long Island Tourism Office (242-338-8668; www.longisland.bahamas.com) Office in Deals, North Long Island.

Other Out Islands

Berry Islands Tourism Office (242-367-8070; www.berryislands.bahamas.com)

Inagua Tourism (www.inagua.bahamas.com)

Mayaguana Island Tourism (www.mayaguana.bahamas.com)

San Salvador Tourism (www.sansalvador.bahamas.com)

INDEX

A

Abaco, 37, 109–32; beaches, 115–16; car rentals, 46–47; don't miss, 111; eating, 125–29; emergencies, 248–49; ferries, 44, 117; information, 252; lodging, 122–25; map, 108; nightlife, 114–15; shopping, 129–31; sights/activities, 112–20; special events, 131–32; suggested reading, 111–12
Abaco: The History of an Out Island and its Cays, 111
Abaco Art Festival, 131
Abaco Bahama Amazons. *See* Bahama parrots
Abaco Beach Resort & Boat Harbour, 123; eating, 127; nightlife, 114; special events, 131; water sports, 117, 119
Abaco Beach Resort & Boat Harbour Marina, 117, 119
Abaco Christmas Festival, 132
Abaco Dorado Boat Rentals, 118
Abaco Gold, 129
Abaco Journal, 111
Abaco Life, 111
Abaco National Park, 20, 120
Abaco Neem, 129
Abaco Vacation Resorts, 125
Abaconian, The, 111
Above & Below Abaco, 120
Acklins, Brendal, 121
Acklins Island, 38, 239; emergencies, 250; ferries, 45; special events, 245; water sports, 242
Adderley's Plantation, 21, 225–26
Adelaide Village, 53
Agro/Expo & Muttonfest, 236

AIDA Freediving World Championship, 236
air travel, 23, 39–41
airlines, 41
airports, 39–41; taxis, 47–48
Albert Lowe Museum, 20, 112–13
Albury, Annie, 130
Albury Sail Shop, 129–30
Albury's Designs, 129
Alec's Caverns, 142
Alice Town, 157–58; beaches, 161; church, 159; eating, 168–70; emergencies, 249; lodging, 165–67; museum, 159; nightlife, 160; shopping, 171; water sports, 162
All Andros Crab Fest, 152, 153
All Tackle Fishing Tournament (Long Island), 236
Allen's Cay, 62, 208, 212–13
Alton Lowe Studio, 112
ambulances, 248–50
Amici, A Trattoria, 71–72
anchorages. *See* boating
Andros, 37, 135–53; beaches, 139; car rentals, 47; don't miss, 137; eating, 148–51; emergencies, 249; ferries, 44; information, 252; lodging, 142–48; map, 134; naming of, 137; nightlife, 138; shopping, 151–53; sights/activities, 138–42; special events, 153; suggested reading, 138; taxis, 47
Andros Barrier Reef, 136, 141–42
Andros chickcharnie, 142
Andros Island Bonefish Club, 143, 145
Andros Lighthouse, 138
Andros Town, 137; art galleries, 138; biking, 139; eat-

ing, 149–50; fishing, 140; lodging, 143; museums, 138; nightlife, 138; water sports, 141
Androsia Batik Outlet Store, 151
Androsia Batik Works Factory, 138
Androsia Steak & Seafood, 72
Angel Fish Blue Hole, 212
Angie's Bread Baking, 151
Angler's Restaurant, 127
Anna's Sweet Pot, 129
Anthaya Art Gallery, 13–14, 58
Anthony's Grill, 76
Aqua Grille, 168
architecture: overview, 31. *See also* churches; historic sites
Ardastra Gardens, Zoo & Conservation Center, 19, 57–58
area code, 13
art (artists), 13–14, 31–32. *See also* specific artists
art galleries and studios, 13–14; Abaco, 112; Andros, 138; Eleuthera, 189; Nassau, 58–59; Paradise Island, 58
Arthur's Bakery, 201
Arthur's Town, 175
Arts & Crafts Festival (Hope Town), 132
Atlantis, 51, 69–70; art galleries, 58; beaches, 60; casino, 59; for children, 19, 61; eating, 76–79; nightlife, 59; shopping, 80–81; spa, 61; water sports, 62
Atlantis Kids, 80
Atlantis Marina, 62
Augusta Bay, 215
Aura (Atlantis), 59
Austin Smith, 212
Awesome Blossoms, 192, 194

Bacardi Rum Billfish Tournament, 105
Baha Men, 20
Bahama Coffee Company (Eleuthera), 202
Bahama Craft Centre (Paradise Island), 80
Bahama Mama, 63
Bahama Mama Cruises, 91
Bahama parrots, 14, 26, 94, 120, 241
Bahama Sol, 79, 80
Bahamarama (Morris), 189
Bahamas Boating Flings (Bimini), 15, 172
Bahamas Chamber of Commerce, 252
Bahamas Discovery Quest, 227, 228
Bahamas EcoVentures, 91
Bahamas Historical Society Museum, 19, 53
Bahamas International Film Festival, 82
Bahamas Ministry of Tourism, 22, 252
Bahamas National Trust (BNT), 20, 93–94, 120, 240, 241; Ornithology Group, 63
Bahamas Out Island Promotion Board, 22, 252
Bahamas Outfitters (Abaco), 130
Bahamas Wahoo Challenge, 171, 172
Bahamasair, 23, 41
Bahamian Music and Heritage Festival (Exuma), 218
Bahamian people, 30–31
Bailey Town, 158; eating, 167–71; fishing, 161–62; lodging, 167
Bain Town, 175
bakeries, 15; Abaco, 128; Andros, 151; Bimini, 170; Eleuthera, 202; Exuma, 218; Grand Bahama Island, 104–5; Long Island, 235; Paradise Island, 79
Balcony House, 19, 53–54
B&B Boat Rentals, 118
Bannerman Town, 188; beaches, 191
Barbary horses, 120
Barefoot Sailing Cruises, 62
Barracuda Shoals, 63
Barraterre Bonefish Lodge, 210
batik, 80, 81, 138, 151, 202–3
Bay Street Market (Eleuthera), 202
Baycaner Beach Hotel, 243

Beach Club Restaurant (Bimini), 169–70
beaches, 14; Abaco, 115–16; Andros, 139; Bimini, 161; Cat Island, 178; Eleuthera, 189, 191–92; Exuma, 210; Grand Bahama Island, 88–89; Long Island, 226–27; Nassau, 60; New Providence Island, 60; Paradise Island, 60
Beat Retreat, 82
Becky's Bahamian Restaurant & Lounge, 16, 98–99
Behring Point, 137; lodging, 143
Bennett's Harbour (Cat Island), 175
Bennett's Hill (Nassau), 55–56
Berry Islands, 21, 38, 239; car rentals, 47; eating, 245; emergencies, 250; information, 253; lodging, 242–43; water sports, 241
Big Charlie's & Fathia's Fishing Lodge, 143
Big John's Conch Shell Bar, 160
Big John's Hotel, 165
Big Major Cay, 208, 211, 213
Big Shop (Andros), 138
Bight, The (Cat Island), 175; historic sites, 177
biking: Abaco, 116; Andros, 139–40; Grand Bahama Island, 89
Bikini Bottom Bar & Grill, 104
Bill & Nowdla Keefe's Bimini Underseas, 162
Billfish Blast Release Tournament, 183
Billy Joe's on the Beach, 17, 100
Bimini, 37, 156–72; beaches, 161; car rentals, 47; don't miss, 158; eating, 167–71; emergencies, 249; ferries, 44; information, 252; lodging, 164–67; map, 157; nightlife, 160–61; shopping, 171; sights/activities, 159–64; special events, 171–72; suggested reading, 159; taxis, 47–48
Bimini Bay Resort & Marina, 158, 165–66; eating, 168–69; shopping, 171; special events, 171–72; water sports, 162
Bimini Bay Rod & Gun Club, 156, 159
Bimini Biological Field Station Sharklab, 163
Bimini Blue Water Resort, 162, 166–67

Bimini bread, 15, 170
Bimini Craft Centre, 171
Bimini International Airport, 40
Bimini Museum, 20, 159
Bimini Native Tournament, 172
Bimini Regatta, 171
Bimini Road (Paradise Island), 76–77
Bimini Road to Atlantis, 162
Bimini Sands Resort & Marina, 158, 167; beaches, 161; eating, 169–70; nightlife, 161; water sports, 162–63
Bimini Sands Resort Nature Trail & Conch House, 163
Birch, Jeff, 147, 148–49
birds (birding), 14, 26–27; Abaco, 120; Andros, 142; Eleuthera, 192; Exuma, 212–13; Grand Bahama Island, 92–94; Great Inagua, 241; New Providence Island, 63. *See also* Bahama parrots; pink flamingos
Bishop's Beach Club & Bar, 100
Bishop's Bonefish Resort, 95
Bistro, The (Eleuthera), 198–99
Bita Beach, 115
Black Angus Grille, 72
Black Sound Cay, 111, 120
Blackbeard's Cay, 21, 62
Blister Beach, 161
Blue Bird Club, 181
blue holes, 15; Abaco, 119; Andros, 137, 139–40, 141; Eleuthera, 192, 194; Exuma, 212; Long Island, 228, 236
Blue Lagoon Island, 62
Blue Lagoon Seafood Restaurant, 77
Blue Rooster, 202
boat cruises: cruise ships, 41–42; Abaco, 116–18; Bimini, 162; Exuma, 211; Grand Bahama Island, 90–91; Nassau, 62–63; Paradise Island, 62–63
boat travel, 23; around the islands, 43–45; to the islands, 41–42
boating, 15; Abaco, 116–18; Andros, 141; Bimini, 162; Eleuthera, 192; Exuma, 211; Grand Bahama Island, 90–91; Long Island, 227–28; Nassau, 62–63; Out Islands, 241; Paradise Island, 62–63. *See also* kayaking; regattas
Bob Marley Boutique, 80
Bonafide Bonefishing, 227

bonefish: about, 18, 141
Bonefish Ansil Saunders, 15, 161–62
Bonefish Folley & Sons, 90
Bonefish Tommy Sewell, 162
bonefishing, 18; Abaco, 116; Andros, 140, 141, 144; Bimini, 161–62; Crooked Island, 240; Exumas, 210; Grand Bahama Island, 89–90; Long Island, 227
books, suggested, 38. *See also specific destinations*
Booze & Cruise (Nassau), 62
Booze & Screws (Bimini), 171
bread: about, 15. *See also* bakeries
breakfast, 15–16, 34–35. *See also specific eateries*
Breezes Bahamas, 23, 64
Brendal's Dive Center, 22, 116, 118, 119, 121
Bridge Inn Restaurant, 181
Briland Androsia, 202
British Colonial Hilton, 68
Bull Run, 162
Bullion Nassau, 74
Bullock Harbour, 239; eating, 245; lodging, 242
burger: defined, 126
Burial Mound Cave, 16, 93
Burnside, Jackson, III, 13, 58
buses, 48
bush medicine: overview, 16, 25–26
Bush Medicine in Bahamian Folk Tradition, 38
Bush Medicine Trail (Andros), 16, 140

C

Cabbage Beach, 60
Cable Beach, 52; art galleries, 58; casino, 59; eating, 71–73; golf, 60; lodging, 64–67; shopping, 80; spa, 61–62; taxis, 47
Cable Beach Golf Club, 60
Café Skan's, 16, 74
Calabash Bay, 137; eating, 151; grocery, 151
Calabash Eco Adventures, 89
candy, on Paradise Island, 79
Cape Eleuthera Divers, 192
Cape Eleuthera Institute (CEI), 194
Cape Eleuthera Resort & Yacht Club, 197–98; beach, 191; coffee, 202; water sports, 192
Cape Santa Maria, 230
Cape Santa Maria Bay and Beach, 226–27

Cap'n Jack's Restaurant and Bar, 125
Capt. Bali, 162
Capt. Bob's, 168–69
Capt. Rick Sawyer, 116
Capt. Will Key, 116
Captain Bill's, 15, 139
Captain Robbie Gibson, 240
car rentals, 45–47
car travel, 23, 45, 46
Cara's Caverns, 142
Cargill Creek, 137; bakery, 151; fishing, 140; lodging, 143, 145
Caribbean Divers, 92
Caribbean Express Band, 59
casinos, 59, 65, 67, 69–70, 88, 95
Castaway Cay, 21, 42
Castaways Resort and Suites, 95
Cat Island, 38, 174–83; beaches, 178; don't miss, 175; eating, 181–83; information, 252; lodging, 179–81; nightlife, 178; sights/activities, 177–79; special events, 183; suggested reading, 175
Cat Island Airport, 40
Cat Island Rake 'n' Scrape Festival, 183
caves: overview, 16. *See also specific caves*
Caves Beach (New Providence Island), 60
Cavill, Percy, 163
cay: defined, 25
Charlie's Bakery, 170
charters. *See* boat cruises; boating
Chat 'N' Chill, 218
Cheater's Restaurant & Bar, 217
Cherokee Sound, 110
Cheryl's Creations, 235
Chez Pierre, 232–33
chickcharnie, 142
China Beach, 100
Chopstix, 77
Christ Church Cathedral (Nassau), 16, 58
Christmas Festival (Abaco), 132
Christmas Jollification (Nassau), 81
Chub Cay, 239; lodging, 242
Chub Cay Marina and Resort, 241, 242
Chubasco Charters, 60
Church of the Holy Redeemer (Cat Island), 177
churches, 16–17, 58, 159, 177, 225–26

Churchill's Chophouse & Bar, 100–101
Clarence Town, 224; churches, 225; eating, 231–32; emergencies, 250; lodging, 229; special events, 236; water sports, 227
Clifton Heritage National Park, 20, 21, 55, 60
climate, 250–52
Club Amnesia, 87
Club Land'Or Resort, 59, 70, 77
Club Med-Columbus Isle, 243–44
Club Peace & Plenty, 210, 215, 217
Club Washington, 232
CoCo Cay, 21, 42
Coco Plum Restaurant & Bar, 200
Coconut Cove Hotel, 215–16
Coconut Festival, 105–6
Coin of the Realm, 80
Cole's of Nassau, 80
Colors Beach Club, 138
Columbus (Christopher) Monument, 226
Comfort Suites (Paradise Island), 70–71
communications, 17
Compass Cay, 213
Compass Point, 59, 68, 73
conch: overview, 17, 27, 34; souvenirs, 80
Conch Cracking Contest, 87, 106
Conch Fritters (Nassau), 74
Conch House (Bimini), 163
Conch Inn Hotel & Marina, 123–24; eating, 127–28; nightlife, 114; water sports, 117, 120
Conch Pearl Galleries (Abaco), 130–31
conch salad: about, 182
Conch Sound, 137; eating, 150
Conch Sound Resort Inn Restaurant and Bar, 150
Conch Stand (Andros), 138, 151
Conchman Triathlon, 106
Congo Town, 137
Coolie Mae's, 245
Coral Caverns, 142
Coral Harbour: horseback riding, 60–61; lodging, 67–68
Coral Harbour Beach House & Villas, 67
Cove, The (Eleuthera), 195
Cozy Corner, 245
crab: overview, 17. *See also specific eateries*
Crab Cay Ruins, 21, 209

Crab Fest (Andros), 152, 153
crab picker: defined, 227
cricket, 81
Crooked Island, 38, 239; eating, 245; emergencies, 250; ferries, 45; fishing, 240; lodging, 243; special events, 245; water sports, 242
Crooked Island Lodge, 243
Crooked Island Ruins, 239
cruises. *See* boat cruises
Cruising Guide to Abaco, 111
Crystal Palace Casino, 59, 63–64, 67
cuisine, 34–35
Curly Tails Restaurant, 114, 127–28
Curry's Sunset Grocery, 128
Cush's Place, 202
customs regulations, 36

D

De La Salle, 63
Deadman's Cay, 224, 226; eating, 232, 235
Deadman's Cay Cave, 16, 226
Deadman's Reef, 87; beaches, 88; lodging, 97–98
Deal's Beach, 227
Deal's Blue Hole, 15, 227
Dean's Blue Hole, 228, 236
Deveaux Plantation Ruins, 178
Diana's Dungeons, 142
dilly crabs: defined, 209
Dilly Dally, 202
Dips, Sips & Wishes, 129
Dis We Style, 129
Dive Abaco, 120
Dive Cat Island, 179
Dive Exuma, 212
Dive Guana, 116, 118, 120
diving. *See* scuba diving
Dixon, Allan, 235
Dixon Hill Lighthouse, 239–40
Dock & Dine, 127
Dr. Seabreeze, 190
Dog Rocks, 212
dolphin encounters: Abaco, 120; Bimini, 162; Grand Bahama Island, 91–92; Nassau, 62; Paradise Island, 61, 69–70
Dolphin House (Bimini), 159, 160, 171
Doolittle's Grotto, 242
Doongalik Studios, 13, 58
Dornell's Treasures, 202
Double Caves, 242
Drigg's Hill, 137; lodging, 145–46; nightlife, 138
Drigg's Hill Marina, 140
driving. *See* car travel
Dundas Centre for the Performing Arts, 13, 55
Dune (Paradise Island), 77–78
Dunmore Beach Club (Eleuthera), 196
Dunmore Town (Eleuthera), 189
Dunmore's Cave (Long Island), 16, 226
Dunmore's Plantation (Long Island), 21, 226
duty-free shopping, 35–36

E

East Bimini, 157–58; map, 157; water sports, 162, 164
East End (Grand Bahama Island), 86, 87
East Restaurant (Grand Bahama Island), 102
Ebbie's Bimini Bonefish Club, 167
Ebbtide, 131
ecotours: Abaco, 118; Andros, 141; Bimini, 162; Exuma, 211; Grand Bahama Island, 91
Eddie's Edgewater, 210
Edith's Pizza, 169
Eight Mile Rock, 87
Elbow Cay, 110, 117; beaches, 115; eating, 125–26, 128; historic sites, 113–14; lodging, 122; shopping, 131; water sports, 118, 120. *See also* Hope Town
Elbow Cay Lighthouse, 113
Eleuthera, 37, 187–203; beaches, 189, 191–92; car rentals, 47; don't miss, 189; eating, 198–202; emergencies, 249; ferries, 44; information, 252; lodging, 195–98; map, 186; naming of, 190; nightlife, 190; shopping, 202–3; sights/activities, 189–94; special events, 203; suggested reading, 189; taxis, 48
Elkhorn Gardens, 63
Elsie's Authentic Crafts, 22, 235
Elvina's Bar and Restaurant, 190
Emancipation Day, 81, 219
Emerald Bay, 208; golf, 210; lodging, 213–14
Emerald Palms Resort, 145
emergencies, 248–50
End of the World Saloon (Bimini), 160
Erickson Museum & Library, 20, 240
Everglades Souvenir Shop, 235
Exuma, 37, 207–19; beaches, 210; car rentals, 47; don't miss, 209; eating, 217–18; emergencies, 249–50; information, 252; lodging, 213–16; map, 206; nightlife, 210; shopping, 218; sights/activities, 209–13; special events, 218–19; suggested reading, 209; taxis, 48
Exuma Cays Land and Sea Park, 20, 208, 212–13; beaches, 210
Exuma Docking Services, 211
Exuma Straw Market, 218

F

Fan-Ta-Sea, 91
Farmer's Cay Conch Festival, 218
farmer's markets: Eleuthera, 202; Nassau, 79
February Point Resort Estates, 216
Ferguson, Amos, 14, 31, 58
Ferguson, Steve, 210
Fernandez Bay (Cat Island): eating, 181–82; lodging, 179; water sports, 179
Fernandez Bay (San Salvador), 240
Fernandez Bay Village (Cat Island), 176, 179; eating, 181–82
ferries, 43–45
Ferry, The (Exuma), 208; lodging, 214–15
Festival (Nassau), 80–81
Festival Noel, 106
films set in Bahamas, 17–18
fish and sea life, 27–28
Fish Cage, 192
Fish Fry: defined, 103; Eleuthera, 190; Exuma, 210; Grand Bahama Island, 86, 87, 103; Nassau, 75
Fish Hotel, 63
fishing, 18; Abaco, 116; Andros, 140; Bimini, 161–62; Cat Island, 178–79; Crooked Island, 240; Exuma, 210; Grand Bahama Island, 89–90; Long Island, 227; Nassau, 60; Paradise Island, 60. *See also* bonefishing
Fishing Hole Road, 105
fishing tournaments: Abaco, 132; Bimini, 171–72; Cat Island, 183; Grand Bahama Island, 105–6; Long Island, 236
Flamingo Bay Club (Cat Island), 180
Flamingo Bay Hotel & Marina

at Taino Beach (Grand Bahama Island), 97
flora, 25–26
Flying Cloud, 62
Flying Fish Marina, 227
Fort Charlotte, 55
Fort Fincastle, 55–56
Fort Montagu, 56
Fortune Beach: lodging, 94–95
Fowl Cay Preserve, 119
Freeport, 85–106; beaches, 88, 89; eating, 98–100; golf, 90; lodging, 95; map, 84; nature centre, 93–94; shopping, 105; special events, 105–6; water sports, 91
Freeport Players' Guild, 13
Fresh Creek, 137; biking, 139; eating, 150, 151; lodging, 146; nightlife, 138; water sports, 141
Froggie's Out Island Adventures, 120

G

galleries. See art galleries and studios
Gambier Village, 53; eating, 73; lodging, 68; nightlife, 59; shopping, 81
Garbanzo Beach, 115
Garbanzo Reef Bar, 115, 122
Garden of the Groves, 23, 92
gardens, 57–58, 63, 92
Generation Gap, 200–1
Geneva Braynen, 151
Geneva's Place, 16, 99
geography of Bahamas, 24–28
George Town, 207–8; eating, 217, 218; emergencies, 249; historic sites, 209; lodging, 215–16; nightlife, 210; shopping, 218; special events, 218–19; water sports, 211–12
George Town Cruising Regatta, 218
Gibson, Gertrude, 153
Gibson, Robbie, 240
Ginn sur Mer, 86, 87, 90, 97
Glass Window Art Gallery, 189
Glass Window Bridge, 188, 192
Gold Rock Beach, 88
golf: Exuma, 210; Grand Bahama Island, 90; Nassau, 60; Paradise Island, 60
golf cart rentals, 45–47
Goodfellow Farms, 78–80
Goombay Festival (Andros), 153
Government House, 21, 56
Governor's Harbour, 188; eating, 198–99, 202; emergen-

cies, 249; historic sites, 189; information, 252; lodging, 195; medical services, 249; nightlife, 190; shopping, 202–3; water sports, 192
Governor's Harbour Airport, 40
Governor's Harbour Bakery, 201
Grabbers Bar & Grill, 126
Grand Bahama International Airport, 39
Grand Bahama Island, 37, 85–106; beaches, 88–89; buses, 48; car rentals, 45–46; car travel, 45; don't miss, 87; eating, 98–105; emergencies, 248; ferries, 44; information, 252; lodging, 94–98; map, 84; nightlife, 87–88; shopping, 105; sights/activities, 87–94; special events, 105–6; suggested reading, 87; taxis, 47
Grand Bahama Nature Tours, 89, 91, 94
Grand Bahama Players, 13
Grand Bahama Sailing Regatta, 106
Grand Bahama Yacht Club, 90–91
Grand Island Resort and Spa, 213–14
Grant's Town, 53, 56
Graycliff Cigar Factory, 56
Graycliff Hotel, 23, 68–69
Graycliff Restaurant, 74–75
Gray's Plantation, 21, 226
Great Abaco Island, 37, 110–32; beaches, 115–16; don't miss, 111; eating, 125–29; lodging, 122–25; map, 108; shopping, 129–31; sights/activities, 112–20; special events, 131–32; taxis, 47
Great Exuma, 37, 207–8; beaches, 210; eating, 217–18; lodging, 213–16; map, 206; shopping, 218; special events, 218–19; water sports, 211–12. See also George Town
Great Guana Cay, 111, 117; beaches, 115; biking, 116; eating, 126; lodging, 122–23; water sports, 118, 120
Great Guana Cay Beach, 115
Great Harbour Cay, 239; eating, 245; emergencies, 250; lodging, 242, 244; water sports, 241
Great Harbour Cay Marina, 241
Great Harbour Inn, 242
Great Inagua, 38, 238, 240–41;

eating, 245; car rentals, 47; emergencies, 250; information, 253; lodging, 242, 243
Great Inagua Lighthouse, 240
Great Stirrup Cay, 21, 42
Green Turtle Cay, 109, 117; art galleries, 112; beaches, 115; biking, 116; eating, 126–29; historic sites, 113; lodging, 123; museums, 112–13; nightlife, 114–15; shopping, 131; special events, 131–32; water sports, 118–19
Green Turtle Club Resort & Marina, 118, 123; eating, 126–27; Fishing Tournament, 132; special events, 131, 132; Wine Tasting Event, 131
Greenwood Beach Resort & Dive Center, 180–81
Gregory Town, 187–88; art galleries, 189; beaches, 192; eating, 199–200, 202; lodging, 195–96; nightlife, 190; shopping, 203; special events, 203
Gregory's Arch, 56
guava duff, 35
Gully Roosters, 114
gully wash: defined, 89
Guy Fawkes & Bonfire Celebrations, 132

H

hair-braiding: overview, 18
Half Moon Cay, 21, 42
Hamilton's Cave, 16, 226
Hank's Place Restaurant and Bar, 138, 146, 150
Happy People's, 47, 241
Happy Trails Stables, 60–61
Harbour Island, 188–89; beaches, 14, 191; eating, 200, 202; lodging, 196–97; shopping, 202; special events, 203; water sports, 192
Harbour Island Beach, 191
Harbour Island Club & Marina, 192
Harbour's Edge (Hope Town), 126
Hard Bargain, 224
Havana Trading Company, 105
Hawes, John "Father Jerome," 177, 225
Hawk's Nest: eating, 182–83; lodging, 179–80
Hawk's Nest Resort & Marina, 179–80; eating, 182–83; fishing, 178–79, 183; scuba diving, 179
Hawk's Nest Restaurant, 182–83
Haynes Library, 189

Hazel's Seaside Bar, 178
Healing Hole, 162, 164
health foods, on Paradise
  Island, 79
Hemingway, Ernest, 156, 158,
  159, 166
Hermitage, The (Cat Island),
  16, 177
Hermitage Estate Ruins
  (Exuma), 21, 209–10
High Rock, 86–87; eating, 100;
  lodging, 95
hiking: Andros, 140; Bimini,
  163; Long Island, 227
historic sites: Abaco, 112–14;
  Andros, 138; Bimini, 159;
  Cat Island, 178; Eleuthera,
  189–90; Exuma, 209–10;
  Long Island, 225–26; New
  Providence Island, 55–57;
  Out Islands, 239–40
history, 24–30; natural, 24–28;
  social, 28–30
Hog Island. See Paradise
  Island
hog snapper: defined, 199
Hole in the Wall, 192
Homer, Winslow, 13, 31, 112
Homer Lowe Memorial Regat-
  ta, 132
Hope Town, 110; architecture,
  112; eating, 125–26, 128;
  emergencies, 249; fishing,
  116; historic sites, 113–14;
  lodging, 122, 125; shopping,
  129, 131; special events,
  131–32; water sports, 118
Hope Town Annual Heritage
  Day, 131–32
Hope Town Arts & Crafts Fes-
  tival, 132
Hope Town Big Hill Box Cart
  Derby, 132
Hope Town Coffee Shop, 128
Hope Town Harbour Lodge,
  122, 132
Hope Town Hideaways, 125
horseback riding, 60–61
hunting, 18, 140, 236

I

ice cream, 79, 129
Iggy Biggy, 131
Ike's Reef, 192
Inagua. See Great Inagua
Inagua: An Island Sojourn,
  239
Inagua National Park, 20, 241
Independence Day Celebra-
  tion (Exuma), 219
Inside Grand Bahama, 87
International Bazaar, 85, 105
Internet access, 17

Into the Blue (movie), 18, 63
Island Book Shop (Nassau), 81
Island Breezes Motel (Abaco),
  124
Island Gal Charters (Abaco),
  118
Island Girl (Abaco), 131
Island Java Coffeehouse &
  Desserterie (Grand Bahama
  Island), 102, 104–5
Island Made Shop (Eleuthera),
  202
Island Marine Boat Rentals
  (Parrot Cay), 118
Island Roots Heritage Festival
  (Abaco), 132
Island School (Eleuthera), 194
Island Seas Resort (Grand
  Bahama Island), 98
Island Shop (Nassau), 81
Island World Adventures (Par-
  adise Island), 62
Iva Bowe's Central Highway
  Inn, 217

J

Jamba Juice (Paradise Island),
  79
James Bond sites, 15, 208, 212
J&T's Daily Manna, 171
Java (Abaco), 128
Jaws Beach, 60
Joe, Billy, 101
Joe's Studio, 112
John Bull (Abaco), 131; (Bimi-
  ni), 171
Johnson, Grant, 163, 164–65
Johnston, Randolph W., 14,
  111, 112
Joulters Cays, 140
Junkanoo, 13, 18, 31, 33;
  Abaco, 131–32; Andros, 153;
  Eleuthera, 203; Grand
  Bahama Island, 106; New
  Providence Island, 81, 82
Junkanoo Summer Festival
  (Abaco), 132; (Nassau), 81

K

kalik: defined, 35
kamalame: defined, 146
Kamalame Cay, 141
Kamalame Cay Resort, 141,
  146
Kamalame Cove: lodging, 146
Kathy's Bakery, 202
kayaking: Abaco, 118; Andros,
  141; Bimini, 162; Exuma,
  211; Grand Bahama Island,
  91; Nassau, 62
Keasler, Mark, 176
Keefe, Bill & Nowdla, 162
Kidd Cove, 211

Knowles, Elsie, 22, 234–35
Kristina's Café, 149–50
kupunkled up: defined, 192

L

Land Shark Divers Hotel, 69
Landfall Park, 240
language, 19
Laughing Lizard Café, 199
Leadon, Rupert, 144, 145
Lighthouse Marina (Elbow
  Cay), 118
Lighthouse Point Beach
  (Eleuthera), 188, 191
Lighthouse Yacht Club &
  Marina (Andros), 141, 143
lighthouses, 113, 138, 239–40,
  240
Little Exuma, 37, 208; beaches, 210; fishing, 210; historic
  sites, 209–10; map, 206;
  national park, 213
Little Harbour, 110; art galleries, 112
Little Whale Cay, 21, 239,
  242–43
lobster: overview, 19, 27. See
  also specific eateries
Long Cay, 239
Long Island, 37, 223–36;
  beaches, 226–27; car rentals,
  47; don't miss, 225; eating,
  231–35; emergencies, 250;
  information, 253; lodging,
  228–31; map, 222; nightlife,
  226; shopping, 235; sights/
  activities, 225–28; special
  events, 236
Long Island Airport, 40–41
Long Island Breeze Resort,
  229–30; eating, 233;
  nightlife, 226; water sports,
  227
Long Island Breeze Restaurant, 233
Long Island Library, Museum
  and Community Centre, 20,
  226
Long Island Regatta, 236
Long Wharf Beach, 60
Love Hill, 137, 139
Lowe, Alton, 14, 31, 38,
  112–13, 114; Studio, 112
Lowe, Robert, 116
Lowe, Vertram, 112
Lowe (Albert) Museum, 20,
  112–13
Loyalist Memorial Sculpture
  Garden, 113
Loyalists, 28–29, 109, 112–14,
  135, 188–89, 209
Lucaya, 85–86; beaches,
  88–89; eating, 100–103; fish-

ing, 90; golf, 90; lodging, 95–97; map, 84; shopping, 105; special events, 105–6; water sports, 90–92
Lucayan Marina Village, 90–91
Lucayan National Park, 16, 20, 85, 91, 93; beaches, 88; culture tours, 87
Luciano's, 102

M

Mable's Meat Mart, 151
McIntosh Restaurant & Bakery, 127
McKann's: eating, 232
Mackey's Sand Bar, 161
McKinney, Elton "Bonefish Shakey," 240
McLean's Town, 87; Conch Cracking Contest, 87, 106
mailboats, 45
Main House (Great Inagua), 243
Major's Cay: lodging, 243
Mandara Spa, 61
Mangoes Restaurant, 128
Mangrove Cay, 137; nightlife, 138
Mangrove Cay Seafood, 151
Man-O-War Cay, 15, 110–11, 117; art galleries, 112; eating, 127, 129; lodging, 123; shopping, 129–30, 131; water sports, 119
Marian, 142
Marketplace, The (Eleuthera), 202
Marley, Bob, 80
Marley Resort & Spa, 64–65; eating, 72–73; shopping, 80; spa, 61–62
Mars Bay, 137
Marsh Harbour, 109–10; eating, 125, 127–29; lodging, 123–24; map, 108; nightlife, 114–15; shopping, 129–31; special events, 131–32; water sports, 117–20
Marsh Harbour International Airport, 40
Matthew Town, 238, 240; eating, 245; lodging, 243
Max's Conch Bar & Grill, 232
Mayaguana Island, 239; information, 253; lodging, 243
medical emergencies, 248–50
Mennonite Tents, 151
Mesa Grill, 78
Miller's: eating, 232–33
Millerton: shopping, 235
Minns Water Sports, 211
Miss Emily's Blue Bee Bar, 21, 114–15

Miss Gibson, 202
Miss Lola, 128
Mom's Bakery (Exuma), 218
Monkey's Uncle, 131
Moray Alley, 162
Morgan's Bluff, 137; special events, 153
Morgan's Bluff Beach, 139
Moriah Harbour Cay National Park, 213
Moss, Jeff, 240
Mount Pleasant: eating, 78–79; shopping, 79–80
Mount Pleasant Fishing Lodge (Andros), 145
Mount Thompson, 209, 210
movies set in Bahamas, 17–18
Munjack Island, 14, 121
museums, 19–20; Abaco, 112–14; Andros, 138; Bimini, 159; Cat Island, 178; Eleuthera, 189–90; Exuma, 209–10; Long Island, 225–26; Nassau, 53–54; Out Islands, 239–40
Musha Cay, 21, 208
music, 13, 20, 32; Abaco, 114–15; Andros, 138; Bimini, 160–61; Cat Island, 178; Eleuthera, 190; Exuma, 210; Grand Bahama Island, 87–88; Long Island, 226; Paradise Island, 59. *See also* Junkanoo; rake 'n' scrape
mutton: defined, 233

N

Nassau, 36–37, 51–82; beaches, 60; buses, 48; car rentals, 45–46; car travel, 45; don't miss, 53; eating, 71–76; emergencies, 248; ferries, 43–44; information, 252; lodging, 63–69; map, 50; shopping, 80–81; sights/activities, 53–63; special events, 81–82; suggested reading, 53; taxis, 47
Nassau Cricket Club, 81
Nassau Dolphin Encounters, 62
Nassau Farmer's Market, 79
Nassau Glass Art Gallery, 14, 58
Nassau Guardian, 53
Nassau International Airport, 39
Nassau Public Library and Museum, 19, 54
Nassau Race Week, 81
Nassau Regatta World Championship, 81
Nassau Straw Market, 80

Nassau Yacht Club, 81
Nassau's Historic Landmarks, 53
National Art Gallery of the Bahamas, 13, 59
National Centre for the Performing Arts, 13, 56
National Dance Company of the Bahamas, 13, 56–57
National Family Island Regatta, 218
national parks: overview, 20. *See also* specific national parks
Native Creations (Abaco), 131
natural history, 24–28
Natural Mystic Spa, 61–62
Nettie's Different of Nassau, 16, 57, 65, 66
New Bight (Cat Island), 175, 177; eating, 181
New Briland Big Ten Lounge, Restaurant & Bar, 75
New Plymouth, 109; architecture, 112; art galleries, 112; eating, 127–29; museums, 112–13; nightlife, 114–15; shopping, 131
New Plymouth Dock, 129
New Providence Island, 51–82; beaches, 60; don't miss, 53; eating, 71–80; lodging, 63–69; map, 50; shopping, 80–81; sights/activities, 53–63; special events, 81–82; suggested reading, 53. *See also* Nassau; Paradise Island
New World Museum, 240
New Year's Day Junkanoo, 131
Neymour, Charlie, 140, 143
Nicholl's Town, 137; beaches, 139; eating, 151; lodging, 146–47; nightlife, 138; special events, 153
Nicholl's Town Beach, 139
nightlife, 13; Abaco, 114–15; Andros, 138; Bimini, 160–61; Cat Island, 178; Eleuthera, 190; Exuma, 210; Grand Bahama Island, 87–88; Long Island, 226; Paradise Island, 59
Nippers Beach Bar & Grill, 117, 126
Nobu, 78
Nodules, 162
Norman's Cay, 210
Norman's Cay Beach Club at MacDuff's, 210
North Abaco Christmas Celebration, 132
North Andros, 137; beaches, 139; biking, 140; eating, 151; nightlife, 138; produce, 151;

special events, 153
North Andros Conch Stands, 138, 151
North Andros-Berry Islands Regatta, 153
North Bimini, 37, 157–58; beaches, 161; eating, 168–69; fishing, 161–62; grocery stores, 170; lodging, 165–67; map, 157; shopping, 171; special events, 171–72; water sports, 162
North Eleuthera Airport, 40
North Eleuthera Sailing Regatta, 203
North Palmetto Point: eating, 200; lodging, 197
North Pole Cave, 242

O

obeah: defined, 174
Ocean Hole Park, 15, 194
Ocean Wonder, 91
Oceanfrontier Hideaway (Great Guana Cay), 122–23
Off Island Adventures (Exuma), 211
Oh Sugar, 79
Old Bahama Bay at Ginn Sur Mer, 97
Old Bahama Bay Marina, 91
Old Bight (Cat Island), 175, 177
Old Bight Beach (Cat Island), 178
Old Freetown, 88, 93
Oneil's, 224, 234; shopping, 22, 235
One&Only Ocean Club, 71; eating, 77; golf, 60
Orange Beach, 178; anchorage, 178
Orange Creek, 175
Our Lucaya Beach and Golf Resort, 95–96; casino, 88; eating, 100–103; golf, 90; nightlife, 88; shopping, 105
Our Lucaya Beach and Golf Resort Lucayan Course, 90
Our Lucaya Beach and Golf Resort Reef Course, 90
Out Islands, 238–45; don't miss, 239; eating, 244–45; emergencies, 250; information, 253; lodging, 242–44; sights/activities, 239–42; special events, 245; suggested reading, 239
Outriggers Native Restaurant & Beach Club, 87, 103

P

packing tips, 250–52

paddling. *See* kayaking
Painted Fish, The, 131
Palm Bay Beach Club, 216
Paradise Cove, 88, 97–98
Paradise Island, 36–37, 51–82; art galleries, 58; beaches, 14, 60; for children, 19, 61; don't miss, 53; eating, 76–78; emergencies, 248; gardens, 58; golf, 60; information, 252; lodging, 63–64, 69–71; map, 50; nightlife, 59; spa, 61; special events, 81–82; water sports, 62
Park Lane Jewelers, 81
Peace & Plenty Bonefish Lodge, 214–15
peckerwood: defined, 120
Pelican Bay, 96–97; eating, 103
Pelican Cays Land & Sea Park, 111, 120
People-to-People Program, 20–21, 31
People-To-People Teas (Exuma), 218
Pepperpot Grill, 75–76
performance art. *See* music; nightlife
Perfume Factory (Grand Bahama Island), 105
Peterson Cay National Park, 88, 91, 93
Pete's Pub & Gallery, 14, 112
Petite Conch Restaurant, 170
Pier One (Grand Bahama Island), 99
Pillars, The, 118–19
Pineapple Festival, 188, 203
Pineapple Fields, 190, 195, 199
Pineapples Bar & Grill, 115
Pineville Motel, 138, 146–47
pink flamingos, 14, 20, 26, 241
Pink Sands (Eleuthera), 196–97
Pirates of Nassau, 19, 54
Pirates of the Caribbean (movie), 18, 93, 208, 210
Plait Lady, 22, 81
plantations, 21, 178, 225–26
Poitier, Sidney, 175
police, 248–50
Pompey Museum of Slavery & Emancipation, 19, 54
Poop Deck, The (Nassau), 76
Pop's Place, 129
Porgy Bay, 158; eating, 170
Port Howe, 178; lodging, 180–81
Port Lucaya Marina, 91, 105
Port Lucaya Marketplace, 13, 18, 105; eating, 102, 104, 105; special events, 105–6; water sports, 91–92

Port Royal (Cat Island), 175
potcake: defined, 115
Potter's Cay, 80
Powerboat Adventures (Paradise Island), 62
powerboating. *See* boating
Preacher's Cave, 189
Princess Cay, 188
Princess Resort, 85, 94
Prop Club Sports Bar & Dance Club, 88, 102–3

Q

quadrille, 13, 32
Queen's Baths, 194
Queen's Staircase, 55–56

R

Radio Beach, 161
Rahming, Dorothy, 193, 203
Rainbow Blue Hole, 15, 139–40
rake 'n' scrape, 20, 32, 138, 153, 178, 183, 190, 210
Ramsey: eating, 217
Rand Nature Centre, 93–94
reading, suggested, 38. *See also specific destinations*
Red Bays, 22, 135, 152
Reef Rentals (Green Turtle Cay), 118
Reef Tours Ltd., 90, 91, 92
Reel Tight Charters, 140
regattas: Abaco, 132; Acklins Island, 245; Andros, 153; Bimini, 171; Crooked Island, 245; Eleuthera, 203; Exuma, 218–19; Grand Bahama Island, 106; Long Island, 236; Nassau, 81; San Salvador, 245
Reggae Boat Adventures, 211
religious sites. *See* churches
Rich's Boat Rentals, 118
Riding Rock Inn Restaurant, 245
Ritchies, 235
Robert Lowe, 116
Rock Sound, 188; beaches, 191; eating, 200, 202; historic site, 190; lodging, 197–98; nightlife, 190; special events, 203; water sports, 192
Rock Sound Beach, 191
Rock Sound Blue Holes, 192
Rolle, Alston "Rambo," 210
Rolleville Regatta and Homecoming, 219
roundabouts, 46
Rowdy Boy's Bar & Grill, 231–32
Royal Bahamian Police Band, 20, 32

Royal Palm Boutique, 81
Ruby Golf Course, 90
Ruby Swiss European Restaurant, 99–100
rugby, 81
rum drinks: about, 21
Runway Wall, 63
rush-out: defined, 106

S

Sabor (Bimini), 169
Sabor Restaurant & Bar (Grand Bahama), 103
sailing. See boating; regattas
St. Francis Xavier Cathedral (Nassau), 17, 58
St. Mary's Church (Long Island), 225
St. Mary's the Virgin Anglican Church (Cat Island), 177
St. Matthew's Anglican Church (Nassau), 16, 58
St. Paul's Anglican Church (Long Island), 225
St. Peter's Roman Catholic Church (Long Island), 225–26
Salt Pond, 224; beaches, 227; eating, 233; lodging, 229–30; nightlife, 226; special events, 236; water sports, 227
Salt Pond Beach, 227
Salt Water Boutique, 202–3
Sammie Boy's Gift Shop, 131
Sam's Place, 16, 217
San Andros Airport, 40
San Jacinto, 119
San Salvador, 38, 238; eating, 245; emergencies, 250; fishing, 240; historic sites, 239–40; information, 253; lodging, 243–44; special events, 245; water sports, 242
San Salvador Regatta, 245
Sandals Emerald Bay, 214
Sandals Emerald Reef Golf Club, 210
S&M Jerk Stop, 151
Sandpiper Arts & Crafts, 218
Sands, Henry, 201
Sands Bakery, 15, 202
Sandy Cay, 14, 210
Sandy Point, 110, 120
Santana's Grill, 218
Sapona, 162, 163
Sara's (Bimini), 169
Saunders, Ansil, 15, 161–62
Saunders, Ashley, 159, 160, 171
Sawyer, Rick, 116
Schoolhouse Reef, 63
Schooner's Landing, 123
scuba diving, 21–22; Abaco,

118–20; Acklins Island, 242; Bimini, 162–63; Cat Island, 179; Crooked Island, 242; Eleuthera, 192; Exuma, 212; Grand Bahama Island, 91–92; Long Island, 228; Nassau, 63. See also blue holes
Sea Grape Gift Shop, 81
Sea Horse Boat Rentals, 118
sea kayaking. See kayaking
sea life, 27–28
Sea Side Café (Crooked Island), 245
Sea Spray Resort & Marina (Abaco), 122
Sea View Restaurant (Eleuthera), 200
seasons, 250–52
Seaworld Explorer, 91
settlements: about, 21
Sewell, Tommy, 162
Sharklab (Bimini), 163
Sharks Amberjack Reef, 212
Shell Beach (Bimini), 161
Sheraton Nassau Beach Resort, 65; eating, 71–72
shipwrecks, 63, 119, 142, 162, 163, 212
shopping: overview, 35–36. See also specific shops and destinations
shuttle buses, 48
Simmer Down, 72–73
Sip Sip (Eleuthera), 200
Sky Beach Club, 195–96; eating, 198–99
Small Hope Bay: eating, 150–51; lodging, 147–48
Small Hope Bay Lodge, 16, 147–49; biking, 139–40; eating, 150–51; fishing, 140; hiking, 140; scuba diving, 22, 141–42; water sports, 141
Small Hope Bay Lodge Dining Room, 150–51
Small's Variety Store, 170
Smith, Andy, 140
Smith's Point, 86; eating, 103; nightlife, 87
Smitty's Convenience Store, 218
Smuggler's Plane Wreck, 192
snack: defined, 200, 209
Snappas Grill & Chill, 115
snorkeling, 21–22; Abaco, 118–20; Acklins Island, 242; Bimini, 162–63; Cat Island, 179; Crooked Island, 242; Eleuthera, 192; Exuma, 212; Grand Bahama Island, 91–92; Long Island, 228; Nassau, 63
social history, 28–30

South Bimini, 37, 157–58; beaches, 161; eating, 169–70; grocery stores, 170; lodging, 167; map, 157; nightlife, 161; shopping, 171; special events, 171–72; water sports, 162–63; wildlife spotting, 163
South Eleuthera Mission, 190
Southwest Reef, 63
Spanish Wells, 189; beaches, 191; eating, 201–2; lodging, 198; water sports, 192
Spanish Wells Beach, 191
Spanish Wells Harbourside Rentals, 198
Spanish Wells Yacht Haven, 192
spas, on New Providence Island, 61–62
Spider & the Boys, 190
Splash (Bimini), 171
Spook Hill, 161
Stafford Creek, 137
Staniel Cay, 208, 211; lodging, 216
Staniel Cay Marina, 211
Staniel Cay Yacht Club, 216
Starfish the Exuma Adventure Center, 211, 212
Stella Maris, 224; beaches, 226–27; eating, 233–34; lodging, 230–31; water sports, 227
Stella Maris Marina, 227
Stella Maris Resort Club, 230–31; eating, 233–34
Stella Maris Restaurant, 233–34
Stingray Adventure, 62
Stocking Island, 210, 211; eating, 218
Stocking Island Mystery Cave, 212
straw markets, 22, 35; Bimini, 171; Eleuthera, 202; Exuma, 218; Grand Bahama Island, 105; Nassau, 55, 80–81; Paradise Island, 80
straw work: overview, 22, 32. See also specific destinations
Stuart Cove's Snorkel Bahamas, 22, 63
Sub Bahamas, 62
Sue & Joy Variety Store, 170
Sunset Beach, 191
Sunset Souvenirs, 131
Supreme Court (Nassau), 57
Surf Watersport (Bimini), 162
Surfer's Beach (Eleuthera), 192
Surfers Beach Manor (Eleuthera), 196, 199–200
Sweeting's Cay, 87
symbols, key to, 7

Symonette, Nettie, 57, 65, 66

T

Taino Beach, 14, 88–89; eating, 103; lodging, 97; special events, 106
Tarpum Bay: beach, 192; blue holes, 194; special events, 203
Tarpum Bay Beach, 192
Tartar Bank, 179
Tat's Rental, 244
taxis, 47–48
Taylor, Maxwell, 31
Teasers Bar & Grill, 103–4
telephone calls, 17
Thirsty Turtle Yacht Club, 170
Three Sisters Beach, 210
Thunderball (Fleming), 207, 209
Thunderball (movie), 18, 63, 208, 209
Thunderball Grotto, 15, 208, 212
Tiamo, 145–46
Tilloo Cay, 111, 120
tingum: defined, 197
Tingum Village, 197
Tippy's Restaurant, Bar & Beach, 190, 199
TJs Bonefishing & Guide Services, 227
Tommy Bahama (Paradise Island), 81
Tongue of the Ocean, 136, 141
Toni Macaroni's, 17, 89
Top Gun Charters, 42
Tortuga Rum Cake Bakery, 79
tourist information, 22, 252–53
Tranquility on the Bay Resort, 243
transportation, 23, 39–48; around the islands, 43–48; to the islands, 39–42

Travellers' Rest, 59, 73–74
Treasure Bay Casino, 88
Treasure Cay, 110, 115–16; beaches, 115–16; lodging, 124–25; special events, 132; water sports, 118
Treasure Cay Airport, 40
Treasure Cay Billfish Tournament, 132
Treasure Cay Hotel Resort & Marina, 115, 118, 124–25
Treasure Reef, 91, 92
Tropic of Cancer Beach, 210
true true: defined, 169
Trumpet Reef, 141
Tunnel Rock, 192
22 Above (Nassau), 67
20,000 Leagues Under the Sea (movie), 63

U

Uncle Charlie's, 15, 140
UNEXSO (Underwater Explorers Society), 22, 91–92
Unique Village (Eleuthera), 197, 200
up south, down north: defined, 189

V

Valley of the Sponges, 119
Vendue House, 54
Versailles Gardens, 23, 58
Victory Reef, 162
Violet Mitchell, 119
Viva Wyndham Fortuna Beach, 94–95
Vlady's Reef, 179

W

Wahoo Challenge, 171, 172
Walker's Cay National Reserve, 120
Wall in Crooked Passage, 242

Wallace, Henry, 153
water sports, 15; Abaco, 116–20; Andros, 141–42; Bimini, 162–63; Cat Island, 179; Eleuthera, 192; Exuma, 211; Grand Bahama Island, 90–92; Long Island, 227–28; Nassau, 62–63; Out Islands, 241–42; Paradise Island, 62–63
Watling's Castle Ruins, 240
waving: defined, 239
Wax Cut Drift, 212
weddings: overview, 23
Wesley Methodist Church (Bimini), 159
West End (Grand Bahama Island), 85, 87; beaches, 88; biking, 89; eating, 103–4, 105; fishing, 90; lodging, 97–98; water sports, 91
West Side (Andros), 135; fishing, 140
Whale Shark Reef, 212
White Sound: eating, 126–27; lodging, 122–23; water sports, 119
Williams Town (Exuma), 208, 209–10; eating, 218
William's Town (Grand Bahama Island), 86; eating, 104; lodging, 98
Winding Bay, 110
Winter Haven, 229, 231–32
Wyannie Malone Historical Museum, 20, 114
Wyndham Fortuna Beach, 94–95
Wyndham Nassau Resort, 67; casino, 59; eating, 72; golf, 60

X

Xanadu Beach, 89
Xanadu Hotel, 94